Smart ¹

Travel the World Cheap

How To Discover More, Spend Less, and Visit
The Best Places Around The World.

Planning – Organising – Exploring

Daniel N. Silva

Smart Ways to Travel the World Cheap

www.megatraveltips.com

Sponsored by:

PRIMABOINCA is a research project that uses Internet-connected computers to search for a counterexample to some conjectures.

This project concerns itself with two hypotheses in number theory. Both are conjectures for the identification of prime numbers. The first conjecture (Agrawal's Conjecture) was the basis for the formulation of the first deterministic prime test algorithm in polynomial time (AKS algorithm). Hendrik Lenstras and Carl Pomerances heuristic for this conjecture suggests that there must be an infinite number of counterexamples.

So far, however, no counterexamples are known. This hypothesis was tested for $n < 10^{10}$ without having found a counterexample. The second conjecture (Popovych's conjecture) adds a further condition to Agrawals conjecture and therefore logically strengthens the conjecture. If this hypothesis would be correct, the time of a deterministic prime test could be reduced from $O(\log N)^6$(currently most efficient version of the AKS algorithm) to $O(\log N)^3$.

You can participate by downloading and running a free program on your computer.

Please visit **www.primaboinca.com** to learn more.

To God, the Creator of the universe, He created the heavens and the earth and I will be forever grateful for the opportunity to explore such a beautiful creation.

Table of Contents

Introduction

Many people are clueless about what their vacation activities should be. However, it is important to travel to various countries and mix with people of varied cultures. It broadens the mind to many new things, and can help travellers to enjoy life in various exciting ways.

Travelling allows a break from the routine happenings of life. Travellers can forget their issues and problems for some weeks and even find ways to solve them, which they would have been incapable of without the break and experience that their trip offered them. Everyone has a busy schedule, family and work to care about, and travelling with a few friends/family members or even alone can offer a much-needed break. Trippers can also understand how important in their lives these people are. Most people never understand the importance of relations until they end up losing them. Travelling helps relax people as well. It feels beautiful to live life to the full and spend some time alone without any stress. Vacation helps dissociate a person from their mundane life and rejuvenate the mind and body. They come back refreshed and feel more capable of entering the daily grind again. It removes a lot of stress and makes people more willing to undertake routine activities.

Going on trips also helps broaden knowledge and allows one to view the world from a wider angle. Travellers can get exposure to new traditions and varied ways of existence, which can be excellent for their mind. They can develop new habits and change negative ones to emerge as better people. Exposure to new styles of living and accommodation, various faiths and cultures, different foods and clothes, art and culture helps them discover various values. This makes them more open-minded and makes life more exciting for them. Visiting new and exotic destinations helps them know that the world has much more to offer to them. With newer travel experiences, people can become more resourceful and deal with everyday situations with more creativity, which is impossible when living at home. Those who travel frequently are open to change and develop the natural capacity to overcome challenges that other people are scared of.

Travelling is cheaper today than ever before. With the prices of oil climbing, the era of cheap travel might be conventionally nearing an end. Fortunately, many budget airlines companies are falling over each other to offer more competitive flight rates. Nowadays, travellers can use the newest tools and technology, and the internet, to make travel plans as per individual preferences. It is possible choose travel duration, vacation activities, budget, and go through travel blogs as well to be pre-informed about the possible difficulty of the trip as faced by others.

For people having some time off, travel is highly recommended as it can help them understand all that life has on offer. It is not a good idea to put off trips for later. They should take the plunge and use the chance to make travel arrangements and leave immediately. Once travel becomes a habit, travellers look forward to their next trip and then the next.

I have done my very best to write this book for people travelling any length of time, in any continent around the globe. This book will provide readers with cheap ways to travel, strategies to save money, the best credit cards, a list of low-cost airlines, bus and train companies, as well as the best destinations in each continent on this beautiful planet. Let's plan ahead, organise ourselves and explore this beautiful world together.

Sincerely,

Daniel N. Silva

Travel Perception

"Vacation" and "travel" are two words often used interchangeably, but a deeper analysis reveals subtle differences. Vacation means an escape from an existing situation or surroundings, whereas travel might offer the chance to be immersed completely in a widely varied culture. Travel involves two forms of journeys – the outer and the inner. While the outer one reveals the physical journey involving travel experiences, including the destination, activities and sightseeing, the inner travel is about interpreting the travel experiences, the things learned and how they changed life and perspectives.

Improving Language Skills

Travelling frequently improves language skills, given that proper communication is necessary while travelling. You can learn local colloquialisms and new words by interpreting various gestures. It is also possible to undergo some language skills program or 'talk' to local people who understand multiple languages to pick up new language skills. For instance, the IELTS course for English as taught by the British Council in many countries helps people improve their English speaking, reading and writing skills before going to a new country. With enhanced language skills, travellers can get a better idea about the cooking traditions, dressing habits, rituals etc. of other countries.

Travelling helps people experience destinations, people, culture and customers personally and not just read about them in a history or travel book. In some countries, various periods and ages from history are also re-enacted. For instance, in places like Rome and Kyoto, history is re-enacted through light and sound and even with actual people playing historical characters to provide holidaymakers with an idea about the olden days and times. Walking inside ancient palaces and ruins, and along majestic rivers can help travellers get a feel of the place and understand its historical significance. Seeing places and objects in pictures is one thing, but witnessing them personally is another.

Worries about Travelling? Move Over Them!

While travelling, the logistics is not the toughest aspect to deal with. Firstly, it is about finding the inspiration to move. One has to be brave enough to leave the comforts and predictability of everyday life and travel to an unknown world. Most people never travel for this reason; they fail to muster the courage. It is difficult for many individuals to change the status quo. Rather than being urged to make the change, some people need a major thrust for this reason.

A major part of this book will deal with the financial and practical aspects of travel. However, the first thing for a traveller to do is to never fear travelling to other places. Change is the only constant in life, and a traveller must embrace the change to usher in more experiences in their life. Many people ask whether they should travel across the globe. Should they give up their day job and start globetrotting or country hopping? Is this the best stage of their life to do so? Can they bag a good job when they come back? Will everything be in proper order even when they are gone to some other place? The bottom line is that many people want to travel and see new places, but are afraid to take the plunge and want someone to reassure them that everything will be okay.

People are generally curious about travelling and want to explore the world. Yet the fear of being unable to afford their trip, having plenty of household responsibilities, being socially inept to make friends with new people and not wanting to be lonely are a few things that hold them back. All of these doubts and fears make a person likelier to stay at home and not leave their comfort zone rather than going out and exploring the globe. For many people, home is where the heart is as it happens to be the safest place minus any challenges. They dream of that 'someday' when they will be finally able to travel, and try to look deep inside and confess that fear, is what holds them back.

What they do not realize is the fact that household problems, monetary issues and commitments are never going to go away. These often turn out to be excuses to avoid going out and experiencing life with all its new challenges and dimensions. The fear of unpredictability and alien situations holds them back.

If you have read this far, you are possibly interested enough to embark on a trip. Going on a long trip has much to do with the mind. You are probably committed already or are toying with the idea. Irrespective of what your final decision might be, you will find it heartening to know that even highly experienced travellers started their journey with doubts.

It is going to be an amazing experience

In order to get over travel fears, the first thing is to remember that many people have travelled before you, and have come back healthy and hearty. And so will many others who will do so in the future. Many people consider long-term travelling to be slightly off-beat. However, it is very popular for people from many parts of the globe.

Even young high-school graduates go for long-term travel overseas in large numbers. While you are reading this, know that millions are visiting different parts of the planet and exploring foreign countries. If millions of teens can come back home in full health after exploring the world, surely you can do so too. There is little reason to believe otherwise. There is nothing in the world that you cannot do if you believe it, and travelling is just a simple task.

Whether to the forests of the Amazon or the peak of the Everest, you can find trails of other people before you. You will not be the only one to leave home. And there will be other travellers to offer you enough comfort and support too.

Unlike Christopher Columbus, who had every reason to be scared as he was the first person to embark on an unknown voyage, you are not going to be a pioneer. You will simply have to tread the beaten path. Once you realize this, most your fears will be gone. You will be travelling with many other people who will be there to comfort, advise and guide you.

Yes, You Can!

First, you have to believe that you are competent, intelligent and coherent. If so many others can travel so many places, why can't you? Like any other person, you have the capacity to travel around the globe. Many people travel in so many countries without having anyone who knows them and manage to survive there for many days and months. Some people make lifelong friends, learning new languages and skills, falling in love and even ending up marrying and having kids on such trips.

You have to remember something simple. Nobody knows everything when stepping out for travel. However, there is something called learning along the way, and the art of travelling has much to do with being open to picking up skills and other things as you go. So many people become experts at sign language while travelling in countries with foreign languages. View it as a magnificent opportunity to learn new things and emerge as a better, more intelligent, more capable, street-smart person with many life lessons that can help you back home.

The job of media platforms is to highlight social problems, and many media houses such as BBC and CNN show the crimes and troubles of foreign countries, giving prominence to physical violence, natural disasters, religious bigotry, corruption and so on. These end up making people around the world too insecure to leave the borders of their home. One of the biggest problems why things seem so much more dangerous today is the fact that this is the age of instant communication. As soon as anything happens, 24/7 news channels and social media platforms jump in and make everything seem like national news. You end up being scared, very nervous, not knowing that such things have always occurred. It is only that people in older times did not know about them immediately, as there were fewer avenues of information.

Truth be told, many of the problems such as mugging, theft or snatching can occur in Latvia or New York as easily as in London or Namibia. It is simply not true that staying in your home country will save you from these unpleasant circumstances.

It is also important to know that many other countries have electricity, good roads and other infrastructure that people have come to expect in their own country. If you wish to visit a country, read up on the internet about it and you will find it often has enough resources to support you in your trip, such as in the form of well-equipped hotels, public and private transport, hospitals, medical facilities and medicine shops etc.

However, you have to understand that everyone in the world wants the exact things that you need. Other people in other countries also have families, jobs and responsibilities, and laugh and cry at about the same things that you do. They want to earn money, keep their family happy and live safely and with contentment. Most of them do not like trouble and wish to live and let live. Every day, travellers from different parts of the globe cross paths and do not have any hostilities or malice towards each other. You can use street-smartness in any city to get out of messy situations, and will be fine. There are parts of Los Angeles that are as unsafe as anywhere in the world. The point is, you can be unsafe in your home country as much as in any other part of the world. Once you use common sense, you will not come across any problems.

Meet as many people as you can

Being socially reclusive, introverted and tongue-tied happen to be some of the biggest factors for why people hate travelling. Many people wonder how they can strike up friendships with strangers while on a trip. Those who are not too social find it difficult to meet with random people and talk to them. Few people are actually capable of walking up to someone they have never known in their life and striking up a conversation. Initially, you might be unable to make any social contact with a stranger and keep to yourself on your first trip.

When you embark on a trip, you are likely to feel very shy in the beginning. You might be very talkative in your friend circle, but feel tongue tied when you meet a stranger. However, the more you travel, the more you meet with more people. You can learn the art of talking while on the way.

When you travel, you'll always find people to talk to. You can find many solo travellers exploring the world, and many of them being first-time trippers. Many of these people love companionship, and like to talk to new people.

These people love friendship. You may find many people coming up and randomly talking to you. Not all travellers are tongue-tied, and many of them actually like to strike up conversations with other people. While on a journey, you can find many things in common with random people and bond on common ground. It is true that most travellers are friendly and love to make friends even with random people who are strangers to them. You can be one of those friends.

Age is just a Number

Trips around the world, backpacking, budget travel etc., are not only for young people. When you go on trips, you can find many elderly people making a trip to distant countries, embarking on backpacking trips and more. You may even find very old and terminally ill patients going around the world to gather varied experiences from life, knowing that they have little time left to see the world. Many of them live on prescriptions, but still manage to travel.

You can also find many retirees setting up camps atop mountains, beautiful valleys and in forests, and even find families travelling with small children. The bottom line is that there is no age for wanderlust to kick in. You can travel at any age, and even come by travellers who are of the same age as you. There is always a first time for everything, and your first long-distance travel can happen at any age.

Planning Your Travel on a Budget

Travelling is generally believed to be an expensive hobby. However, this is just a myth and a misconception at best. With careful planning, you can reduce your travel budget as much as possible and make a trip to your favourite destination without spending a bomb. How can you do that?

Grab a piece of paper and write all your monthly expenses down. You have to write down your mortgage or rent expenses, cell phone bills, cable and internet bills, car payments as well as groceries. Add these up and get the total amount. Next, write down all the other expenses that may or may not be about the necessities, but something that is part of your life. These should include expenses related to your beverages, cigarettes, shopping, movie nights, food and more. In case you are clueless about what you actually spend money on, tracking your costs for around 2 weeks will help you to learn about the things you spend money on.

Add up the total expenses to get a complete figure every month or year. Many people have low-income jobs that allow them to just scrape by and make a living. They cut corners and try to save every penny to be able to visit their places of interest. This might take them a few months or even a few years. However, they manage to travel and do not wait for the perfect time to go on a trip. As soon as they manage their finances, they go out. Fact is, you do not need to be filthy rich to pick your things up and go on a trip.

Even if you are out of money, you can find many avenues of work overseas. It need not be only about travelling with savings. Even as you travel, you can stay in one place for some time, work in shops, hostels, hotels etc., and offer your services to earn more money. However, if that sounds like a bad idea and you hate being away from home for so long, you can just come back anytime. The choice is yours, but it is important to understand that you should never procrastinate and keep travel plans always for tomorrow when you can do so today with a little planning and fortitude.

Saving Money Smartly and Travelling More

Once you calculate travel costs for travelling around the globe or at least to your favourite destinations, it is a fact that you are likely to feel overwhelmed at the magnitude of expenses. Even a casual estimate will make you wonder how and when you will be able to save so much money. The figures might seem to be too big and scary. However, once you write down all your expenses and find out where your money goes, you are likely to understand that a few changes in your lifestyle can help you save the amount needed. With a steady job and steady payment, all you have to do is reduce your expenses to grow your savings. You should also try to find ways to save more money.

First of all, you have to make a list of all your expenses. It should include everything from movie-watching expenses to car payments and rent per month. Do not leave anything out. Unless you arrive at your total monthly expense, you will not know where you need to save and which expenses can be done away with. You will be surprised at how your money gets drained by small things without being noticeable.

✓ **Walk or Use Public Transportation:** It is expensive to travel by car, which costs a lot by way of gasoline, insurance and repairs. Therefore, try to minimize your car usage. Try to walk, or use public transport facilities such as bus, train or tram. Although it will take longer for you to reach your workplace and other places through public transport facilities, you will soon find that a car is not as necessary as you initially felt. Although this is not a practical suggestion for everyone, particularly those who live in small towns that are lacking in good public transport facilities, it can be a good idea for those living in bigger cities. Even if you are a small-town resident, you can buy a cheaper, second-hand car rather than a brand-new car. You can buy an eco-friendly, smaller car that uses up less fuel. It is also a good idea to use cycles or motorbikes as alternatives. With no repairs, insurance or gasoline expenses, you can save more money, and will also be in better shape.

✓ **Reduce Your Housing Costs:** When you reduce the costs of your housing, you can witness a significant boost in personal savings. You can invite some friends to stay as roommates or even ditch that apartment altogether. If it is possible for you, try to stay with your parents. It might not be fun to be a young 20 or 30 year old living with your mom and dad, but you can save a lot of money that way. You may even transform your living room into a spare room, and then invite a roommate. In many of the bigger cities of the US, such as the Big Apple, people often set up a folding screen through the middle area of the room and transform living rooms into studio apartments and bedrooms. Living like this might not be the best idea, but can help save a lot of money. In case your rent gobbles up hundreds of dollars every month, this type of living can halve that figure or even eliminate the entire costs for you. This will make your savings take a jump.

✓ **Exploit Credit Card Benefits:** With a travel credit card, you can get free flights, free rooms and free money. Your card can let you accumulate miles and redeem reward points on them for the purpose of free travel during your travel. You need not go on a long trip either to use up those points. You may use the points on a 2-week to 2-month long trip. A free flight is a flight that is, well, completely free of cost. The best method of saving money is undoubtedly avoiding expenses in the first place. If you start early, you can reap the maximum benefits from this practice. The moment you decide to go globetrotting, it makes sense to opt for a travel credit card that lets you accrue free points on your purchases every day.

✓ **Earn Interest on Savings Account:** While saving money, you can make it grow slightly more if you put the saved money in an online, high-yield savings account that lets you earn interest. When you do this, you will find that you have got a few hundred dollars more in your bank account.

✓ **Skip Dining Out:** Eating in a restaurant can give you a high and save the hassles of cooking up food at home, but can turn out to be a huge expense for you. Rather than spending 20 USD on dinners and at least 10 USD on lunches, you can take lunch to work in a brown bag and cook up foods to dine at home at night. You can save close to 100 USD by spending on groceries for making foods at home. You can cook for dinner one day and live off leftovers the following day. Although cooking can look boring and appear a hassle, it can be invaluable in saving you money for your trips. While you travel, it can be one of the best ways to reduce your trip expenses.

Ask any frequent traveller and you will see how much they stress being economical. Clip food coupons to reduce food expenses, watch matinee shows while movie-watching, shop when it is sale season and walk for short distances rather than taking a cab. The practice can seem 'ordinary' and none of them will give you a high, but the sacrifices will indeed be worthwhile when you find that you have saved enough cash to last during your trip abroad. Set small financial goals and they will keep you inspired on your journey to save money for your traveling expenses. You can set an annual goal to save a few thousand dollars by paying off your credit cards. Work backwards and then set smaller goals for every month. Write down your goal on a piece of paper and keep it where you will see it every day, such as next to your bedroom wall. The more you see it, the more you will be motivated to become a habitual saver. Over time, you will find the humble savings adding up to thousands in figures. You may also try some side endeavours, such as buying a few stocks of a company as an investment for the short-term. The bottom line is that the more money you can save, the more you will be able to travel with comfort. You can take part in more travel plans and activities. Once you see the rewards in a single trip, you will be motivated to make more of these sacrifices. When you sail past the Sydney Harbour or take a hike on the Swiss mountains, you will hardly ever regret missing lavish dinners or the night shows of the latest blockbusters.

Start Freelancing to Earn Extra Money

Freelancing is another useful and practical way to earn some money on the side. There are many freelancing websites, and the number is constantly growing, which makes it more convenient for you to earn some additional money beside your main income. As a freelancer, you will be a self-employed individual offering one or more services – to multiple clients or a single business or client at a time. The kind of freelancing work that you can do can vary. Today, a freelancer can be hired to perform any type of service needed by a business. These can include, but are not limited to:

- ✓ Bookkeeping, and other financial support services
- ✓ Writing, like blog posts or articles
- ✓ Publicity services, such as internet marketing or social media marketing
- ✓ Marketing services, like copywriting
- ✓ Web programming and design
- ✓ Creative services, like graphic design
- ✓ Technological support, like software support

Some popular freelancing websites that you may try are:

- www.fiverr.com
- www.konker.io
- www.seoclerks.com
- www.99designs.com

Smart Banking While Abroad

You will enjoy a smoother trip if you make a proper budget and can arrange the money prior to going out for travel. All of that begins with an account in a good bank. Keep in mind that you will have to access money from various locations across the globe multiple times every week. Naturally, it makes sense to have an account in a reputed, professional bank that has few transaction fees and can easily be worked with.

You must have already picked up tips about how to save money for your travel by reducing your everyday living costs. Next, you will learn how you can make your savings stretch as far as possible and have some extra cash to last for your trip. Most trippers make the big mistake of not making their money grow while they are out on travel.

Convenience of a Savings Account Online

Before going on a trip, you would also like to open up a money market savings account online for earning interest on the saved sum. Once you have saved quite a lot of money before going on a trip, keep in mind that the pile will soon be depleted as you hop from one location to another. However, you can take steps to ensure that not all of the money is spent.

Although you will not be working as you travel, you can still go on earning some money in the form of interest on savings. Financial websites report that the majority of conventional banks pay interest lower than 0.30%. At that measly interest rate, you will soon have to come back home without seeing much of the world. You can get significantly higher interest rates with online money market accounts, given that these do not have to pay the overhead expenses like traditional, land-based banks.

How to Reduce Penalties and Exchange Fees

You would also like to reduce the exchange penalties and conversion fees involved in using your credit card abroad. Each time your card is used overseas, your bank has to transform the foreign currency charged on the card to your local currency for billing. You will be charged a small amount, generally 3%, for the same.

Given that banks pocket a small sum for every transaction, you will always be unable to get the exchange rate that is officially listed online over currency rate websites. Unless you open up your own bank, it is impossible to get rid of these extra charges.

✓ **Change Only the Amount of Cash Needed:** It is never a good practice to change cash, particularly at the airport. Unless you find that the exchange rate going to be changed abruptly or you have much cash to get rid of, do not change money – ever. The majority of exchange bureaus lack the network to offer significant currency conversion rates. Non-banking institutions, moreover, charge high fees and commission rates for monetary exchange. Even those that do not charge such fees make money by offering an exchange rate that is even less. To put it simply, unless you are in dire need of exchanging cash, never do so – whether you are in a small town or in an airport. You should simply draw money out of the nearest ATM.

✓ **Avoid High Fees of ATMs:** It is never a good idea to use the ATMs in hostels or hotels, or even in any of the random places. Although using them is convenient, you will hate paying the high transaction fees for that ease of use. These ATMs frequently charge high fees and the conversion rates are pathetic too. Even when the fees are waived, the conversion rates are much worse when compared to that of any major financial institution or bank. You should always avoid such ATMs at all costs.

✓ **Withdraw after Taking Conversion Rates into Account:** In case you find the exchange rate to be at your advantage, for instance the foreign currency of the place of your visit has fallen against the currency of your country, you can withdraw more than needed as you will be able to get 10 times more the sum. Thus, when the exchange rate climbs again, you will manage to get some additional money without any extra work.

✓ **Do not use Airport ATMs / Exchange Bureaus:** Most of the airports are notorious with exchange rates for currencies. You may be in for a shock when you personally witness the conversion rates. You should never withdraw money from an exchange bureau. If you are in dire need of exchanging currencies, try using a bank where you can get a better deal.

✓ **Choose Local Currency Every Time:** Whenever you use a credit card overseas, you will often get the chance to be charged in the currency of your country. For instance, you will be charged in USD rather than in Euros. You should not agree to this option. The current rate of currency conversion always tends to be worse than the conversion rate offered by a bank. Choose your local currency and allow your credit card-providing agency to make the conversion. This will offer you a better exchange rate.

Choosing the Best Credit Card

Travel credit cards are vital for lessening your travel expenses and offering you greater convenience. With such credit cards, you can avoid fees, save on currency conversion rates, avail cheap flights and get more free stuff, thus getting the chance to make money. You can find plenty of travel credit cards that come with various types of rewards, from airline cards and branded hotel to general points programs. These are excellent when you use them properly and pay the balance when every month comes to an end. These are better than cash, particularly when you can avail plenty of free items and rewards from these cards.

Regardless of the duration of your trip, you need to get a special credit card for your travel purposes. There are simply too many benefits offered by travel cards to ignore them. You can accumulate more than a million points with bonuses.

Selecting a Credit Card with Top Benefits

Now that you have learned why these cards are essential for travellers, it comes down to how to choose the best one for your needs. It is important to have credit cards related to travel for two big reasons.

Firstly, you can get huge bonuses involving a minimum of 20,000 points with most of these cards just for registration. Do not register for a card that comes without such generous offers, given that without these offers you will need a long time to redeem reward points on air travel, restaurants or hotel fares or getting them in the form of cash. It is better to begin at 20,000 points than at 0.

Other than sign-up bonuses, you can get many other perks with travel credit cards. You can enjoy elite loyalty status with many of these cards. Few things are better than elite status, as you can get attractive perks without doing anything special. You can get huge travel credit worth hundreds of dollars, airport lounge access, free checked bags, priority boarding and more freebies.

Most of the reputed credit cards offer additional points to help you shop free at particular retail stores. If you opt for a credit card from a major brand, you can get additional points with that specific brand. If you have to shop, it is better that you earn something special in the process. The reward points are meant to ensure customer loyalty, so that users do not opt for a card from a competing business. Some airline credit cards offer the chance to buy clothes with their use, while others allow using their credit card for direct flight booking on their website. If you do not like to be stuck with just one agency, you may opt for a general rewards credit card such as one from American Express or Visa. You can still be able to get cashback offers as well as reward points for discounts and free flights. You will not get any of the benefits from elite status membership as offered by a credit card from a major brand. However, you can still get access to offerings from many companies and brands while also getting redeemable points for free trips.

In case you are just looking for 2 – 3 cards, do not care which brand you opt for and just need ones that offer the most value for your money, you have to use some important criteria to make the right choices.

Wonderful Advantages for an Applicant

As you must have understood, most of these cards come with huge sign-up bonuses consisting of 20,000 miles or points. Never go for a card that does not offer this, as you will waste a long time in bagging a free flight. These days, many hotel and airline-specific credit cards are offering huge sign-up bonuses between 60,000 – 100,000 points to attract more consumers to their card programs. It is important not to go with a card company that does not offer 20,000 points at sign up at least. Most of these cards offer a daily sign-up bonus of about 30,000 points.

Extra Points and Additional Retail Partnership Points

Most of the credit cards come with 1 point for every spent dollar. Reputed credit cards, however, offer additional points when customers shop at particular retailer stores or with a specific brand (if the credit cards happen to be branded). This can help in earning points much faster. If you are not content with a single point for each spent dollar and want more points per dollar that is spent, choose cards that come with the scope of retail partnerships. That way, you can earn more points faster while going for shopping. You can get thousands of additional points with some credit cards in this way.

Choosing the Right Credit Card Option

There are plenty of credit cards to pick from, but you should always try to pick the best one. The answer to which of these is the best is not easy to offer, and you should try to grab as many as possible. Why should you go for a card that comes with limits regarding the number of points you can get?

Some Excellent Credit Cards Options Are:

✓ **American Express Platinum (Global):** The last few months have witnessed major changes in the area of premium travel rewards cards. With stiffer competition, the Platinum Card from American Express comes with new features and a new bonus. Customers can earn 60,000 Membership Rewards points once they spend $5,000 USD in the initial 3 months of owning the card. You can get Uber Credit worth $200 USD and the new bonus is worth $600 USD while redeeming gift cards or points for air travel. There are 5 times more rewards on hotel stays and airlines rates.

Although the membership fee is higher at $550 USD per year, there are plenty of advantages. There are immense travel benefits such as airline credit worth $200 USD on in-flight purchases or checked bags with a specific airline. You can get access to more than a thousand airport lounges such as International American Express lounges and The

Centurion Lounge Network. There is free credit worth $100 USD for Global Entry or TSA Precheck. For every stay in Staywood, you can earn 3 Starpoints. There is upgraded hotel loyalty status in the form of Complimentary Hilton Honors Gold Status and Upgraded Rental Car Membership Status, Secondary Rental Car Collision Coverage and Boingo Wi-Fi Access. However, it cannot be used for ticket purchases.

✓ **Halifax Clarity Credit Card (United Kingdom):** Halifax Clarity credit card has minimum fees, and does not charge any commission or fees on foreign currency transactions. There are no fees charged on usage abroad or for cash withdrawals. You do not have to pay any annual fee. It converts currencies at the same rate offered by MasterCard. Even the fee that is charged on cardholders by most card providing companies at the ATM is absent here. The interest rate for cash withdrawal transactions, generally referred to as cash advance transactions, are the same for purchases. All of these factors make it one of the most low-cost options for overseas cash withdrawals and local as well as overseas credit card purchases. Keep in mind, however, that some fees are involved with surpassing the credit limit or not making any monthly repayment. The interest rate for this card is the same as for cash advances, purchases and balance transfers.

✓ **Chase Sapphire Preferred Card (USA):** For any traveller, the Chase Sapphire Preferred Card is a great option. It is available with a large sign-up bonus, bonus points on dining and travel expenses and plenty of flexibility with benefits over the usual penny for each point. The card helps you to get a point per dollar and two Chase Ultimate Rewards points for every dollar that is spent at restaurants on dining and travel. There are no foreign transaction fees on this card. As a new member holding this card, you can gain two major bonuses. Spending $4,000 USD in the initial 3 months of registration on purchases can help you earn bonus 50,000 points. Adding an authorized user during this time can also help you to get 5,000 more points. You can get the chance to redeem these points for gift cards or cash at 1 cent for each point value, and can avail a discount of 20% when you redeem the points through Chase for travel booking.

Finding Cheap Flights

With oil prices climbing up, routes being cut, fares being raised and airlines lowering capacity, availing low-cost flights is no longer a possibility. It is getting tougher by the day to get low-cost flight deals. Those sweet days, when you could fly cheap to any exotic location, are gone.

However, if you intend to travel to a city like London or even go to destinations across the planet, you would have to find a way to fly without spending a bomb. The more you pay for flying, the less you will have money to travel and the more quickly you have to come back home. The biggest complaint for travellers is always that flight rates are so high and unaffordable these days.

But things are not completely hopeless for you, and you can indeed find some easy ways to avail cheap flights to go to your chosen destination. Before discussing the specifics, you need to understand what makes flight rates cost so much more these days. If you have been a regular flier for the last few years, you must have seen how flight costs are nearly as high in the cheapest ones as in the most high-end carriers. When they are not part of a promotional offer or flash sale, ticket prices are much more these days than they used to be.

What is the explanation? First of all, the airline industry has undergone consolidation in the last few years. Due to mergers and bankruptcies, USA has just 3 major airlines while Canada has only two. Two major airlines, Lufthansa and Air France-KLM, control most of the European market. With most airlines companies going bankrupt, merging or forming partnerships, there is a lower need or incentive to reduce fares to win over customers; the number of options for them is less anyway.

Secondly, airline fuel costs have also skyrocketed in the last decade. The cost of aviation fuel was around 1.50 USD per gallon in July 2017. Contrast this with the mid-90s, when each gallon cost around 60 cents. Airline companies cannot soak up all that inflation, and their inability to adjust has continuously been passed on to the customers, thus pushing the ticket costs up. Security fees and airline taxes have soared too, and base fares have witnessed increases of hundreds of dollars.

Demand for flights also dropped in the aftermath of the World Trade Center attacks in 2001 and the 2008 recession. Airline companies, in a bid to compensate, lowered the frequency of flights as well as the total number of routes that they operated on. This helped them fly to full capacity and save money. With fuller flights, there were lower expenses and more in terms of ticket revenue. This should help you understand why people living far from big cities find the number of flights reducing and the fares soaring up. This strategy has helped airline companies fly to about maximum capacity, and keep their business up and running.

Understanding Price Variation

Flight rates reduce or climb up due to numerous factors. It is impossible to predict when exactly the ticket rates are going to come down or go up. It can only be stated by the airline company, which decides the rates. However, 4 major factors tend to influence the costs:

- Oil prices
- Demand
- Supply
- Competition

These 4 important factors constitute something known as the "load factor", which is the total % of seats sold on a specific flight. Airline agencies like to make optimal profits by filling up their planes to maximum capacity. These companies do this through proper calculation of the load factor of a plane.

A domestic flight ticket in the USA might have 10 – 15 various price points. Airlines agencies like to fill a flight up with those who pay the highest price, and obtain optimal revenue. This makes them change their costs frequently, in a bid to get more people on every flight. An airline agency will offer more low-cost tickets if the demand and the load factor are low for any flight. Ticket prices are raised in case both of these are high for any flight.

The advanced computer systems installed in the offices of airline agencies continuously compare the current trends in flight booking to previous sales histories, and prices are consequently changed depending on factors such as competitor behaviour, time of year and of course – the load factor.

You can get two flying options as a traveller. You may pay for flights while moving from one destination to another, or purchase a ticket that allows round-the-world flight trips. Each option comes with its own strengths and weaknesses, and the best one for you is one that matches your travel plans and style of travelling.

Best Options for RTW (Round-the-World) Travel

RTW (Round the World) tickets can be wonderful ways to fly across the globe. You can go wherever you like without being concerned about flight bookings. You can book every ticket in advance and frequently save money on your total individual ticket prices when you make ticket purchases in a single, big package.

Round the World tickets are Airline Alliance passes in reality. You purchase a ticket from an airline that you can use with the company as well as all its alliance partners. Each alliance lets you travel across the globe on the partners of that airline. For instance, if you book a ticket with United Airlines, it will only be usable with its partners.

The term "Airline alliance" refers to a type of partnership where seats are shared by airline companies on elite status benefits, passengers and planes. For instance, you cannot fly to any destination on Earth with United Airlines. You might have to fly from Miami to Lisbon, which is not directly connected by the airlines company. Booking that route with United Airlines will make you fly with its alliance partner TAP Portugal.

Most alliance partners for major airline companies are small carriers that do not fly too many routes over long distances.

Every alliance partner for a major airline company comes with its own rules regarding the working of RTW (Round-the-World) tickets:

The Oneworld (rtw.oneworld.com/rtw)

You can get two varied types of passes with Oneworld: Mileage based / Segment based, or Global Explorer, which is the mileage-based, more traditional RTW ticket for Oneworld. It has 3 levels of passes in economy class:

- 26,000 miles
- 29,000 miles
- 39,000 miles

There is a 34,000-mile ticket for first class and business class. Every mile, including overland segments, are counted just like in the mileage-based RTWs from Star Alliance. The rules for this pass are similar to the above.

The other pass from Oneworld is significantly better, and possibly the best RTW pass available for purchase. The

Oneworld Explorer includes the total number of continents that is visited. It does not have any maximum limit for mileage, and as many as 16 segments can be on the ticket. Given that a flight segment is regarded as a single flight, a ticket having 16 segments would be regarded as 16 flights, including any connections. If you wish to travel from New York to New Delhi, and there is a stop in London, two segments will be counted. There are no mileage limitations or overland penalties with the Oneworld Explorer. You can avail a total of 16 flights.

There are various factors as to why this is the best pass. Overhead segments, compared to other tickets, involve no mileage criteria and are not counted against customers. Each segment is counted similarly, which is one of the major advantages of the segment system, even destinations that fall out of the way and are distant to any major airport count similarly as a flight for 2 hours. Every flight is equal.

The Star Alliance
(www.staralliance.com/en/round-the-world)

The Star Alliance has an attractive Round the World Fare that can help you to travel throughout the world very easily.

It covers 191 nations, 1300 destinations and a single Round the World Fare.

The flexible Round the World Fare from The Star Alliance offers you the best bang for your buck, and you can make a trip to 98% of the countries in the world. The Star Alliance network has as many as 28 member airlines and helps connect different continents smoothly and comfortably. You can plan multi-destination trips as well as make online booking for fares with the unique Star Alliance Book and Fly tool.

Star Alliance passes depend on the total number of miles travelled. Passes are offered in increments of 29,000, 34,000 and 39,000 miles. You can roam 3 continents for 29,000 miles, 4 continents for 34,000 miles and 5-6 continents for 39,000 miles. The higher the number of miles, the more destinations you can visit and vice versa.

Every pass allows a total of 15 stopovers. A stopover is regarded as 24 hours in a single destination. You can avail the ticket in economy, business or first class. The special Starlite economy-only pass demands fares for a total of 26,000 miles, although it is restricted to up to 5 destinations. You have to pay more to increase the number of miles and the number of destinations that you can visit.

As a Star Alliance passenger, you are required to begin and end your trip in the same nation, although you do not need to do so in the same city. You may backtrack across continents, although not across oceans. In other words, you may fly from Italy to Indonesia and then Indonesia to Hong Kong, but not from Hong Kong to Italy. While crossing an ocean, you need to continue flying in your actual direction. Keep in mind that surface sectors and backtracking that are parts of the trip are taken not with a plane but over land, and all the connections count against the total mileage.

There are some conditions to consider: RTW (Round the World) tickets are available with various terms and conditions. This type of ticket has 1-year validity from the date of commencement, as it typical in all alliances, and needs you to end the trip in the country where you started journeying from. Although you do not have to end the trip in the same city, it is required that you end it in the same nation you began from.

All RTW tickets also need you to travel in a single direction, and cross the Pacific and Atlantic oceans just once. In other words, you cannot take a flight from Miami to Lisbon and then go back across the Atlantic to Rio De Janeiro, then go on journeying to Istanbul and Seoul, before finally flying back to the United States. This is backtracking and not one-way flying, and backtracking between two or more continents is not allowed in RTW tickets.

Round the World tickets also need a specific number of stopovers, with every one specified as a stay over 24 hours. You need to make at least 3 stops and up to 15 stops. Oneworld allows a maximum of 2 stopovers in the continent where the trip starts from.

Trippers can change the times and date on their ticket for free, as long as they do not change the names of destinations. If you intend to change a NYC to New Delhi flight, you can only change the time and date at no additional charge. However, in case you intend to change the destination names and fly from New Delhi to Beijing instead, you will need to pay a fee. You have to pay a fee of about $130 for any changes to your ticket destinations.

A Different Option for RTW

You can view all the destinations listed on an airline's website, and directly book the RTW tickets that they offer. However, you can come across a better deal at times by using Airtreks.com or any other third party. The mode of operation of these third parties differs a lot from airline alliances. Airtreks, rather than creating a RTW ticket, pulls individual airline tickets together depending on the lowest fares available. These do not deal only with a single airline alliance; instead, these companies tend to combine results from every airline available to come across the lowest rates, excluding budget airlines. Due to this reason, there are no rules that are generally expected from alliance tickets. You may fly to any destination in any direction of your choice. Given that there are no mileage restrictions, the overland mileage is not counted against your own flight.

The fees charged by Airtreks can be in the range of 50 – 250 USD, based on the type of airline you have chosen for travel. You will have to pay charges for changing travel and date times, as compared to airline alliance tickets. Given that conventional airline tickets are booked by Airtreks, standard airline ticket rules apply to them. Although fares are lower in cost, given that Airtreks has to follow standard airline rules, there are greater change fees. Booking with Airtreks or any other third-party booking website is a more convenient option due to more flexibility. However, nothing is 100% obtainable in travel. It is essential for you to use all available options and price your ticket out.

RTW Tickets Prices

The average cost of RTW tickets is generally in the 1,500 – 10,000 USD range, based on the number of stops, mileage and route. However, the cost of a regular 2 – 3 stop RTW ticket can be as low as 1,400 USD.

Check out a sample of RTW 5-stop ticket prices, including fees and taxes, depending on a search conducted in May 2017 to travel from 5th June 2017 to 20th July 2017:

London – Dubai – Bangkok – Singapore – Manila – Los Angeles – London

- **Airtreks:** $2,204.02 USD
- **Star Alliance:** $2,852.59 USD
- **Oneworld:** $3,225.69 USD

You can understand that booking directly with the alliances tends to involve significantly higher costs than booking via Airtreks or some other third-party agent, when you use Flight Centre (flightcentre.com) or STA Travel (statravel.com), or opt for direct booking with an airline. If you buy a Round the World ticket directly through the airlines, you should do that with the miles obtained through the methods and credit card bonuses mentioned in the following section. This will help you to reduce the expense by hundreds of dollars.

As you can understand, you have to spend a lot for these tickets. For most flyers, spending thousands of dollars for RTW trips is out of the question. It is obviously not cheap travel. In case you wish to buy a RTW ticket, you should do it on the number of miles if possible.

Round the World Tickets Main Advantages

Round the World tickets are ideal for those with a set itinerary. You can save plenty of money and time if you know about the destinations and travel dates, and do not plan to make significant changes to your trip.

However, these come with inflexible terms and conditions. Given that the dates are set already, it can be often difficult to change these. The availability is only limited. In case you want to change the times and dates, you can find that no flight is available for you. While making changes to time and date can be free of cost, as long as you fly to the same destination, other changes involve some fees. You will need to pay up to 130USD as a fee if you want to change your flight route.

Given that Round the World tickets normally have 1-year validity and you have to end your trip where you began from; you will be throwing away the last leg of the journey in case you want to travel for longer. After 1 year, any non-used flight loses its validity and you end up wasting money.

Round the World tickets can be a good option. These are the right options for those having a set time schedule and itinerary. However, these are not sensible options for those with unpredictable or variable travel plans. If you belong to the latter category of travellers, you will possibly be able to get a low-cost ticket with budget airlines, wait for ticket sales and apply flier points often. There are plenty of ways to avail cheap and free flights. Any individual who is even slightly flexible should try to avoid a RTW ticket.

Alternative Ways to Fly Inexpensively

If a RTW ticket will not satisfy your needs, you will have to find some other way to fly all around the globe. Purchasing single point-to-point tickets is one way to do so. With this way, you can save more due to various reasons. If you are not sure about your itinerary and tend to change your plans numerous times before deciding on a final destination, a

RTW ticket is not the best option. This is because you will have to pay up to 130USD to change your route every time.

You can avail many fights for free by using your travel credit cards' frequent-flier points. Travel credit cards are a great way, given that you can earn sufficient points for one or more free flights after some usual spending and the sign-up bonus. You can also try flying with budget airlines. The fares of these airlines are half the fares of big international airlines, and you cannot ignore these. Although travelling in these flights can be slightly inconvenient, you can get from point to point in a very cost-effective manner.

Many people do not like budget airlines due to the hidden charges. These airline companies, in a bid to keep fares very low, add fees that come with rigorous rules – with the hope that customers will break them and they can be charged as a consequence. Some of these need you to pay a fee or bring along boarding pass copies. You will have to check in using their website or have to pay more if your bag surpasses the weight limitation, and more. Such fees are nothing but an inconvenience. It is never suitable to charge a "convenience fee" for making payment with a credit card. However, it is a fact that being a little mindful and following these rules can help you actually avail the low fares. The cost of these tickets is much less than those from major airline companies.

Ticket prices in budget carriers can cost 3 to 4 times less, or more, depending on which airline company you are flying with. That said, you will find it more convenient to travel with point-to-point tickets.

Flexibility Can Bring Great Opportunities

Based on the oncoming holidays and the times of year or day, there can be great variations in ticket prices. You can expect to pay higher fees if your children are on a school break. The fares can climb on a holiday or when more travellers wish to fly.

If you want to take a break in the Alps in the peak of summer, when your kids have their school holidays, you have to remember that many other people also find it a convenient time for them. Airline ticket prices are the highest during such times due to a higher demand. You can save more by travelling during the off season. It is not advisable to travel to the mountains during peak winter; however, you can try vacationing there during the colder season.

You can save a lot of money if you are flexible with your times and dates. Travelling on weekdays can help you to save hundreds of dollars. Try to fly when few other travellers want or try to board a flight. You can save by flying midweek rather than boarding a plane on weekends given that most fliers travel during the weekends due to the holidays, and the cost of those flights are raised by airlines.

Flying just after a big holiday will help you to avail slightly cheaper rates. For example, Thanksgiving falls on a Thursday and people fly back home on the Tuesday or Wednesday of that week, which pushes up flight rates. Even on normal weekends, the rates for Friday and Saturday is higher as people fly back home to be with their families during the weekend. Midweek fares are less costly. Unless you are flexible about the times and dates that you wish to fly in, you will be unable to avail a low-cost flight.

You may also go to a place with the cheapest flight rates rather than travelling to a destination with a costly flight. Use the "Explore" tool offered by Kayak, where you can type in your airport name and find route costs all over the globe. Look at it to find the cheapest destination. You can also use the Google Flights tool (google.com/flights), which works better and is used by many people. If you are flexible with your vacation destination, it can be very useful for you to research about destinations and choose one that is cheaper.

Fantastic Options Using Low-Cost Airlines

You can find only a few budget airlines in America. There are dozens of airline companies in Europe and the rates have been pushed down due to competition. SpiceJet has pushed down flight rates significantly in India, and flying with this budget can be a generally good experience. These cheap carriers come with no-fare tickets and all you have to pay is the taxes. Flying with these low-cost carriers is a good substitute for flying with the major airlines companies. Although the perks are fewer, you can save a lot when it comes to ticket rates. Make sure that you check the distance of the airports from the city centre. At times, a budget carrier can be costlier during transportation to the city from the airport.

The number of LCCs (low-cost carriers) growing in number is a recent phenomenon in the aviation industry. Things do not change very quickly in the industry, especially among the bigger airlines. However, it is clearly accepted that even companies such as Air Asia hold influence today. Companies like Ryanair and EasyJet have the biggest short-haul networks. In most cases, these yield more revenues on a per share basis than larger, older rivals. Low-cost carriers, these days, are usually the most convenient ways to move between various points.

More LCCs such as WOW Air (wowair.com), Norwegian Air Shuttle (www.norwegian.com), and Air Asia (www.airasia.com) are now offering cross-continent tickets, and you can save a lot with these airlines by using their long-haul flights.

Low-Cost Airlines Advantages

Low-cost flights come with immense advantages. You could have many reasons to travel from one spot to another, such as a business trip, a honeymoon vacation or a family vacation. Irrespective of the reason however, you would always like to save on your travel costs. The higher your savings, the more money you can have for the rest of your trip. If you are a usual traveller who is adventurous but likes to travel on a budget, it will be a good decision to travel with a LCC (low-cost carrier) and save money.

These days, airline companies across the world offer cheaper flight rates to help travellers get more convenience in tripping and fly more. In the last few years, air travel has become more popular given that travellers find flights more affordable. Browsing the web will help you note a sharp fall in travel costs in the recent years. Low-cost air travel is possible today, and anyone can benefit from it.

It is natural that most people love to travel to far-off countries. Unfortunately, even a few years back, travellers had to reconsider their itinerary due to steep flight rates. These days, most airline companies have low-cost options to offer to budget fliers. It is easier to avail low-cost flights today than was possible earlier, due to many flight booking websites and engines operating nowadays. This has consequently pushed up competition between various carriers and they have reduced their flight rates due to this. As customers, you can derive advantages from the higher competition in the shape of lower flight rates.

There are many advantages of low-cost flights and the cost-effectiveness is possibly the most vital advantage. Air travel through cheap flights has become low-cost for honeymooners and vacationers as well as for frequent flyers. If you belong to any of these types of flyers, you would obviously like to reduce your flight expenses. Nothing beats the benefit of a low-priced flight ticket in these situations.

In cases where you did not have the time to make a timely air travel flight booking, you will have to pay a lot for traveling even for a short distance with a standard carrier. You can improve the situation by going for cheap airlines companies or budget carriers. If you wish to spend a vacation in an overseas destination, you can spend more on your vacation by availing cheaper flights. As a smart traveller, you should always try to save your air fare and have more fun on your holiday. If you wish to get maximum advantages out of LCCs, go online and look for low-cost flights. You can find the cheapest flights as well as compare airline fares. On specific websites, you can also find huge discounts on air travel rates. However, you should carefully check all the important details while looking for inexpensive flights. Check your flight schedule down to the last added detail. It is important not to ignore the fine print, as doing so will only cause you to land in hot soup.

Discover Different Routes Options

Other than being flexible with travel dates, you should also try to be very flexible with your chosen route. Many people take advantage of wonderful travel deals from low-cost carriers to fly to some other city. With online tools such as Google Flights and Skyscanner you can come across low-cost airlines and get more flight time.

You can save a huge amount by looking for different offers from various airline companies. This is a more workable method, as it lets you know about various routes and the deals offered by various carriers. You can save plenty of money on your flight rates, and spend more on your actual travel. You can see more places and even use the extra money for fine dining, staying in more lavish hotels and buying more things for your friends and family members back home.

Most flyers tend to use the 3 major websites: Orbitz (www.orbitz.com), Expedia (www.expedia.com) or Travelocity (www.travelocity.com), when trying to find cheap airline tickets online. However, depending on only these tools is an error. You have to explore as many websites on flight search as possible, to make sure nothing is left unexplored. Many budget carriers do not wish to pay any booking commission, and are not listed by many websites as a consequence.

It is essential that you check more than one flight booking website, given that all sites come with their negative points – such as not mentioning every airline. On major websites, you will not often find budget carriers such as Ryanair or Air Asia. There are issues in every booking website given that they do not cover all carriers and all parts of the globe equally. When you are looking for a flight ticket, you should check multiple websites – such as the ones mentioned here.

- **Kayak:** kayak.com

- **Matrix Airfare Search:** matrix.itasoftware.com

- **Google Flights:** google.com/flights

- **Skyscanner:** skyscanner.com

- **Momondo:** momondo.com

It is not established 100% whether airlines and booking websites change flight rates by tracking visitor cookies. However, it is generally well-known that if you check prices over a few days, it is better to clear your cookies every time. This can maximize your chances of a better deal. If you happen to be a student, you can find numerous discount offers available. Visit the STA Travel (statravel.com) and check its search engine. You can come across student flight tickets at flexible rates on this website as well as its agency stores. You can find numerous students codes on the site, and can get assistance in finding a low-cost ticket from many tourist agencies in backpacker regions.

Benefit of Airline Rewards Programs

You can get free companion tickets, free flights and free upgrades with airline rewards programs. Irrespective of your frequency of flying, you should register for the reward program of the airline. Try to sign up with the airline companies as these are involved in every major alliance. You can get the chance to earn many miles on partner flights. While flying, you would benefit with these companies as you can go on earning miles.

There are many other ways for you to earn miles even if you are not a frequent flier. For large retail stores, every airline company has special points offers. When you shop at these stores, you can earn up to 4 miles for every dollar that you spend. You will only need to shop online using the links present on the website of the airline, and that will immediately add additional points to your account. It is much better than directly visiting the store and earning a point per spent dollar. There are no extra costs for the products either. Many people shop at these websites just for those additional miles.

The Best Time to Buy Tickets

It is best to book a ticket 6 – 8 weeks prior to your flight. When booking in peak season, book 12 – 16 weeks ahead. Airline companies, during this period, find out whether a flight will be a sell-out and start to raise or reduce fares depending on demand. Do not wait until the last minute, given that the carrier will understand that you will possibly board the flight in case you are booking near the time of departure. Then again, you should not book too far in advance as the carrier will wait for as long as it can before publishing lower fares.

Look Out for Offers from Airlines Companies

It is a good idea to sign up for newsletters and subscriptions from search engines and airlines. This means that you will be sent updates about offers and last-minute deals. In many cases, ticket sales are only available for just one day. You will be missing out if you are not constantly browsing the web.

It is important to subscribe to mailing lists and newsletters from airlines companies. Websites such as The Flight Deal (www.theflightdeal.com), HolidayPirates (www.holidaypirates.com) and Airfare Watchdog (www.airfarewatchdog.com) are wonderful, and can offer you notifications about special offers and last-minute deals. Airlines companies that draw fares from meta search websites like Kayak and online travel companies can lead to bigger problems for customers that try to do price comparison. This can actually affect competition. However, the ability of consumers to get detailed price comparison is going to be unchanged.

The fewer numbers of carriers has made the direct channel more dominant. The airlines companies can now use the stronger market position for pushing out all competitors. Robust, independent distributors are needed for ensuring that carriers put honest fares on their official websites as well as other offerings for customers. Comparison websites use their online comparison-shopping tools to offer fare information to customers, and ensure there is some discipline and decorum in the fare system.

You should sign up for official airline newsletters, given that these often include deals that are absent on the website of the airline company. It can be triple miles on any chosen route, taking part in a contest on Facebook, completing a survey or just setting up an airline shopping toolbar in the browser. These are not high bonuses, but these add up over the course of time and take much less effort.

Pay the Best Price

Fliers who want to avail the lowest rates end up waiting for too long and paying more than needed. Flight rates tend to waver, but holding out for longer will make most people miss the lowest fares. It is naturally essential for you to decide about the amount that you wish to pay, what counts as the lowest fares for you and what you are actually comfortable paying. Wait for the rates you are willing to pay, and not the so-called "perfect" rates.

Indeed, you should have practical expectations. In case the average rate is $1,300 USD and the lowest rate available is $900 USD, you should not wait until the rate goes down to $700 USD. Flight booking is best made about 8 to12 weeks before you fly, and you should start looking for tickets about 3 months before time. This will give you enough time to find out where the rates are going. In case the rates begin to threaten to go out of your expected margin, check the seats available on the flight that you wish to board. If there are not many seats remaining, make your booking as you can be assured that the rates are not going to plummet further. When a plane is mostly booked, the carrier does not have any urge to reduce the price further. At times, you might not find a comfortable price. You should look for a seat in some other flight or carrier.

The costs of flight tickets cannot be expected to reduce in the coming months. When compared with inflation, flight rates are cheap – as has been seen throughout history. Although you cannot turn back time, you can use the tips mentioned here and hope that you avoid higher flight rates for as long as possible.

Learn From Airports' Information

A smart tip for you is to visit the website of the airport and find which carriers are flying to it. At times, you can come across small carriers not listed on Skyscanner, Momondo, Expedia, Kayak and other flight search aggregators. It is important that you browse the websites of all airlines and subscribe to their newsletters for possible offers. This will ensure that you do not miss any cheap flights from an airline that was not listed on the website.

You should use point-to-point tickets between every destination that you visit, as this can help you to be unpredictable in your travel habits. In case you have already signed up for any frequent-flier program, you may pay for flight tickets with reward miles while going. You may even use LCCs (low cost carriers) or wait for budget flights.

If you wish to save the most on flights, it is advised that you combine your frequent-flier miles with the point-to-point method to get a free flight. In case you get a travel credit card with a huge sign-up bonus, you may use the miles for availing a flight for free. With a low-cost carrier and using the above tips, you can further lower your flight expenses.

Using Discount Cards
Available To You

Youth Hostel Association (YHA)

With an YHA card, you can access more than 4,000 Hostelling International Youth Hostels in more than 80 nations across the globe. Also, whenever you reside at a Youth Hostel in Wales and England, you will pay a lower rate.

This is a hostel discount card, and is perfect for members of Youth Hostels Association or Hostelling International Association. This is actually the same organization, and which name is used to refer to it depends on the country. With this card, you can avail a 10% discount on the rates at the YHA worldwide hostel chain.

You can buy the card while checking into any hostel that is a member of YHA. The prices can differ depending on the nation where you buy the card. The cost of the card is always in the local currency. Given that anyone can be a member, it is ideal for you to become a member in the U.S itself before going on a trip. This will help you to avoid paying more for membership in other nations. Once you get the membership, you can be relaxed with the knowledge that it will have global validity.

Availing this card will also get you discounts on bus tours and train passes. Members can get the basic travel insurance. However, this insurance is not much to talk about. It covers only $1,250 USD in trip interruption and $1,400 USD in medical bills. Yet based on which country you visit, you will also get discounts for local destinations. A complete list can be found at www.hiusa.org/membership benefits.

Without question, the primary attraction of this card is the 10% off on accommodation. For further information, you can visit hihostels.com, the prime international website of the company.

International Student Identity Card (ISIC)

As a full-time school, college or university student aged 12 years or more, you can use ISIC to apply for a student card. This card lets students across the globe prove their official status as student, and access more than 150,000 student offers and discounts across the world.

The ISIC card is a student-only card, and offers discounts on transportation, tours and hostels. You can only buy it through the official website, isic.org, or via STA travel and other travel agencies. The card has no upper age limit, and you will only have to fulfil the criteria of being a full-time student. You cannot use the card as a part-time student.

With the ISIC card, you can avail 40,000 discounts in total. These can include discounts on tour deals, transportation costs, free tours, accommodation sites' booking fees and museums. As an ISIC cardholder, you can avail exclusive youth/student fares from many carriers. It is wonderful to have this amazing card, as it can help you save on various things, particularly attractions and accommodations. The card is especially great for Europe, where you can get a huge discount of 50% on museums. You can also avail discounts on online booking fees on Hostelworld and other websites, Skype credit and magazine subscriptions.

IYTC For Anyone 30 Years Old or Younger

Even if you are not a student, you can use the International Youth Travel card (IYTC). You should not be over 30 years old in order to be eligible. The card will help you to be a part of the worldwide ISIC community and gain from numerous discounts and benefits offered by the ISIC student card.

The ISIC Global Office lets individual card issuers lower the IYTC sales eligibility to 26 years or less in the market, given that many carriers offer discounts to young travellers less than 26 years of age.

Travel Costs and Saving Strategies

When you go out on a trip, you will have plenty of opportunities to spend cash. Unless you are prudent with your expenses, you will end up spending every last dollar you have. There are many attractions to spend money on while travelling, but you need not splurge on all of them. You can always find an enjoyable activity, delicious foods and wonderful beverages, so may quickly find your pockets running dry with uncontrolled spending habits.

If you want to make your money last for some time, you have to know about careful spending tips as well as ways of finding excellent travel deals. You can do this by being practical and intelligent about spending money, given that everything begins with making a proper budget.

Before travelling, you have to assign a specific budget for transportation, foods and accommodations. You have to look for the cheapest services or accommodation while you travel. Try to walk as much as possible, and avoid expensive modes of transport. Make a proper budget for foods and beverages, and save the rest to personally witness the different places, cultures, sights and sounds. There are people who have little money for travel and do not mind spending the night sleeping on a floor.

Once you make up your mind about exactly what you need on your trips, you will spend practically. With practical planning guided by needs and not temptations, you can set a realistic budget and have proper spending goals for your journey.

There will of course be those unpredictable times when you have no choice but to loosen your purse strings – such as buying a new pair of beach slippers when the ones you own get washed away by the sea or splurging on that exquisite delicacy you never knew existed. Such things are common on trips, and you have to set some money aside for these as well.

However, there are many expenses that you can actually predict and spend more carefully on. With proper research, you can understand how much every item actually costs. If you understand your habits well enough, you can spend with more prudence. You should also exercise excellent control on your spending, and make it a point not to splurge too much on foods, drinks and clothes. Keep in mind that transportation and accommodation are the main things to spend on if you are serious about visiting new places. Those who return home sooner are those who are clueless about what to spend their funds on while on the road.

The following sections will provide you with some general tips that can be used for short as well as long trips and for any type of destination. With these tips, you can stay exactly on budget. Most of this book discusses making a trip, but the following chapters have universal resonance. It hardly matters whether you are taking a week-long trip to South Africa or going on a month-long trip to Japan.

Once you have developed the approach of saving money, you can find wonderful deals for all kinds of holidays.

The Money-Saving Approach

If you wish to save money while travelling, you have to move away from the traditional mindset that travel is costly and you have to reside in 5-star hotels, go on premium tours and dine at plush restaurants to enjoy your trip.

You live economically while at home, so why should you change the habit while travelling – when everything is often extremely expensive? Living on the road is more difficult that it is at home, and you should avoid everything expensive or unaffordable. Spending more money than you earn can only bring about disastrous consequences for you. Keep in mind that the people who live at the places of your visit also live frugally, to enjoy a good lifestyle within their means. They are not enjoying gourmet dinners at 5-star hotels or buying luxurious apparel every night. Many of them have a similar lifestyle as guests to their country, and shop for groceries and cook them at home. You do not have to spend a lot every day to 'feel' the place. If you wish to make the most of your trips, live within means just like the natives of the place.

Change the perception that you can only enjoy travel if you spend much. You can absolutely enjoy even a cheap vacation. Just like you live happily at home without going overboard with your expenses, you can be happy during a trip. It is important to do some careful planning and research, and decide on travel plans only after a lot of deliberation. This will help you save a lot of money on your trip, but manage to see the exotic destinations.

Strategic Places of Stay

The biggest share of daily costs while travelling goes on accommodation. When you reduce that cost, you can have the maximum positive effect on your finances.

You can save the best on accommodation expenses when you do not need to pay for staying at all. This is possible with a hospitality exchange. With hospitality exchange services, travellers can be in close contact with locals offering a free place where they can reside without any issues. At times, it can be a couch, a bed or even a floor. This will immediately reduce your daily expenses, and you can save a lot of money at the end of every month.

A home-stay network or hospitality exchange organization can put travellers in touch with the locals in the places of their visit. When trippers get in touch with the right locals at an appropriate time, they can avail a room and stay there at a major discount or even for free. The size of the network can range from 1,000 to 100,000 depending on the country that you visit, and most of these networks are steadily growing.

There are pros as well as cons in home-stay options. You can obviously enjoy paying much less for the accommodation expenses than youth hostels or hotels, as staying comes free of cost with most networks. There is also the added benefit of being able to establish personal rapport with individuals from various social classes and cultures, and visit the destinations with the help of locals who can act as your guides. Also, while you have a pleasurable trip, the exchange of ideas and pleasantries can also make intercultural bonds and understanding stronger.

Intolerance and prejudice can be reduced as a by-product of such stays.

The cons are obvious as well. You need some extra planning before the trips, and it is expected that you try to abide by your original schedule as much as you can. Generally, there are strict limitations on how long you stay as well as the type of activities you can indulge in at such a home. While warmth from both guest and host can make the connection instantly pleasant, lack of emotion from either side can lead to an awkward relationship and its effects can mar the joy of the trip.

Such networks require users to register and create profiles on their websites, and connect with each other with the expectation that the person who enjoys staying in a foreign place will pay the courtesy forward and be a host to a guest to their place. Although it is not necessary for you to be a host in the future, most travellers like to be a host themselves sometime and welcome a guest from another place.

Hospitality Networks

Various networks are available that connect guests with hosts, and there are varying requirements for geographical spreading, number of members, restrictions for guests and participation. Two of the largest online organizations are CouchSurfing and Hospitality Club, and these have more than 300,000 members. It is not known how many active members are in various networks, given that it is not properly defined which type of user is actually classified as an active member.

For many people, signing up simply involves filling in an online form. Some websites do not need more verification while others need so. A printed book or online listing of available hosts is generally offered, at times with reviews styled like those of eBay by trippers, or vice versa. Every network that is listed operates globally.

The Hospitality Club (hospitalityclub.org)

This is a major website for hospitality exchange that was set up in July 2008. The network has around 400,000 members in over 200 different countries across the globe. It comes with free membership, and a volunteer team verifies every member.

A member has to type in their full address and name for registration, and volunteers verify the information. Potential visitors can make use of the advanced search feature or use geographical navigation of the host database. They can use a built-in message sender system, while keeping their email IDs private and block spam with the help of volunteers. Members can arrange their own conditions free of cost, for exchange to happen with HC rules that state that free hospitality exchange should be the norm. However, the rules allow members to come to a private agreement regarding the associated expenses such as phone calls and food.

Once you use the service, you can post a comment for every member that can be seen by every user. The website also consists of groups, highly active forums and travel guides in a wiki style that can be updated by members with local information. Hospitality Club also boasts the most active group that takes part in activities like huge camps and regional meetings, with attendances of more than 400 members at times. This club depends on volunteers working from across the globe with the same belief that such networks can promote peace through intercultural understanding.

The CouchSurfing Project (couchsurfing.com)

This is the biggest non-profit hospitality exchange network, consisting of hundreds of thousands of members in over 220 nations across the globe. It was established in January 2004 and offers free membership. You can optionally be a "verified member" for a one-time fee of 25USD. This can be a good way to improve safety and keep the network operational.

There is Vouching, another safe verification system, which lets a member vouch for some other person and express reliability for them. A person can be regarded as reliable if they have 3 other members vouching for them. This system was developed to let core administrators and founders vouch for others from the very beginning, and the practice is spreading quite well.

You may choose verification or vouching. However, it is good to try vouching if you are unable to transfer or even afford the fee for verification. Extended profiles are offered to ensure extended search. Once you have used the service, you may leave a comment about your guest or host as a reference. Those with very bad references, as in cases of sexual abuse or harassment, are immediately deleted from the website. You can check whether people are travelling themselves and how many messages have got responses. In June 2006, a major system failure occurred. Most of the data was recovered before long, and the whole system became functional again. The website also has a wiki page dedicated to it, with useful notes about cities, countries, safety and various other topics related to CouchSurfing.

GlobalFreeloaders (globalfreeloaders.com)

This is a web-based hospitality network. It has more than 30,000 members, as was last counted in December 2005. The network represents Australia particularly well.

Servas (joomla.servas.org)

This was set up in 1949 by an American, Bob Luitweiler, based in Denmark. The network spread very fast across the globe and has numerous travellers and hosts in over 120 different nations. Even the United Nations (UN) recognizes Servas. The organization recommends that people apply for its network program a minimum of 4 weeks before travelling. If you want to take part in Servas as a traveller, you need two reference letters and have to pay a membership fee – with the amount differing by country – as well as appear for a personal interview with a local coordinator of Servas. Once the interview is successfully completed, a letter of introduction will be handed to you that would be valid for a 1-year travel period and for a list of countries that you intend to visit.

As a traveller, you have to get in touch with prospective hosts sometime in advance. The lead time can differ, as specified by every host. You have to inform them about the estimated travel date, and might have to reconfirm this 1-2 days before visiting. You can stay for up to 2 nights and 3 days with your host. If you develop a warm relationship with them by that time, you can stay full time.

You can get sleeping space from the host, which can be a guest room at times. You might be offered meals as well to assist you with visiting the local area or city. Once the trip ends, you will be expected to report to your local Servas coordinator and offer updates to the host list, such as a change of phone number, address or any other important detail.

TravelHoo (travelhoo.com)

This is one of the oldest hospitality exchange organizations based online, and has been running since 1997. As counted in December 2005, the organization had over 6,000 members spread over as many as 114 nations, with particular representation for Asia and Eastern Europe.

Pasporta Servo (pasportaservo.org)

Its name stands for "Passport Service", and it serves as a home-stay organization for people who speak an auxiliary international language known as Esperanto. The network is funded by the World Organization of Young Esperantists called TEJO, who are known to publish an annual book containing thousands of hosts spread over 80 varied nations.

Travellers have to pay a fee for this annual list. Rooms from hosts come free, although every host has their own requirements specified for advance notice before trip, whether foods have to be provided, number of visitors, time for duration etc. Some hosts demand money for food. The host list is offered free of cost to every host.

Every traveller is expected to use Esperanto to talk to their host. Service coordination should occur in Esperanto, and even the host list is expectedly printed in Esperanto. In case you cannot use Esperanto for speaking or are not actually interested, this is not a home-stay network that you will want to sign up with.

BeWelcome (www.bewelcome.org)

The service was established in early-2007. This is a non-profit organization that was set up by former HC volunteers, and is based on the Rox Open Source Project of BeWelcome. All the features and membership come free of cost. Prior to approval, the applications of new members are checked in order to avoid fake profile or duplicate subscription issues. Once they are approved, travellers can contact hosts requesting accommodation with the help of the internal email system. This keeps the privacy of emails intact. As soon as even a single member registers a complaint, the system removes spammers.

Members of BeWelcome can post comments about others who they meet or know. If bad or negative comments are useful for other BeWelcome members, they are allowed and not removed.

The BeWelcome site consists of a forum. It also boasts traditional features for exchange of hospitality, such as groups, links between profile, a sophisticated search for hosts, Google Maps and contacts management. Members can also have different versions of their own profile translated in more than one language, which can assist them in finding a host in an overseas location.

Organic Farms Worldwide (wwoof.net)

Do you wish to live in organic farms across the globe and learn how organic farming is done? Do you want to share your own life with other people who have the same mindset as yours? A global movement, WWOOF connects growers and organic farmers with volunteers and promotes academic and cultural experiences depending on trust. There is no exchange of money involved. This helps lay the basis for a global, sustainable community.

You are supposed to live as a WWOOFer or volunteer along with your host, and assist them with everyday operations and learn what the life of an organic farmer is like. When you are a farm host, you can welcome visitors from abroad or your own nation to your home and give them a chance to be unified with your place and offer support to your organic movement.

WWOOF or World-Wide Opportunities on Organic Farms has hosts in as many as 99 nations across the globe. It is a hospitality service that is run by an informal group of national organizations that encourage and assist home-stays on various organic farms. While the US has 2,052 hosts, New Zealand has 2,340 hosts, the UK has 688 WWOOF hosts and Australia has 2,600 hosts. All WWOOF hosts are not encompassed by any central organization or list. When it comes to an international WWOOF membership, there is actually none. Every recognized WWOOF nation's organizations attempt to maintain the same standards and they work closely to advance the objectives of WWOOF.

The organization tries to offer first-hand experience to volunteers, often referred to as woofers or WWOOFers, in ecologically safe and organic growing techniques, and contribute to the organic movement. This helps volunteers experience what life is like in some other country or in a rural backdrop. Typically, WWOOF volunteers do not get any money for the services that they render. Hosts offer them lodging, food and a chance to learn organic farming in exchange for help with gardening or farming activities. Visitors can stay with hosts for anywhere between a few days to a few years. The workdays range between 5 and 6 hours on an average, and participants get an opportunity to connect with woofers from various other nations. WWOOF farms consist of private gardens via commercial farms, allotments and smallholdings. Farms enlist with their respective national organizations to become hosts for

WWOOF. Farms located in countries without any WWOOF organization can get enlisted with WWOOF independents.

Getting a Hotel Deal

Many websites offer deals on rooms at the last minute or allow customers to let know their comfortable price point, which allows as much as 60% savings on the usual rate. The sites include:

- **Hotwire (hotwire.com)**

- **Priceline (priceline.com)**

- **Hotel Tonight (hoteltonight.com)**

- **Last Minute (lastminute.com)**

- **LateRooms (laterooms.com)**

Websites like Hotwire and Priceline are among the best as these have the lowest rates and the biggest inventories. Searches on other sites do not throw up so many results.

Priceline and Hotwire have 2 booking sections. One of these allows you to bid on discounted hotels while another allows bidding on hotel rooms. Go to the auction side of the site and pick your city, the location you wish to stay in, the class of service (1-star, 2-star, 3-star etc.) that you wish to enjoy, along with your bid price.

For instance, if you need a 3-star New York hotel at 150USD, you have to place a bid. In case Priceline finds a suitable match, you can book into an appropriate hotel in that class. Once you pay the money, you can get the deal. This is a blind auction, as you cannot find out the same before payment. In case no match is found, you can search with a different bid once more – and as many as 3 times like this. After this, you need to try again in 24 hours or search again in other areas.

A similar system, although slightly different, is used by Hotwire. Rather than allowing you to bid on a hotel, you can get a price quote for a hotel with "Hotwire Hot Deals" in the city or area that you want. Until you book, you cannot find out what you exactly will get from a list of hotels in a class that you are shown. Although there are risks in booking for a hotel you have not heard of, there is a golden prospect of having 60% shaved off the listed price.

You can have more profitable bids with Better Bidding (betterbidding.com), a forum where users can post about their latest successful bids as well as the most current deals on hotels. You can find out about the going rate, and thus will not end up overbidding or paying more than another person. The forum lets you book a hotel at cheap rates even during peak holiday seasons, such as Christmas. You have to be a member to make posts on Better Bidding, although no membership is necessary to view the bids placed by other people. Bid on Travel (bidontravel.com) and Bidding on Travel (biddingtraveler.com) are two other websites that allow the same, although these focus exclusively on Priceline.

The other side of Hotwire and Priceline lets you book hotels at discounted rates, just like on any other website for hotel booking. You will not gain the huge savings possible through bidding, although you can find out where you will be staying. You can find the Hotwire and Priceline rates to be similar to the popular Hotels.com (hotels.com) as well as the aforementioned booking websites.

Every hotel rates online search engine is different, similar to the airline websites mentioned in Part One. Although Hotwire and Priceline have good rates and a huge inventory, Last Minute and LateRooms also have an appreciable inventory that focuses on Europe. You should check quite a few airline sites and check prices at least 2 times on a minimum of 3 websites before conducting a purchase.

Hostel Stays

One of the cheapest paid accommodations on the planet, a hostel mainly offers shared rooms to travellers who need low-cost rooms. At times, private rooms are offered as well. Shared rooms are mostly dormitories with 4 – 20 beds. The more the number of beds, the lower the room costs are.

The rates of hostels are around 1/3rd of those of hotels. In London, a cheap hotel costs around £50 GBP, whereas a hostel room will cost you about £23 GBP.

Hostels in America are notorious. These are generally thought of as stinky and dirty, unsafe and with poor beds, much like Hollywood movies like Hostel show them to be. The reality, however, is something different. You can enjoy comfortable beds, bed lights for night reading, individual lockers on rent to keep your things safe, bars, hot showers, free breakfast etc. Most hostels have offer Wi-Fi, and common rooms with kitchens and pool tables, as well as some type of community space. You can also get assistance with organizing and booking trips.

Although dirty hostels exist much like dirty hotels, you have to understand that what you are offered depends on how much you pay. However, when you stay at a hostel that is highly rated, you can expect a generally comfortable and clean place.

If you want to save on accommodation costs, it is best to live in a hostel and pay for the stay. Although hostels do not come free like house-sitting or CouchSurfing, if you are a single individual in a major city such as Paris, living in a hostel will cost you a fraction of living in a hotel. Rooms in dorms are cheaper than those in hotels.

You may use Hostelbookers (hostelbookers.com) and Hostelworld (hostelworld.com), two of the biggest hostel booking websites. Hostelworld has a more user-friendly interface for booking, and a larger inventory of hostels.

House-Sitting Practices

House-sitting refers to the practice of homeowner or landlord leaving their home for some time, leaving its safety and responsibility in the hands of one or multiple house-sitters. As per a mutual agreement, the house-sitters are supposed to live in the home free of rent while they assume all the homeowner's tasks such as readdressing the mail, preventing the entry of trespassers into the property, carrying out general maintenance – such as that of AC systems, lawns and pools, looking after pets etc. Overall, the house-sitter has to ensure that everything goes on as smoothly as when the owner was undertaking all the responsibilities. Below are some of the best house-sitting resources:

The Caretaker Gazette (caretaker.org)

This is a print and online newsletter that was established in 1983. It publishes a job listing in the style of classified advertisements. This is the largest and oldest house-sitting agency. The online membership subscriptions cost only 69.95 USD for 3 years, 49.95 USD for 2 years and 29.95 USD for 1 year.

Mind My House (mindmyhouse.com)

This is a smaller website with a lower membership fee of just 20USD for joining and a more inviting user interface. It has a very good inventory in Australia, United States and Europe.

House Carers (housecarers.com)

This is one of the biggest house-sitting websites online, having a sizeable inventory in New Zealand and Australia. This site has been running for over 10 years. You can begin with a free limited membership. A full membership, which lets you apply for house-sitting and respond to messages, costs 50 USD annually.

You have to be committed to house-sitting for the long-term, about 1 month or even more. These are perfect for travellers who wish to stay in a particular spot for a longer duration.

In case you are interested in house-sitting, it is essential to conduct some research and make sure that your home is in your desired spot and you know all the responsibilities clearly. It is important to have a legal agreement, where your responsibilities are clearly mentioned.

Renting Apartments on Airbnb (www.airbnb.com)

Apartment rentals are a major option for single or apartment rentals who do not like living in hostels. These are furnished apartments that are owned and maintained by some other person, and you have to rent it similar to a hotel room.

Owners list an additional property, room or couch, with the intention to earn from it.

A hospitality service and marketplace based online, Airbnb lets people rent or lease short-term lodging, which includes hotel rooms, hostel beds, homestays, apartment rentals or vacation rentals. No lodging is owned by this company. Instead, it simply acts as a broker and obtains commissions or a part of the service charges from hosts as well as guests with each booking. The agency has listings consisting of more than 3,000,000 lodging in 65,000 cities spread across 191 nations. The host sets the lodging cost. Airbnb, similar to any other hospitality service, acts as a type of collaborative sharing and consumption.

Both travellers and hosts can benefit from Airbnb. Hosts can meet many travellers from across the globe while they make some additional money. Travellers, for their part, can find accommodation for a fraction of what hotel rooms cost. Many trippers also love the different experience of staying in an accommodation that is very unlike typical hotel rooms. Numerous travellers enjoy the personalized service, both from the Airbnb customer service and the hosts.

Although the customer base of Airbnb mainly comprises of budget travellers, many business travellers are attracted as well. This is partly due to the cost factor, and businesses find that they can save on retreats, conferences and meetings. There is also the attraction of living in a home-like ambience, which means the savings are not the only factor. These properties let travellers choose a comfortable, unique and more informal space over the standard hotel experience. Tourists, whether budget-conscious vacationers or business travellers, can also get the chance to meet and stay with other people. However, travellers might be concerned that hosts might not attend to their needs and the property might be quite different from the description. However, both guests and hosts can reduce the risks through the use of various Airbnb tools.

Food and Beverages Savings

Food is the next major expense after accommodation costs. You have to eat something. Although you may survive on canned food if you so wish, you would probably enjoy tasting local cuisine. You can try the following methods:

Save with Free Breakfast

Staying at a guest house or hotel with breakfast included will leave you with more to spend on your dinner and lunch. You can also eat more during breakfast to keep yourself filled for longer. This will ensure that you do not have to purchase plenty of snacks to last all day long.

Plan a Big Meal Daily

If you want to save, be smart and plan your meals out. If you wish to try out a costlier eatery, make it your big meal for the day. Eat something cheaper and lighter for the other meals. This can be done often. You can also buy some smaller items at a bakery or grocery store to satisfy your appetite as well as budget for a bigger meal.

In case you prefer to have a big lunch, spend on the same but keep your dinner light. If you follow this plan, it will make a major difference to your budget.

Avoid Hotel Restaurants and Tourist Zones

If you intend to use the entire day to visit historical spots or museums, do not starve yourself. Eat before leaving, so that you do not have to purchase overpriced foods from tourist destinations. For example, buying even a sandwich from any shop near the Eiffel Tower will cost much more than from a side street. Restaurants inside hotels or in-house cafes in museums charge much more than those on the street.

In case you are very hungry and want to have a bite at the popular restaurant close to a tourist spot, you have to move just a few blocks farther to find the same foods being offered at half price or even lower. You will find that the further you move away from a tourist attraction, the better and cheaper the foods are. In high-traffic tourist spots, restaurants do not need to stress on quality as most visitors tend to visit just once while going. They do not need to depend on repeat visitors, and you can find that reflected on the menu.

Foods are generally costlier and inferior in hotel restaurants, particularly at chain hotels. Although a few hotels have amazing restaurants that offer delicious foods worth the money, it is best that you check one out after conducting proper research.

Lunch Deal or "Plate of the Day"

You can eat at lunch-special rates on dinner menus in various parts of the globe, particularly in Europe. The "plate of the day" is undoubtedly the most wonderful bargain. You cannot find any website that offers information about lunch specials from every restaurant on the planet. The deals differ across cities, states and countries. You may either hop across restaurants in the city, ask your hotel/hostel staff, or enquire at the local tourist office to know which restaurants offer lunch specials. You can find worthwhile information regarding deals on foods.

The internet, similar to hospitality networks, help connect travellers with local people in different countries who are ready to play hosts and treat them to a nice dinner party – offering them the chance to relish mouth-watering local cuisine.

Availing Discounts on
Activities and Attractions

Would you like to pay the full rate for a tour or spend 20 USD each time you walk into a museum? At such prices, you will spend all your money before long and can only see the museum from a distance. Fortunately, there is no need to pay the whole price every time. Find out how this is possible.

Local Tourism Offices and Tourism Cards

As a traveller, you should use your tourism card frequently. London Tourism, Rome Tourism, Barcelona Tourism and many other local tourism offices issue tourism cards to travellers that help them enter all the local restaurants, go on tours and visit every attraction at cheap rates. You need to pay a one-time fee with such cards to gain free entry as well as avail huge discounts at chosen shopping malls and restaurants. You can avail major discounts on tours and attractions within a city and also get free local public transport. These cards are generally valid for 1 – 7 days. Day 1 starts when you use the card for the first time, whether for a train or a museum.

Most tourists never consider these special cards or passes as these are not promoted or advertised very well. It is only extensive travellers who "somehow" come to know about these. Buying a tourist card, as a matter of fact, helps save a lot of money if you intend to go on much sightseeing.

Discount Cards Advantages

With discount cards, you can avail major deals at local attractions and museums, as well as on various activities across the globe. It is essential for you to avail these cards, given that most of the tourist attractions allow their use. You can use these cards to shave 50% off your standard admission fees, which can help you earn significant savings during the entire trip.

You should also make it a point to check out the local tourist office. These generally issue discount cards for the most visited tourist destinations and keep you abreast of deals offered at specific times. When you visit a tourist office, take a few advertisement brochures offering discounts. Most of these, particularly the maps, have advertisements for meals and tours available on discounts.

You can come across local tourist offices close to the city centre, at major railway stations or at airports, where the major tourist spots are located. Whenever you travel to a new city, check out the information kiosk at the transport hub that you come to. Ask about the location of the tourism office, and you can get guidance from the staff present there.

Travel Insurance is a Must

The idea of spending a large amount of money on something that you may never use may seem a little crazy. You may have travelled a lot and have had awesome experiences every time, so it's natural to dismiss the idea of purchasing travel insurance. However, you may not be so lucky every time. Whether you are travelling domestically or internationally, taking travel insurance is highly recommended. Travellers must understand that without travel insurance, an emergency evacuation can cost more than USD $100,000.

There are some highly trusted companies offering travel insurance; a few options to consider are:

- **Travel Insurance for Coverage Options:** Travelex (www.travelexinsurance.com) and Travel Guard (www.travelguard.com).

- **Low-priced Travel Insurance:** Seven Corners (www.sevencorners.com) and World Nomads (ww.worldnomads.com).

- **Travel Medical Insurance:** IMG (www.imglobal.com) and HTH Worldwide (ww.hthtravelinsurance.com).

Travel insurance is actually a legal contract created by lawyers. It is important that you read and understand the fine print and description of coverage thoroughly. Be sure to ask questions if you don't understand the policy wording. Travel insurance normally ends soon after you arrive home, so if your policy is for a year and you come home after 2 or 3 months, you won't be eligible for a refund for the unused portion of the policy. However, some policies do allow you to resume travel using the same policy.

Buying travel insurance is often considered an unnecessary expense, even though it can save you a fortune, should something go wrong while you are abroad. From providing 24-hour emergency assistance to covering the expense of accidents, travel insurance is a must-have for frequent travellers.

Travel
By Region

North America

The continent of North America falls in the Northern Hemisphere, and almost all of it is in the Western Hemisphere. You may also regard it as a northern subcontinent of America, bordered by the Arctic Ocean to the north, by the Caribbean Sea and South America to the south-east, by the Pacific Ocean to the south and west, and by the Atlantic Ocean to the east.

North America has a total area of around 9,540,000 square miles (or 24,709,000 square kilometres), which means around 16.5% of the entire land area of the earth and 4.8% of the full land area. After Asia and Africa, North America happens to be the 3rd largest continent in terms of area. By population, it ranks 4th after Asia at the top followed by Africa and Europe. The population of North America was estimated to be around 565 million from 23 independent states, or around 7.5% of the global population when the population from adjoining islands such as the Caribbean is also taken into account.

Canada Travel

Canada is the 2nd largest nation on the planet, and you have to spend quite a few days to explore even a small part of the country completely.

Canada by Plane

If you travel to the country during a gap year, it is best to travel by air as you will have to travel very large distances to reach destinations located very far away from each other. In Canada, there are quite a few varied options as far as airline carriers are concerned.

- WestJet is a wonderful travel option from big city centres, and offers flights at very affordable rates.

- AirCanada is the national airline company, and a Star Alliance member with the widest network. When compared to other Canadian carriers, it offers flights more often.

The flight rates in Canada are costlier than those of other nations such as China, Australia and the US, given that the policies of the Canadian government are protectionist. At times, flying in the US can be lower in cost than a domestic direct flight.

Most of the major air terminals are well connected to public transportation facilities. Generally, buses run on 5-15 minute schedules or even less in big Canadian cities. Services can significantly differ or be absent during weekends or at night, particularly in areas out of city centres. If you want to make a trip to the city centres directly from the air terminal, right after landing, you have to take a public transport system in most cities. In cities like Ottawa, Winnipeg, Montreal and Vancouver, you have to think about other options such as shuttles and taxis.

List of Low-cost Airlines in Canada:

- ✓ Air Canada Rouge: flyrouge.com
- ✓ Sunwing Airlines: www.flysunwing.com
- ✓ WestJet: www.westjet.com
- ✓ Canada Jetlines: www.jetlines.ca
- ✓ NewLeaf: gonewleaf.ca

Hitchhiking in Canada

This is one of the most low-cost ways to travel in Canada. Hitchhiking is traditionally defined as wooing drivers by standing at the edge of any road, facing cars coming towards you, with a thumb extended or pointing upwards.

There are many types of people you can come across in Canada, as in other countries. There are risks of facing dangers and annoyances along the way, which makes many drivers hesitant to give lifts to hitchhikers these days. However, it feels great to get a lift after standing and waiting for a long while. Those who give lifts to hitchhikers often happen to be extremely friendly in nature. Of course, it is a fact that hitchhikers are in danger of being picked up by drivers who are malicious or even dangerous.

However, when you are planning hitchhiking in Canada during the winter you have to consider more risks. The temperature frequently drops below -30° C and you need not pass over 15 minutes outside. It is essential for you to wear proper gear and take enough care to avoid standing outside in the freezing cold.

The roads can be frozen or narrowed due to snowbanks during the winter season. Cars often find it difficult to stop by and safely pull over in order to pick up hitchhikers.

Drivers avoid doing that as the risks of accidents are very high, and there can be risks of skidding or toppling over, in which case drivers need to bear the entire burden of vehicle insurance. It is very important for you to find a good hitching spot where drivers can enjoy better visibility and can pull over safely.

Hitchhiking through air transport

You can easily travel from one place to another free of cost in Canada when you hitchhike by air. There are float planes, small planes which fly in northern Canada from one lake to another. You can fly free of cost from different airports by accessing pilots who generally deliver air mail from one lake to another. It can be tough to find such pilots, but like many others you can easily talk to a few when they are not flying and resting while grabbing a drink or a quick meal. At times, you can meet them in airports when they walk in and out of the weather offices of Environment Canada.

Bus Travel Around Canada

Many tourists commonly take buses to travel between the major cities of Canada. The most inhabited service plies in the corridor of the Windsor-Quebec City, which includes Ottawa, Toronto and Montreal.

The major bus companies include Canada (www.coachcanada.com), Greyhound (www.greyhound.com), Orleans Express (www.orleansexpress.com) and Megabus (ca.megabus.com), which offer frequent schedules and can be availed at reasonable rates.

- Toronto – Montreal routes – From Megabus and Coach Canada.

- Toronto - Ottawa route; Montreal - Ottawa route; Toronto - southwestern Ontario route, Toronto – west of the major corridor route – Greyhound

- Montreal-Quebec City route; Montreal – East Corridor (via Acadian) - Orleans Express

The competition is very little between these companies, given that just one company operates on one route. American bus companies generally operate on the routes to Niagara Falls passing to the US and New York.

Bus tours through the prairies can be arduous and long, and the routes are often more than 48-hours long – with only a few stops to allow travellers to take rest and eat food.

It is generally much safer to travel by Intercity buses. However, it is essential to be alert and always keep an eye on your belongings. Municipal governments generally operate the bus routes, with stations to be found in areas with the most population in every city.

Canada by car

Tourists, particularly solo tourists, love car rentals – although the charges can be quite high. When compared to other transportation methods, group travel in a car can be a better alternative – although these come with some limitations:

- No rentals for manual transmission can be found at all.

- Driving is generally allowed only on paved roads, and off-roading is not allowed here.

- No limit on km in the province in your rental. Number of km can be highly reduced out of the province, generally under 200 kilometres daily with most agencies.

- Higher surcharges for dropping the vehicle at some other area than the pickup location.

It is most convenient to use a car to go around Canada, other than in urban centres such as Vancouver, Toronto and Montreal (where it is more practical to take public transport facilities) and areas without any paved roads.

The price of gasoline generally ranges between 1.20 and 1.35 USD per litre in the primary Canadian regions, around 50% higher than prices in the U.S. The prices can rise in the travel season in March during the summer season.

You should try to avoid speeding and running red lights, as anywhere, given that you can be penalized for these. Your rental agency might charge you additional fees for doing so.

Canada Train Travel

Touring Canada via train is obviously a good option, given that various locations can be accessed. However, there is often lower convenience and higher expenses than with various other methods of transportation, such as buses and flights. However, train rides allow you to enjoy plenty of sights and sceneries, such as during the 3-day train ride through the Rocky Mountains and the prairies in the Toronto – Vancouver route. You can avail a domed car in this particular route, and enjoy panoramic sights of some of the loveliest landscapes of Canada.

The primary rail service in Canada is the VIA Rail (www.viarail.ca). You can enjoy much lower air travel rates with an advance booking.

Ride sharing in Canada

If you wish to travel to a place that is not on the routes generally serviced in Canada, you can ask around in the hostel or hotel you are staying in and find out whether anyone would like to share rides with you. By doing so you will be able to share fuel costs as well as make new friends.

Top Places to Visit in Canada

Canada has become a popular travel spot due to its inviting ambience, amazing sceneries and wonderful cities. It is the largest nation in North America, and comprises of the Arctic tundra, vast prairies or grassy plains, virgin forests, spectacular coastlines and huge mountains. Most of the inhabitants are French and British in origin. However, Canada is a country boasting a multicultural community. Find out about some of the best tourist spots that you can check out in Canada:

- **Toronto**

    This is the capital city of Ontario, and happens to be the Canadian city with the most population. It is one of the largest cities in North America. Toronto has many ethnic districts, such as Little Italy, Chinatown and Little India. Indeed, it is one of the most culturally diverse cities on the planet. The main tourist attractions of the city include the majestic architectural wonders such as the Casa Loma fairy-tale castle and the iconic CN Tower. The Toronto Islands are also very popular, and have quite a few beaches where you can take part in many outdoor activities.

- **Quebec City**

    This is located in eastern Canada and is the capital region of the Quebec province. Its French language, heritage and architecture make it look more like a wonderful village of Europe. The Vieux Quebec is the heritage district of the city and is set atop a hill that overlooks the St. Lawrence River.

Take a walk along the Old City's cobblestone streets, and you can come across various attractions such as the Place-Royale and the Citadel. It is the Place-Royale where the first ever North American-French settlement was founded by Samuel de Camplain, the famous explorer.

The elegant Chateau Frontenac is the most photographed North American hotel that offers the option of tours without any option for overnight staying. It is an iconic area of the city.

- **Whistler**

  The Whistler resort happens to be the most popular and the largest North American alpine ski destination, due to its wonderful mountains, Blackcomb and Whistler. It is situated in British Columbia, in the Coast Mountains. It is located 2 hours away from Vancouver along the Sea-to-Sky Highway, the most beautiful drive in Canada. Three beautiful villages, Upper Village, Creekside Village and Whistler Village, are located at the base of the Blackcomb and Whistler mountains. Travellers are transported to the mountains from the villages by the Peak 2 Peak gondola.

- **Montreal**

This is the biggest Canadian city after Toronto, and serves as the financial and cultural capital of the Quebec province. It has the largest French-speaking community outside of Paris in France. It serves as a highly populated metropolis that consists of various distinctive neighbourhoods, an entertainment district, an iconic quarter and a downtown district. Some of the major attractions in Montreal include various family attractions such as water parks and theme parks, ancient buildings in Old Montreal, Olympic Tower and other skyscrapers in downtown.

- **Banff National Park**

This is the first national park in Canada, situated in the Alberta province. It is also one of the most visited and largest national parks in the country. Throughout the year, the diversity of wildlife and amazing sceneries in the park draw numerous tourists along the Trans-Canada Highway passing through this park. The Banff National Parks have many wild animals, including animals such as bighorn sheep, bison, grizzly bears, black bears, moose and wolves. There are bald eagles as well.

- **Niagara Falls, Ontario**

  The Niagara Falls consists of a breath-taking waterfall series, located on the border of New York in the U.S and Ontario in Canada. The Horseshoe Falls is on the side of Ontario and consists of the biggest attractions as well as offering the best sights. The region immediately adjoining the Falls is a prominent tourist area, consisting of high-rise hotels, casinos, souvenir shops, restaurants and observation towers. The Ontario side is one of the best vantage points to get the greatest views of the Niagara Falls. Stand in the Queen Victoria Park, and you will see an illuminated Falls. During the summer months, you can find fireworks being displayed during the night.

- **Vancouver and Vancouver Island**

  Vancouver is located between the Pacific Ocean in British Columbia and the Coast Mountains, and is popular for its amazing landscapes. You can go snow skiing in the mountains, enjoy rollerblade trips through beautiful parks or try swimming in the ocean. It is the 3rd largest metro in Canada and is one of the most famous tourist destinations in Canada. The Stanley Park is the chief attraction of Vancouver, and covers a vast area comprising of green spaces, woodlands and gardens. The wide array of shops in the vibrant Chinatown and the mouth-watering food market in the Granville Island are some other attractive sites in the city.

The Vancouver Island is the largest island in North America, located off the West Coast. It owes its name to George Vancouver, the famous British explorer. It is situated across from the Washington State, and can be accessed in the following ways:

- From Vancouver on mainland British Columbia

- From Port Angeles on the Olympic Peninsula of the state

- Through the San Juan Islands via Anacortes

Vancouver Island is popular for its northern wilderness, Tofino – the surf town, the stunning Butchart Gardens, the old-time city of Victoria. You can board a ferry to Alaska or to Prince Rupert from this northern wilderness.

- **Ottawa**

  It is situated at the meeting point of the rivers Rideau, Ottawa and Gatineau in the south-east region of Ontario. It is the capital city of Canada, and consists of many federal, financial and commercial establishments. You can visit Parliament Hill, the government establishment that sees the ceremonial Changing of the Guard occurring every day during the summer. The Rideau Canal, which runs exactly through the middle of the city, is the main attraction of Ottawa. During the winter months, it transforms into the biggest ice-skating rink on the planet.

- **Calgary**

  Located between the foothills of the Canadian Rockies and the Canadian Prairies, Calgary is the largest city in Alberta. After the discovery of oil during the early 1900s, the city transformed into the largest metro in Canada. Thousands of travellers flock to the city every year to witness the Calgary Stampede, the rodeo event held here that has become globally famous. This is an Old West celebration organized for more than 10 days in the month of July. It is a celebration witnessing delicious foods, amazing crafts, competitions, parades, chuck wagon races and rodeos.

United States of America

The United States of America is the official name for America and is often abbreviated as U.S.A. or U.S. It is a nation in North America, and a federal republic consisting of 50 states. Its variety is possibly the most defining attribute of the United States. Its physical area spans everything from moist rainforests, rugged mountain peak and the Arctic to the arid desert, flat prairie and the subtropical area. The entire population in the U.S might be large by global standards. However, its overall population density happens to be low when compared to other highly populated countries. The nation witnesses some of the largest concentrations on Earth in its urban areas, yet there are many vast areas that are almost uninhabited.

Travelling across the United States

If you are prepared to travel over 5,000 miles across the U.S.A., you will have multiple options for the trip. The options include driving your own vehicle or travelling by bus, train or plane. The most cost-effective and convenient option for you obviously depends on the number of people in your group and the total number of stops you would like to have. It also depends on which spots you would like to start and end your travels with. However, when it comes to comparing, you have to compare the expenses of travelling to Seattle, Washington from New York City.

It can be very costly to travel in the U.S, and when you exhaust your budget you'll have to change your travel plans. This is not a cheap option. However, if you are smart and are adventurous enough to travel with some inconvenience in your stride, you can make a trip across the U.S. at an affordable cost.

Is flying the best and most cost-effective travel option?

Although it might appear to be an improbable proposition, flying can indeed be the most cost-effective option for travel – particularly when you are flying only one way. These days, flying from Miami (MIA) to Los Angeles (LAX) can cost you under $150 USD. Flying happens to be the quickest way to move across destinations. However, you might not like this option if you wish to halt at different stops and view the sights. Also, keep in mind that flight rates can significantly differ, depending on your starting point, time of the year and baggage fees. You should be prepared to pay much more if you are not starting your journey from a location with close proximity to a big airport.

List of Low-cost Airlines in the USA:

✓ **Allegiant Air** (www.allegiantair.com)

✓ **Frontier Airlines** (www.flyfrontier.com)

✓ **JetBlue** (www.jetblue.com)

✓ **Southwest Airlines** (www.southwest.com)

✓ **Spirit Airlines** (www.spirit.com)

✓ **Sun Country Airlines** (www.suncountry.com)

✓ **Virgin America** (www.virginamerica.com)

Cheap Airport Options in USA

The US Airport Affordability Index lists 101 popular US airports and ranks them according to average flight costs.

The cheapest US airport is Long Beach Airport, having an average flight rate of $210 USD. For a short time, the airport lost its crown, although it topped the list twice previously.

The Dallas/Fort Worth Airport comes in second position, with an average flight rate of $215 USD. It has moved up 27 spots in the list to reach this position.

By contrast, you would probably like to stay away from flying to Honolulu, Hawaii. This airport in America is still the costliest air terminal in the country, with average ticket rates being $650 USD. It shows a standard trend: an overall reduction in flight costs is one of the major inferences to draw from the index.

The index also reflects the fact that the location might not necessarily matter, with famous air terminals such as LaGuardia in NYC beating those like McGhee Tyson that are less frequented.

Top 10 cheapest airports in the United States:

- ✓ Long Beach (Daugherty Field), CA (LGB)

- ✓ Dallas/Fort Worth International, TX (DFW)

- ✓ LaGuardia, NY (LGA)

- ✓ General Mitchell International, WI (MKE)

- ✓ Minneapolis-St Paul International, MN (MSP)

- ✓ Denver International, CO (DEN)

- ✓ Fort Lauderdale/Hollywood International, FL (FLL)

- ✓ Chicago-O'Hare International, IL (ORD)

- ✓ Atlanta International, GA (ATL)

- ✓ Philadelphia International, PA (PHL)

Bus Travel in the United States

Bus travel is the travel option that comes next in terms of affordability. In almost every midsized and major town in the US, including many of the smaller ones, you can come across Greyhound buses (www.greyhound.com) stops. You have to spend about $320 USD to travel long distances, such as New York City – Seattle, with a bus. The rides are almost 3-days long, so you'll have plenty of time to enjoy the amazing sights through your bus window. Given that you have to spend much time in a small space, you need to take along packed food or purchase meals whenever your bus comes to a halt. You may even arrange a stop off for 1 – 2 days in any of the cities with a Greyhound stop and then board the following bus. However, this means you have to opt for more expensive accommodation options such as booking campgrounds or hotels.

BoltBus (www.boltbus.com) is the low-cost express city-to-city service from Greyhound, which rivals Megabus (us.megabus.com) on the eastern US coast for the big cities. It is thus possible for you to book trips for a surprisingly low 1 USD with both companies. Greyhound set up the Yo! Bus service in collaboration with Peter Pan Bus (peterpanbus.com), to compete with the basic and low-cost Chinatown Bus Services.

Jefferson Lines (www.jeffersonlines.com) and Trailways (www.trailways.com) are the two bus service companies to be found prominently in the middle region of the US. Buses from these companies serve the routes between rural areas and regional cities. Each company accepts the tickets of the other and often have their schedules aligned to help travellers switch easily to a Trailways bus from a Jefferson Lines bus.

Red Coach (www.redcoachusa.com), a premium bus provider in Florida, also offers rides in 3 varied classes. On most U.S buses, you can come across reclining seats, restroom, AC, power outlets and free Wi-Fi as some of the standard features.

United States Train Travel

At 35,000 feet, you cannot see much of the USA. An Amtrak train will be much better, although slower, and can allow you to enjoy amazing sceneries across the land. If you make an advance booking, you have to pay just $190 USD to travel across coasts – nothing short of a wonderful deal. There is a wonderful rail network available for travellers in the USA. Although it does not quite match up to the lofty European standards, it can help you see about all the cities and towns affordably and in proper comfort. The National Railroad Passenger Corporation aka Amtrak (www.amtrak.com) operates all the trains for long-distance rides in the USA.

Driving across the United States

Driving can be the most cost-effective option if you travel with over two other riders. Your gasoline expenses depend on how fuel-efficient your car is. For instance, driving a fuel-efficient car from New York to Seattle can cost you around 600 USD for gasoline expenses these days. Gasoline costs widely fluctuate through every season and in various regions of the nation, so it is best that you make a decision only after using a trip cost calculator.

This kind of tour can take at least 2-3 days, and you may even find good places for accommodation and meals. You can spend as low as $115 USD for accommodation and food if take your own packed food along and lodge at National Forest Service campgrounds (www.forestcamping.com) that is very low cost or even free of charge. If you travel with 3 or more people, this can be the most cost-effective way to travel from one place to another and indulge in sightseeing.

Hitchhiking in the USA

Hitchhiking, contrary to popular opinion, is legal in every state in the USA. However, there are small variations in the laws about roadways in every town, state and city. You can hitchhike legally in most states if you are in a spot where cars can pull over safely and you manage to stay away from the highway.

You can get details about every state law from the website hitchwiki.org. Before travelling, you should read up about the area where you wish to travel. With a lighter pack, you will be in a happier state. Ensure that your backpack contains sufficient supplies and equipment, which can come in handy if you are stranded. Pack your backpack as if you intend to go on a hike for 2 days.

Toss in more socks than you will use along with a raincoat, a stocking hat, long underwear, a light jacket, an additional set of clothes and a strong and comfortable pair of boots. Place suntan lotion, a few snacks and 2 jugs of water in your own backpack. You should also take along a tent and a small sleeping bag, allowing you to be more peaceful in case you need to create a warm, makeshift shelter at any spot.

Do not carry along anything that is very precious to you, or if its loss might seriously depress you. Waiting for hours by the side of the road can make you tired, and many people can look down on you. Consider this a challenge and ignore this attitude. Continue to believe in your wanderlust despite what much of society might think.

Hitchhiking to a destination can be tiring and frustrating, but you can travel cheap. Once you are successful in hitchhiking, you will be content with your trips and get accustomed to travelling for long periods. Try to dress like local people, given that drivers pick up hitchhikers who dress like them. You can get a better chance of being picked up if you dress like locals. While hitchhiking in a blue-collar area, wear a flannel shirt and a pair of jeans and maintain a clean appearance.

The Legendary Route 66

Travellers across the globe continue to be in love with the very attractive Route 66. As the famous R&B anthem goes, the Route 66 runs between L.A and Chicago and goes more than 2,000 miles all the way. This old, iconic route moves diagonally through the middle of the U.S, and you can see some of the most typical scenes of the country while travelling along this road.

However, the major reason to travel through this route is to personally experience the history of modern America along the way. Before it got its present name and even before it was paved in 1926, this road was crossed by one of the first transcontinental highways of the country, the National Old Trails Highway.

The road came to be known as the "Main Street of America" for 30 years before and after the Second World War, as it wound through various Southwest and Midwest small towns, lined by scores of tourist destinations, gas stations, motels and cafes. You can find complete information about Route 66 trips on www.historic66.com, whether you wish to travel for only a small stretch along this iconic road or move to L.A from Chicago.

Top Destinations in United States

The U.S., with its national icon being the Statue of Liberty, is known across the globe as the Land of Liberty. The last 200 years have witnessed many people from across the globe coming to this country, attracted by its democracy and prosperity, in search of a better life. This big nation is a potpourri of religion, politics, cuisine, cultures and landscapes. It is a land of diversity.

Some of the best places to visit in the USA are:

- **New York City**

  This is the largest city in the United States, as well as most populated. It is continuously abuzz with people and activities, and is hence often referred to as the "city that never sleeps". The city stands on one of the biggest natural harbours of the world in the state of New York, and consists of 5 boroughs:

  - Staten Island
  - Queens

- Manhattan

- Brooklyn

- Bronx

The city, with its various attractions and skyscrapers that are popular across the globe, is often what first comes to the minds of foreigners whenever they think about the U.S.A.

- **Boston**

One of the oldest US cities, it is best known for its rich American heritage, academic institutions and architecture. It is the largest city and the capital of Massachusetts. It is also the largest city in the area of New England. It presents wonderful sights during autumn and spring, with beautiful foliage in autumn and flowering trees in spring. The city is closely related with the early history of America, and it served as the backdrop for numerous events of historic importance that resulted in the American Revolution. The Boston Harbour, which served as the scene for the Boston Tea Party, is popular for its festivals and lighthouses.

- **Miami**

    One of the most attractive US cities, and known best for its attractive nightlife, sun-kissed beaches and Latin culture. It is situated off the Atlantic coast, in south-eastern Florida, and serves as a big port city that manages the largest number of passenger cruisers on the globe. It is famous for its Miami Beach, which is situated on a barrier island across the Miami Bay, and is popular for its stunning South Beach and the amazing Art Deco architecture.

- **Seattle**

    This coastal seaport city is the largest city in the Pacific Northwest area of the U.S. It has the nickname "Emerald City" owing to its lush green beauty due to rainy weather conditions. The majestic Space Needle is the most popular landmark of this city, comprising of a revolving restaurant and an observation deck. It is also home to Starbucks and Boeing aircraft.

- **San Francisco**

    This is a gorgeous city located in northern California, and is located on a peninsular tip in the Bay area of San Francisco. The city is most popular for its rolling, steep streets, cable cars and the famous Golden Gate Bridge – which is of course the top attraction of the city. Across this wonderful suspension bridge, tourists can walk, drive or go on bike rides. They can enjoy grand views from this bridge and photograph them to savour for a lifetime.

- **Las Vegas**

Las Vegas is a big city in the U.S.A and is located in south-eastern Nevada, in a desert location. The city is famous for its extravagant shows, musical productions, comedy acts, luxury hotels and casinos. The "Strip" is an area where most of the major attractions of the city are focused in. Las Vegas, other than gala performances, gambling activities and showgirls, has a lot to offer to people of any age as well as interest level.

- **Grand Canyon**

The Grand Canyon is one of the most popular spots in the USA and attracts scores of visitors throughout the year. This gigantic natural wonder is situated in northern Arizona and has been carved into its present shape over millions of years by the Colorado River. It might not be the longest and deepest canyon on Earth, but its unique landscape and gigantic size makes it an irresistible attraction for visitors from across the globe. It is a natural wonder of matchless beauty.

- **Orlando**

  This is situated in central Florida, and is a spot where reality meets with fantasy. It is home to various amusement parks and theme parks such as Universal Studios, Walt Disney World and SeaWorld. Families love to visit Orlando during vacations. This is the place where kids and even adults can meet with their most loved characters from storybooks, watch amazing tricks being performed by dolphins, ride wonderful roller coasters, re-enact scenes live from popular movies and do much more.

- **New Orleans**

  This is located in south-eastern Louisiana and is considered to be one of the most outstanding cities in America. It is the largest city of the state and serves as a major seaport in the U.S. It enjoys wide popularity for its annual Mardi Gras celebration, jazz music, architecture, cuisine and prominent

French Creole culture. New Orleans was destroyed in 2005 due to the Hurricane Katrina that resulted in heavy flooding, but has mostly recovered from the ravages now to continue being regarded as one of the topmost cities to visit in America.

- **Honolulu**

  The capital and the largest city of the state of Hawaii, a tropical paradise, and serves as a gateway to it. For most travellers, it serves as the point of entry to the U.S. The city is situated 2,400 miles to the west of California and stands in the Pacific Ocean, on Oahu – a Hawaiian island. The city is known best for its historical Pearl Harbor. The most attractive destination in this city is undoubtedly the Waikiki Beach.

- **Denali National Park**

  A large area that is famous for outdoor adventures, amazing sceneries and abundant wildlife. It is home to the highest peak in North America, Mt. McKinley. It stands in the Alaska Interior, and serves as a paradise for people who love outdoor activities and nature, located among the jagged Alaskan mountains.

- **San Diego**

  This is a famous tourist destination that is known for its amazing family attractions, lower crime rate, perfect weather conditions and stunning beaches. It is situated in southern California to the northern part of the Mexican border. This vast coastal city is loved for its small-town ambience, and its famous attractions include the Balboa Park zoo.

- **Los Angeles**

  L.A. is situated in southern California and is lined by beautiful valleys, mountains and the Pacific Coast. It is often referred to as the "Entertainment Capital of the World", and serves as the world-famous centre for music recordings, motion pictures and TV productions. This major cosmopolitan city has many ethnic neighbourhoods and districts. Although the smog issues of the city are infamous, L.A. continues to be a favourite destination for many tourists due to its mild and sunny weather conditions throughout the year.

- **Washington DC**

  Located on the east coast of America and famously known across the world as the U.S. capital and headquarters of the federal government of the U.S.A. Washington DC is where different cultures co-exist, and this cosmopolitan city is visited by millions of tourists every year who stand amazed before its architectural attractions like the Lincoln Memorial, the Washington Monument, the Capitol Building and the White House. Many such monuments can be found in the National Mall, a park land that is wonderfully landscaped.

- **Chicago**

  This is the 3rd largest city in America, and is situated on Lake Michigan in north-eastern Illinois, in the middle of the Midwest area. The city is known best for its one-of-a-kind style of pizzas and hot dogs, majestic skyscrapers and sports teams. It is home to the Willis Tower, one of the tallest buildings standing in the Western Hemisphere and O'Hare International – one of the busiest airports of the world.

- **Yellowstone**

  Famously known as the first national park in the world, the Yellowstone National Park was established in 1872 to protect the large number of hot springs and geysers, the rugged landscape and the fantastic wildlife. The Old Faithful Geyser, known to erupt after every 91 minutes, is the most popular geyser in this park. Yellowstone Park is where you can find one of the best North American wildlife habitats.

Mexico
Touring around Mexico

Mexico is frequented by tourists from the Canada and the United States, due to its convenient position with continuous flights from almost every major U.S.A. hub to Mexico City, the capital of Mexico, and various other major destinations along the coast of Mexico.

The vast region of Mexico, with its diverse areas, can pose various challenges for tourists who want to visit various destinations. The state has more bus services and domestic flights than most areas of the U.S, which can make transportation more convenient by comparison. Read on to learn about some of the most amazing ways to travel to Mexico and get to various destinations in the state.

Low-cost Airlines in Mexico

Some of the major beach destinations in Mexico, including Puerto Vallarta, Cancun and Los Cabos, are particularly well connected from numerous major cities in Canada and the U.S.A. This makes travelling comparatively easier. However, you will want to shop about and compare – given that the best fares are frequently on connecting airline flights. It might be necessary for other destinations to change flights in either Mexico or the United States.

Many of the connecting domestic and international flights to various parts of Mexico traverse Mexico City. The largest national airline is Aeromexico (world.aeromexico.com), which runs its busiest air terminal from this location, with flights to around 20 U.S.A. destinations, along with extra cities in Asia, Europe, South America and Central America.

Due to the huge size of the state, flights are often the easiest and fastest way to travel from one point to another in Mexico. Flight rates on a few routes can be often too high. However, it would be sensible to do some comparison shopping of airfares and book ahead of time.

With the rising popularity of budget airline companies like Volaris (www.volaris.com), VivaAerobus (ww.vivaaerobus.com) and Interjet (www.interjet.com), flight rates have been reduced on some of the most popular air travel routes. However, the services and amenities from the airlines can widely vary. Mexico City and to some extent even Guadalajara are the common connecting cities.

Travelling around Mexico by Bus

Mexico boasts a wide network of bus routes run by quite a few big companies. Here, unlike in other parts of the U.S, you can generally avail long-distance bus service in more than one class of service. There is a single class in every bus, and you can pick the level of comfort and price range that best suits you.

The best service is often known as ejecutivo (executive) or de lujo (deluxe) service, and it mostly operates on the most famous routes, with on-board lavatories, extensive leg space and reclining seats, and often even movies, snacks and beverages. You can find similar services in the Primera clase (first class) bus service, with relaxing seats and movies. It is a good idea to bring a pair of earplugs if you do not like to watch the flick being shown on the route.

Segunda clase (second class) buses, which offer a more cost-effective touring experience, are not very comfortable and make more stops. Travellers often tend to stand in the bus during some sections of the trip. Estrella de Oro, ADO and Primera Plus are some of the biggest long-distance bus lines.

The website Mi Escape is involved in the online sales of tickets for different bus companies across the nation.

Bus Companies in Mexico

Autobuses del Oriente ADO (www.ado.com.mx)

Estrella de Oro (www.estrelladeoro.com.mx)

Primera Plus (www.primeraplus.com.mx)

Mi Escape (www.miescape.mx)

Train Travel around Mexico

At one time, the whole of North America was connected by passenger trains. Unfortunately, that is no longer the case. However, you can find some amazing individual rail routes – especially designed for travellers, and enjoy stunning sceneries while on your way to world-famous destinations.

A passenger service, El Chepe (www.chepe.com.mx) passes through the iconic Copper Canyon, and lets tourists feast their eyes on beautiful scenes in northern Mexico. The train runs from Chihuahua to Los Mochis, and most foreign tourists purchase tickets on this route as part of a package including hotel stays.

If you love travelling by train, you might also like to get a taste of the urban train networks operating in Monterrey, Mexico City and Guadalajara, three of the major cities in Mexico.

Mexico Travel by Ferry and Boat

Boats and ferries along the coastline of Mexico offer easy and comfortable transportation. These are the most widespread services in the most famous tourist destinations of the country. For tourists, it can a wonderful option to see multiple destinations in one area.

On the Caribbean coast of Mexico, Cancun and various other mainland points to adjacent islands like Holbox, Isla Mujeres and Cozumel are connected by ferries. Ultramar (www.ultramarferry.com) is a company offering scheduled service to Cozumel and Isla Mujeres. Trips can be arranged to faraway Holbox with the help of local travel operators.

Baja Ferries (www.bajaferries.com) is a company operating scheduled services between the port city of Topolobampo on the Gulf of California, the famous beach resort Mazatlan and La Paz that is located on the peninsula in Baja California. These trips include overnight travel and the ferries have enough space for the transportation of passenger vehicles. These consist of private sleeping cabins as well as lounges, shopping, bars and restaurants.

Hitchhiking in Mexico

Mexico might be slightly infamous, but it is possible for travellers to hitchhike here and have a lot of fun in the process. The country has a vast expanse, and it is impossible to rate how good it is to hitchhike across all its areas. The general experience can differ from one state to another. As is the case with any other country, you can go slow on roads with less traffic and fast on the highways.

The omnipresent pick-up trucks are one of the singular factors of the hitchhiking experience in Mexico. You have to hop into the back of the trucks, bear the wind and grab your hat with both hands. It is not possible to talk to the drivers due to the high wind. Many locals are ready to offer beverages and foods to hitchhikers for free, particularly Coca Cola. At times, they expect you to pay. Ordinary pickups can magically transform into shared taxis, referred to as 'collectivos' by locals.

However, hitchhiking on small roads can make you end up wasting time unnecessarily. It is common for travellers to wait for 2-3 hours. You should have patience, a couple of water bottles and sun-screen lotion. In many areas, however, even local people hitchhike to return home from grocery stores. Mexicans are not used to hitchhiking as a way of travelling long-distance or do not view it as a lifestyle habit, and few locals can actually understand why you choose to hitchhike rather than take public or private transport facilities. However, on mountainous tracks you might be more willing to hitchhike and soak in the stunning views that the road offers. The journey might literally seem more beautiful for you than the destination, and you might not be too concerned about how much distance you really cover when you feast on the stunning sights and sounds on offer.

Most travellers who prefer to hitchhike in Mexico never come across any major issues. Although this is a vast nation and the experiences might differ across states, hitchhiking is more or less safe here. However, if you wish to avert risks, you would do well to avoid the states near the US border, such as Durango, Chihuahua, Coahuila and Tamaulipas.

Veracruz, Guerrero and Michoacán can be other risky states. You should board "collectives" and buses while making trips north of the line between Mazatlan, Tampico and San Luis Potosi.

Mexico Top Destinations

Mexico has been a destination of choice for North American travellers for a long time. It is also steadily becoming popular with European travellers who want to soak in the always sunny climate of Mexico and enjoy its lovely sandy beaches and wonderful sceneries. The country is also attractive due to its rich heritage and culture. The primitive Mayan and Aztec sites and colonial cities from history have earned recognition as World Heritage Sites from UNESCO. These are sure to remain the same for many decades to come.

The heritage sites, including spots such as Uxmal, Guanajuato and Chichén Itzá, often enjoy as much popularity as Cancún, Playa del Carmen and Puerto Vallarta, the standard beach vacation destinations. The rich culture of the country also makes the entire experience more beautiful. You can find a wonderful combination of local influences as well as strains of Spanish people, which are apparent in almost every aspect of the country – whether the bright song and dance customs or dishes. Mexico is rich in fauna and flora, and it is spread across various climate zones including lush green tropical rainforests, arid deserts and more.

- **Puerto Vallarta**

  This city is located in the Pacific coast and is another of the beach destinations in Mexico that is steadily growing in popularity. It is often abbreviated as Vallarta. Many areas of this city are left unaffected by modernization. It was in the 1960s that the country first became popular as a vacation spot, when it served as a playground for the elite members of the North American community and society. Since then, it has become a favourite destination for many foreigners who view it as a second home in a warm-weather area. These days, the city attracts older travellers who love to swim with dolphins as well as younger tourists who like to go on adventure trips and participate in activities like jet-skiing and paragliding. If you like to spend your vacation in a less hectic way, you can visit destinations in the city that are known for art and craft shops. You can just walk along the wonderful public spaces on the beachside, with many sculptures and green spaces.

- **Historic Centre in the Mexico City**

  Mexico City (Ciudad de México) is the most famous alternative tourist destination, and is not just the seat of the federal government and the capital city of the nation. It boasts many tourist attractions, art galleries and world-class museums. Do not ignore the place because of its small size. Its historic city centre (Centro Histórico de la Ciudad) is spread of 15-square-kilometers and consists of over 1,400 well-known colonial buildings dating back to the 16th – 19th centuries. It is regarded as a World Heritage Site by UNESCO. You can find most of the biggest attractions of the Mexico City in this place, many of which are just a walking distance away from the Templo Mayor known for its Aztec-era souvenirs, the Metropolitan Cathedral, the National Palace and the energetic main plaza, the Constitution Square (Plaza de la Constitución). The entire experience is enhanced by majestic volcanic mountains Iztaccíhuatl and Popocatépetl, each of which is more than 5,000 meters high, and overlooks Mexico City. This area of the Mexican Highlands offers a perfect chance to travel and enjoy wonderful sceneries.

- **Chichén Itzá: The Mayan Metropolis**

  This is a famous destination that is a part of the day trip for travellers visiting the wonderful Mayan city of Chichén Itzá, the Yucatán capital of Mérida, the Playa del Carmen or Cancún. Chichén Itzá is one of the most frequented, best restored and biggest archaeological sites in Mexico. There are many reasons why you should visit this place, designated as a World Heritage Site by the UNESCO. You can come across the wonderful Caracol, which is the tallest structure of the site at about 30 meters high and is an observatory dating back around 1,000 years in time. It stands as proof of the advancement of the Mayans in architecture and astronomy. The building has walls with narrow slits that let sunrays enter only two times every year, so that priests could determine dates accurately. There are other attractions as well, such as the popular Mayan

Chacmools holding sacrificial vessels while keeping the old temples protected and the majestic Pyramid of Kukulkán or El Castillo.

- **Los Cabos Corridor and Cabo San Lucas**

  Los Cabos, often known only as Cabo, is located at the southernmost point of the lovely Baja Peninsula. It is one of the best beach destinations in Mexico. This is a vast stretch spreading for 30 km and consists of pristine sandy beaches known across the planet for clear waters and activities such as fishing, snorkelling and diving. The largest marlin fishing contest of the world is organized here. It consists of a vast stretch of coastline extending from the twin towns of San José del Cabo and Cabo San Lucas and it is referred to as the Corredor Turistico or Los Cabos Corridor.

  Many resorts have come up on this stretch, catering to people of all budgets and tastes. You can find golf courses, luxurious spas and various other properties that offer some of the most attractive programs in North America. You can get the chance to spend some enjoyable time on its beaches and take part in the Cabo San Lucas, one of the most famous snorkelling and swimming activities around the El Arco de Cabo San Lucas, the vast archway that serves as a popular natural landmark. It is at the coastline where the Pacific connects with the Sea of Cortez.

- **The Mayan Riviera and Cancún**

The destination resorts of the island of Cozumel, Cancún and Playa del Carmen, known together as the Mayan Riviera, lie along a wonderful coastline stretch on the Gulf of Mexico. This is a stunning spot on the Yucatán Peninsular tip that draws in around 5 million visitors annually, and makes up for around 20% of the total travel revenue of Mexico. Even with such big numbers, the vast expanse of clear water and wide beaches will help you to avoid the crowd, if desired. This is also the region where you can come across many enjoyable activities to indulge in, like scuba diving in the largest underwater museum in the world where you can see a wonderful collection of sculptures that are submerged around 8 m deep, snorkelling among tropical fishes and reefs, swimming among stingrays and dolphins and more. You can also visit the numerous old Mayan ruins, which happen to lie very close to the beaches. The most amazing and the largest ruins, the Tulum and Chichén Itzá, are located at a distance of only a few hours.

- **Mexico's Grand Canyon: The Copper Canyon**

One of the northernmost states of Mexico, Chihuahua shares its border with New Mexico. It is where you can find one of the most thronged natural attractions of the nation, the breath-taking Copper Canyon (Barranca del Cobre). The Sierra Madre Occidental is what the area is referred to as, and it comprises of a wonderful cluster of deep canyons. It is deeper and larger than the Grand Canyon, its more famous cousin.

This natural wonder owes its name to the unique copper green hue along its steep walls. The wonderful natural structures of the canyon were created by 6 rivers coming together to meet at the Rio Fuerte before pouring to the Gulf of California. With the region steadily becoming more famous as a tourist spot, you can find many options for exploring this beautiful place. You can ride the Ferrocarril Chihuahua al Pacífico and take rail trips amidst scenic locations. You may even ride on horseback or go on bike excursions if you need more thrills.

- **Guadalajara**

  The capital of Jalisco, it is next to Mexico City in terms of size. You can find a distinctive blend of native and colonial Tapatíos influences. It is popular for its wide roads lined by wonderful old buildings and scenic parks that are known for their European style. This is a place where you can witness Mexican tradition and culture, in the form of Charreadas, a kind of rodeo generally accompanied by singing, dancing and other celebrations along with numerous culinary delights and the Mariachi music that appear to be ubiquitous.

  The city is wonderful, and you will love exploring it through walks. It consists of 4 vast squares that create a cross-like shape and consists of the old city centre. The Plaza de Armas is the best of these and is exactly the spot where you should start your trip. There are important buildings like the Catedral de Guadalajara or Baroque Guadalajara Cathedral that was constructed during 1558 – 1616, or the Palacio de Gobierno or Government Palace that was built in the 17th century.

- **Mérida: The White City of Yucatán**

  Merida is the capital of Yucatán, and is laid out in a grid-like shape. This makes it more convenient for travellers to explore its many old buildings and stunning parks. This is one of the most beautiful colonial cities in Mexico and has a perfect location for being a base to explore many of the amazing Mayan sites of the region, such as Tulum and Chichén Itzá. The Spaniards set it up in 1542. The European influences can be seen even today, especially in the old plazas and city squares where French architecture is still evident. It is a popular stopover for overnight or day trips from the Mayan Riviera resorts. The city is very tidy and neat, and acts as a certificate for its residents who love to dress up in white clothes. This gives Merida the name "white city" or Ciudad Blanca.

- **Oaxaca: Experience Mexico at its Truest Best**

  Oaxca is the capital of the eponymous state and serves as one of the most popular travel destinations for people who want to get a feel of true Mexico. The city has an exciting combination of native Spanish and Indian elements. Even with modernization and huge developments in recent times in the other famous destinations of the country, Oaxca has largely been unaffected. Naturally, UNESCO has designated it as a World Heritage Site. Other than its old-styled architecture and the famous city centre, the city is known for being a cultural centre that attracts people from across the globe for its many festivals and events, such as the native festival Guelaguetza that is held in every July. It consists of food, music, crafts, costumes and traditional dancing. The Monte Alban is the place where travellers can explore the primitive ruins and the amazing natural sceneries all around.

- **Guanajuato**

  The place has many beautiful museums and fine galleries. This is where you can find the world-famous Museum of Quixote, which is in memoriam of Miguel de Cervantes, the Spanish writer behind the comic work Don Quixote. Every year, the city witnesses the most important festival of Latin America, the International Cervantino Festival, being organized – which is dedicated to the writer.

The city has been designated by UNESCO as a World Heritage Site. It is known for its narrow alleys, winding lanes and numerous old colonial buildings. It has numerous plazas, such as the amazing Jardin de la Union, which serves as the main square of the city and is known for its magnificent ancient architecture. You can also see the big Juárez Theater, with its flower bed, restaurants, cafes and fountains, and the old, majestic San Diego Church. You should explore this city on foot, which is how it should be enjoyed. You should walk to the subterranean streets of the city, and experience the underground network of tunnels where a river once used to flow. Today, pedestrians and car drivers use it to quickly get around the Guanajuato. If you love creepy stuff, you must visit the awesome Mummies of Guanajuato exhibit that consists of the remains of locals who died in the mid-1800s due to a cholera outbreak and were mummified naturally.

- **Ixtapa and Zihuatanejo**

The attraction factor of the larger beach resorts of Mexico cannot be ignored. However, there are plenty of smaller vacation spots as well that deserve to be seen in the country. Ixtapa and its neighbouring town Zihuatanejo, which was a tiny fishing village at one time and is located on the Pacific coast of the nation, are two extremely popular smaller destinations in the country.

Ixtapa is the larger town, and was known earlier as the town producing mangrove and coconut. It has been designed with a lot of care as a tourist centre. The beaches and streets of the town are un-crowded and you can easily get about. When compared to the traditional beach resorts of Ixtapa, the amazing Zihuatanejo stands as a contrast. The small-town feel has been carefully and painstakingly kept intact here. This safe and beautiful town lies along a well-protected, small bay, and consists of many fantastic restaurants and hotels. There are many fun activities always occurring here, such as fish market shopping or fishing excursion where you can hope to catch something that you like.

- **The Ancient Fortress of Tulum**

Tulum is an ancient city and is popular as the sole fortified Mayan settlement with a coastal location. It was constructed as long back as the 13th century, and is one of the most popular tourist spots in the

Yucatán Peninsula. The Cozumel and the Playa del Carmen are two well-maintained ruins in the Mayan Riviera that can easily be reached from the Cancun beaches. One can easily see the ruins from many miles around as these are situated on top of cliffs with a 12-meter height, and looking over the lovely Caribbean Sea.

The city is also popular for its high walls, which make it look like a fortress of religious and military importance. Occupants inhabited it until 1544, when the Spaniards came. The city also comprises of numerous other archaeological discoveries, such as the Castillo, which is the largest building in the spot and is known for its wonderful location by the side of the cliff. You will also love the Templo de los Frescos or Temple of the Frescoes that is famous for its relics and sculptures.

Central America

Travel in Central America

Central America (Panama, Nicaragua, Honduras, Guatemala, El Salvador, Cuba, Costa Rica, Belize) is known for a lot more than its lakes, trees and rivers, where trips can be quite low cost. It has a population of around 41,739,000 people. The region boasts of a rich history and has a colourful culture and nice forests that contain many attractions, which any traveller would love to know about. Central America is loved for its azure water, flavourful foods, friendly local people, relaxed laidback lifestyle, warm climate and jungle treks. The place holds more attraction for tourists as there is no spot in this continent for over 200 kilometres or 125 miles from the ocean.

While travelling through the cities, you can go around in the most cost-effective way when you board city public buses. Within the city, the fares can be lower than a dollar.

Train Travel in Central America

Train travel is not popular in Central America. The place does not have any consistent international rail network here, unlike in Europe or in sections of Africa or Asia. Most trips are usually made by plane or long-distance buses. However, the lack of consistent rail connectivity is true for most nations. You cannot come across any extensive network for passenger train in any nation. In places like Belize, there is not even any train line of any type. Trains, when present, often happen to be commuter trains that run to any major city from the capital. You have to wait for a long time for trains to more faraway destinations.

However, if you do not mind travelling by odd rail routes, you will probably find this type of travel in Central America to be quite interesting. It is worthwhile knowing about the place in this way. You can find a few freight trains that shift cargo. The Panama Canal Railway (www.panarail.com/home) offers a daily train Monday-Friday between Ciudad Panama and Colon. The Panama Canal Railway offers one of the best train-riding experiences in the world. The railroad has a colourful background and moves across the Panama Isthmus with a stunning natural backdrop. You can find Executive class AC coaches with nice refreshments.

Cuba's rail network runs along the entire island's length, connecting the main towns and cities. It is a wonderful method of travel, particularly if you like to travel just like the Cubans and not take a tourist bus. The train experience will be strictly Cuban and not as per western standards of quality. However, there can be breakdowns from time to time. You should also take along your own toilet paper. The Tren Francès especially offers an interesting, safe and comfortable trip Havana to Santiago, from one end of Cuba to another. The experience is significantly better than that of a flight or what you feel while sitting cramped in a Viazul bus that travels a long distance.

Bus Travel in Central America

Inter-country and countrywide buses happen to be the easiest and most popular way to travel around the area. You may catch most of the buses for about $25-45 USD. Overnight trips and longer bus rides usually come at about $35-60 USD. It is the most common method of travel for most people — tourists as well as locals.

Many travellers like to visit just one nation while visiting Central America. However, cross-country trips are comparatively easier. Although flights are the quickest modes for travel, they can be quite expensive. In Central America, people frequently travel by bus, which is the most efficient and low-cost way of making trips. It is best to opt for tourist-class companies for bus travel in Central America. It is advised that you reserve 2-3 days before your date of departure while making a seat booking on a Central American bus of tourist class.

Tideca Corporation (www.platinumcentroamerica.com)

The Central America King Quality bus service of Tideca Corporation provides travellers with international routes, having stops in every capital city of Central America, as well as in Tapachula and Mexico. Belize is the only exception. The King Quality bus service offers service in 3 levels on various routes:

- Quality level
- King level
- Platinum level

The Quality level is the standard one, and decent enough. You can avail Wi-Fi, leather armchairs, refreshments and movies.

Tica Bus (www.ticabus.com)

Tica Bus is sort of the counterpart of the U.S. Greyhound bus system in Central America. Travellers use buses from this bus company to go on cross-country travels across Central America. You can find routes going as far to the north as Tapachula, as far as Panama City to the southeast area and as far as Mexico when it comes to the southwest area. The buses tend to stop in every capital city of Central America as well as numerous big cities along the route, although with the exclusion of Belize.

The buses also serve Guatemala, Honduras, El Salvador, Costa Rica and Nicaragua, and make overnight stops in San Salvador and various other locations. You can get simple accommodation facilities right at the terminals. You are allowed up to 2 luggage pieces for each passenger, with maximum weight of 66 pounds or 30 kilos. Kids under 3 years of age can ride free.

Transnica (www. transnica.com)

This bus company has buses running between Costa Rica, Honduras and Nicaragua. These are high-quality buses consisting of fantastic features in even standard service, such as TV/video, health service, reclining seats and AC. The Executive service offers TV, free Wi-Fi access, bigger spaces and lunch. There is a luxury fleet offering trips to Nicaragua. You may use the official website of Transnica to make an online ticket booking. The website accepts PayPal.

Other Central American Bus Companies

Most people in Central America use buses for travel. However, unless you are looking for a first-hand experience of local culture, you will not like to board the "chicken buses" or the local buses that ferry people as well as produce and poultry. These serve as the sole mode of travel to some of the Central American areas that are more remote. If you do not wish to travel so far, you may try these bus companies:

Confort Lines (www.comfortpremium.com): Costa Rica, El Salvador, Guatemala, Honduras, Nicaragua

Pullmantur (www.pullmantur.com): Guatemala, El Salvador, Honduras

Hedman Alas (www.hedmanalas.com): Guatemala, Honduras

You can also avail tourist shuttle buses in many cities. However, you can always also ride taxis for locally going around.

Central America Hitchhiking Rides

In Central America, hitchhiking happens to be a very popular way of travelling around the place. The area is heavily serviced by bus but much of the travel occurs by hitchhiking. Expect the buses to be sporadic or late, and they can be highly crowded at times. Given that bus travel is simply unaffordable for many people, you can find hitchhiking to be comparatively safer and more widespread. It is a common sight to find old grannies, kids, families and even single women standing by the roadside and waiting for a ride.

Although hitchhiking is quite common in many areas of the place, you should exercise caution while accepting being picked up, particularly if you happen to be a female who is travelling alone. It is advised that you stay away from Honduras or El Salvador as a hitchhiker given that these nations are not regarded as very safe. You should be cautious, use prudence and wait for another pickup if your intuition sends warning signals.

Flights in Central America

Central America has only a small air network, which is dominated mostly by:

COPA airlines (www.copaair.com) - The airlines is headquartered in Panama.

TACA (taca.alternativeairlines.com) – Flights are available to numerous destinations through hubs in San Salvador and San Jose. However, not many direct flights are offered between destinations. You need to travel through their hubs. For instance, you need to fly to Belize City from Guatemala City and must connect through San Salvador. There is no direct flight available.

If you wish to fly between various nations, you can opt for various small carriers that serve every individual nation. These are very small airports that are located outside international air terminals and out of capital cities. Usually, small propeller planes are found to fly to these airports.

Unless it is highly necessary, it is advised that you avoid flying from the area. Flights are very costly. Generally, a flight to Belize City from Guatemala City is around $330 USD, while you have to pay only around $50 USD for bus service. Such a major difference in price is typical of the region. Although bus rides can take you longer, you should avoid flying if you are short on funds and wish to see the entire area.

Fantastic Places to visit in Central America

Not every traveller is likely to be excited by the mention of Central America. However, this is exactly your type of place if you love outdoor activities and nature, taking a tour through ancient ruins of old civilizations, hiking through rainforests and tropical jungles, relaxing on sandy white beaches, windsurfing, scuba diving, snorkelling, enjoying gorgeous nightlife and fine dining in big cities and learning more about local cultures and people.

Central America comprises of 7 nations connecting South and North America. Although some nations might not be too large, that just means that travellers with small pockets can see more of the nation. However, travelling though Central America should not be done hastily, as the remote areas are some spots that intrigue travellers the most. In some locations, hiking might be needed. Travellers have to ensure that they are in sound health, considering how strenuous hitchhiking tends to be.

However, travelling need not be too laborious in Central America. Had that been the case, the region would not have been such a favourite of elderly people looking for a nice spot to retire in. You can find amazing beaches, perfect just for sunbathing purposes, on the Pacific as well as the Caribbean sides of the area.

The region boasts of some of the most amazing cloud and tropical rainforests on the planet, which serve as a home to wildlife and plants that are impossible to find in any other place. This is also the sole region consisting of many awesome archaeological sites that date as far back as the times of the Mayans, one of the greatest human civilizations. Other popular attractions include the volcanoes that caused the destruction of old towns.

You can still witness many elegant and majestic colonial buildings from the time when many of the Central American nations were colonized by the Spanish and the British. There are also many beautiful European style cathedrals that deserve to be seen. Some of the best places to visit in Central America are:

- **Tikal**

  This can be found in northern Guatemala, in the lowland rainforest area. At one time, this was one of the largest cities that Mayans used to inhabit. However, the present times only find some majestic ruins of the ancient Mayan metropolis. Tikal is most popular for its 5 giant pyramids and the diversity in the flora and fauna of its rainforests.

- **Lake Atitlan**

  Located in the Guatemalan highlands, this deep blue lake is well known for its breath-taking sceneries and Mayan villages. The region is thronged by many tourists, but has not changed as much as quite a few other travel destinations in Central America. Even today, you can find native women using their traditional colourful attire for everyday wear. There are famous attractions such as a nature reserve, butterfly sanctuary and museums dedicated to the Mayans. You can also walk around the famous San Pedro Volcano, which is regarded as a difficult hike.

- **Antigua**

  Located in the highlands of central Guatemala, this city is well-known for its majestic architecture from the times of Spanish colonization, which have been preserved well enough. Antigua was established in 1524, although it has been destroyed repeatedly by avalanches, fires and earthquakes. The city is a major centre for many people to learn the Spanish language. It offers wonderful sights of popular landmarks, such as the Santa Catalina Arch, historic churches and other beautiful architectural structures.

- **Copán**

  Another exquisite instance of the wonderful Mayan civilization, which stands in western Honduras. You can find two majestic archaeological museums as well as ancient Mayan sculptures. If you love bird-watching, this is the place to be in, as it is the site of one of the best Central American aviaries. There are all kinds of facilities and accommodations for travellers in the town Copán Ruinas, located close to Copan.

- **Roatan**

This is the largest island you can find in the Honduras Bay. The bay was first visited by a European traveller in the form of Columbus, although he never stepped on the island. It was only in 1510 that French buccaneers first landed here physically. This is a wonderful site for tropical vacations, and the island has served as a concealed gem for travellers for many years.

- **Ruta de las Flores**

  Its name stands for Flower Route and this 22-mile long road passes through the countryside of Salvadore. The road winds through scenic colonial towns with amazing galleries and culinary delights. It is a heaven for people who love horseback riding, off-road mountain biking and hiking. This is also where the first coffee plantations of the country can be found. You can join in a food festival on this route held every week, and purchase native handicrafts.

- **Caye Caulker**

  This tiny island is located close to the Cayo Hicaco or Belize Barrier Reef. It is probably named after the ships that stopped in this area to caulk the boats or to get a fresh water supply. The last few years have seen this Belize island being transformed into a haven for tourists and backpackers due to the cheap rates, plenty of bars and restaurants and laidback lifestyle. You can bird-watch, cavort on the beach or go snorkelling.

- **Havana**

This is a city of indulgence, in an exciting way. The decrepit buildings standing here would look ugly in any other city, but not in Havana. Curiously, these have not replaced or restored. These evoke a mysterious feeling in Havana, and are a favourite subject for photographers. You can walk through Old Havana, past its attractions like Capitol Building, Plaza Vieja, Plaza de Armas and Plaza de la Catedral, and see wonderful vintage cars polishes and parked by owners at traffic lights. This is the site of the Museo de la Revolución. Havana is situated in the former presidential palace, and offers a better knowledge of Cuban history and culture.

- **Ambergris Caye**

The most popular Belize island, it is the largest island of the nation as well. It once served as the hub for coconut growing and fishing, but its proximity to the Belize Barrier Reef makes it more popular now for its snorkelling and scuba diving activities. It offers superior relaxation, wonderful dining and world-class accommodation, and can be accessed from Belize City by a short ferry ride or flight. The only place where people live here is in San Pedro Town.

- **Xunantunich**

  This has existed from 900 BC at least, and its dark grey, huge structures set against the blue skies of Belize makes for wonderful photographs. The ruins of the Mayan era are situated over a ridge above the River Mopan. These are close to San Ignacio and can be seen from the border of Guatemala. It is advised that you bring plenty of water and wear comfortable walking shoes.

- **Belize Barrier Reef**

  This is a 190-mile long stretch of the world's 2nd largest coral reef system, the Mesoamerican Barrier Reef System. Around 50% of all tourists visiting Belize come here for snorkelling and scuba diving activities. The reef has the Great Blue Hole, a popular diving destination in Belize. The deeper you go into this hole, the clearer you find the water to be. The unique limestone and stalactite structures here are well worth seeing.

- **Flores**

  This island town stands on Lake Petén Itzá, in northern Guatemala. It served as the final bastion for the Maya Itza Indians. Many tourists who flock to Flores like to visit the popular Mayan ruins located at Tikal. Flores has an old-town charm, and consists of attractive restaurants, shops, cobblestone streets and Spanish colonial churches.

- **Ometepe Island**

  This is situated in the centre of Lake Nicaragua, and consists of two volcanoes. One of these is the active volcano Concepcion, which spreads ash over a large area. It comprises petroglyphs and other artefacts of the pre-Columbian era. You can see some of the best rock art in the world. Many colourful folk and religious festivals are observed here.

- **Santiago**

The second largest Cuban city, it is Cuba at its hottest. Despite the high number of scammers out to con people, the place has a bright culture and lifestyle. This is a place where tourists are drawn to beautiful music, interesting people and amazing architecture. You can visit many interesting spots, such as the heart of the town Parque CŽspedes with music and lively activities, the Casa de la Trova, where Eliades Ochoa and other popular artists perform traditional music, and Calle Eredia.

- **Granada**

This is the most ancient colonial city in Nicaragua that draws many tourists due to its nearness to freshwater Lake Nicaragua and the all-year balmy climate. Nature lovers, spa lovers, shoppers and many other types of travellers love to come here and go lake sailing, hiking to the dormant volcano Mombacho and zip-lining through forests. The lovely cathedral Iglesia de la Merced is the best attraction here.

- **Leon**

Established by Spanish adventurers, this is the 2nd largest Nicaraguan city and a university town. It consists of colonial architecture, art galleries, museums and the largest Central American cathedral. In 1610, the first city was destroyed by a volcanic eruption. Leon is home to 8 volcanoes. The famous Pacific beach Las Peñitas is located near to a nature preserve.

- **Corcovado National Park**

This is situated in southwestern Costa Rica and is regarded as the crown jewel of the national park system of the nation. It is one of the best wildlife destinations in Latin America, and is liked by nature enthusiasts and backpackers. It consists of 13 prominent ecosystems, including highland cloud forests, swamps and various threatened species such as scarlet macaws and jaguars.

- **Trinidad**

It is probably the most attractive tourist spot in Cuba. This is a well-maintained and stunning colonial city, and UNESCO has designated it as a World Heritage Site. No car entry is permitted in this centre, and you have to walk around the markets, artesian shops and studios of various painters. It is home to many museums, including the most exciting Museo Histrico Municipal, which offers a magnificent view of the city from its tower. Many ancient colonial homes house restaurants here, and you can appreciate antique furniture in the properties while waiting to be served.

- **Arenal Volcano**

This is a volcano located in the northern lowlands of Costa Rica. Until 2010, it used to be active. Today, it might not spew lava and ash, but it still offers picturesque sights to travellers while they do river-rafting or mountain hiking. It is a must-visit tourist destination in Costa Rica, and is one of its most accessible and gorgeous attractions.

- **Manuel Antonio National Park**

This is situated on the Pacific Ocean, 82 miles from the capital of Costa Rica – San Jose. There are forests and white sand beaches that attract visitors. The park consists of lush green forests and is home to whales, dolphins and 109 varied mammals.

- **Monteverde Cloud Forest Reserve**

  This is possibly the most popular cloud forest on the planet. It is traversed by the continental divide, and travellers can stand with a foot on the Pacific side of Costa Rica and another on the Caribbean side. The primary way to pass through the cloud forest and the amazing jungle is to hike. Canopy tours and zip-lining are two other famous activities in this place.

- **Panama Canal and Panama City**

  This is a huge canal system created to let ships between the Pacific and the Atlantic oceans. It is considered to be one of the Wonders of the World of present times. The canal comprises 3 sets of locks and artificial lakes. You can look at the locks and watch ships passing through the waterways from different locations. The Miraflores locks is a popular spot and consists of a museum that teaches visitors about the canal's history and its operations.

  Panama City, regarded as the most cosmopolitan capital in the whole of Central America, is situated at the entry point of the Panama Canal. It is the largest city in the whole of Panama, and is an international finance hub. Rainforests surround this place. The city has mild weather conditions and is a favourite spot for residing in for expatriate retirees. The old city has modern boutiques and restaurants, as well as charming buildings.

- **San Blas Islands**

  This is an archipelago consisting of around 400 islands situated immediately off the coast of the Caribbean Sea in Eastern Panama. Most of these islands do not have any inhabitants. The native Kuna Yala tribe present on the islands preserve their environment and culture by managing tourism. You can find very basic and small hotels on a few islands, which provide travellers with all-inclusive meal packages as no restaurants are present here.

- **Bocas del Toro**

  This archipelago consists of six forested islands as well as many smaller islets with a laidback lifestyle and without any people. It is situated on the west coast of Panama in the Caribbean Sea. Bocas del Toro on Isla Colon is the capital city of the province, and deserves to be visited for its ancient Caribbean architecture. Many beaches have white sands and wonderful activities such as sailing, fishing, diving and snorkelling in the Caribbean.

South America

South America is an American continent, bordered by the Atlantic Ocean on the east and north and the Pacific Ocean on the west. The entire land area in South America spreads over 17,840,000 square kilometres, or around 3.5% of the land surface of the Earth.

This is a continent where you can find many adventures, such as dance, music, treks in jungles, beaches, mouth-watering foods, beverages such as coffee or wine, football and more. All these are available at a deal, and you do not often have to share the bargain with other travellers. For backpackers, this can be a heaven.

South America is immensely likeable for various reasons, such as the cheap alcohol, party ambience, friendly local people, Latin culture blended with the individual history of every region and more.

Although first-time tourists might feel slightly overwhelmed by this vast continent, and more so due to the notoriety of some parts in kidnappings, petty crimes and gun crimes, the place mostly gives no reason for worries. With some smartness and alertness, you can remain safe in most South American nations. Avoid wearing costly jewellery and do not travel with loads of cash in your pocket or wallet. Do not wear flashy clothes that draw attention upon you. Finally, do not walk at night down the dark and deserted alleys. These basic tips can prevent you from being singled out by troublemakers.

South America: Flying around the Continent

A continent consisting of artificial and natural wonders, South America is known for its amazing diversity and natural beauty. You can fly to the continent to see the largest waterfall in the world, the Iguaçu falls, and the highest waterfall in the world, Angel Falls located in Venezuela. Visit the ancient Inca cities of Machu Picchu, located in Peru, the river Amazon in Brazil and the Andes. There are unique wildlife specimens, with 60% of the Earth's biodiversity being only in the jungle of Amazon.

Flying about this continent can be costlier than living expenses. However, with distances between destinations being vast, flights are often more sensible options for travellers who are short on time. Bus rides can span over 18 hours here. It is often worthwhile to spend more on flights, in order to avoid long travels.

Colombia based airline company Avianca (www.avianca.com) and the carrier Latam (www.latam.com) based in Chile/Brazil are the major airline companies in South America. Some low-cost carriers also operate here quite successfully.

List of low-cost airlines operating in South America:

Brazil

- Azul Brazilian Airlines (www.voeazul.com.br)
- Gol Transportes Aéreos (www.voegol.com.br)

Chile

- Sky Airline (www.skyairline.com)
- Jet Smart (www.jetsmart.com)
- LAW Airline (www.vuelalaw.com)

Colombia

- EasyFly (www.easyfly.com.co)
- VivaColombia (www.vivacolombia.co)
- Wingo (www.wingo.com/en)

Peru

- Viva Air Peru (www.vivaair.com/pe)

Bus Travel Around South America

For travelling around South America, local buses happen to be an effective way. Broad rail systems for commuters and travellers are lacking in most cities, even in the major ones. In South America, the most famous international and intercity travel option include superior tour buses with toilets, beds, reclining seats, AC etc. The trips take more than 24 hours. The prices and quality of the buses tend to differ, based on the nation you travel to.

You can usually find school buses or old tour buses from the U.S being used there. Within the city, buses cost about $1 USD. Taxis are ubiquitous and can be availed between $3 and $10 USD for each trip within the precincts of the city. Subway systems in capital cities and larger metros cost about $2 USD for each ride.

In South America, bus travel rates usually vary from $7 USD to $90 USD for each trip. Domestic buses charge about $9 USD, whereas fancier or international buses charge $95 USD.

Argentina has a wonderful bus network for long and short distance. Costlier bus services are usually of superior quality and commonly offer food, alcoholic beverages and Wi-Fi for distances over 200 km. the leg space is usually good enough. Many of the buses have seats that can be horizontally reclined into camas or beds, which makes the overall experience similar to travelling on a plane in business class. The best bus services have seats that can be reclined completely. These are generally referred to as cama suite, or also known by other names like salón real, executive or tutto leto. Seats in slightly cheaper services recline only partially, known as "semi-camas". The normal seats are known as "servicio común".

In Brazil, long-distance buses offer more convenience. These are highly affordable and even going for expensive bus services means the most comfortable yet affordable way to make a trip between areas. While travelling within Brazil, you have to check the time and distance. It will take over 24 hours to travel to the south from Rio de Janeiro. Naturally, it is worthwhile to fly to areas between Brazil. Sometimes, when you purchase tickets in advance, you will find flying to be a cost-effective mode of travel.

In Colombia, bus ticker rates are quite high. However, long-distance trips generally cost over $60 USD in one way. The speed of long-distance bus travel is very slow, given that main highways have plenty of truck traffic due to bi-lane roads. At times, the bus ticket rates can be more than $90 USD. The ticket rates for budget airlines are frequently lower than bus tickets in Colombia. You should check the websites for the airlines given below, to get more information about fares.

No single bus company serves the entirety of Brazil, and you have to find one that connects two cities of your choice. Major cities such as Rio and São Paulo have multiple bus stations, and each cover specific sections of the city. You should check in advance to find which bus station can satisfy your needs.

Some bus companies in South America:

- **Auto Viação 1001 (Brazil):**
  www.autoviacao1001.com.br

- **Berlinas (Colombia):** www.berlinasdelfonce.com

- **Bolivariano (Colombia):** www.bolivariano.com.co

- **Click Bus (Brazil):** www.clickbus.com.br

- **EGA (Uruguay):** www.ega.com.uy

- **Itapemirim (Brazil):** www.itapemirim.com.br

- **Omnilineas (Argentina):** www.omnilineas.com

- **Pullman del Sur (Chile):** www.pdelsur.cl

Train Travel In South America

As compared to Europe or parts of Africa or Asia, you cannot find any international rail network in South America that is consistent. Most of the long-distance trips have to be done with plane or bus services. Most nations, as such, do not have any consistent rail network serving all parts of the country. However, you can come across odd rail routes that offer a different and exciting method of travel.

- **Argentina**

  You can find InterCity services on many rail routes. Argentina is witnessing a sort of revival in trains, given that the Government wants to revive passenger trains on long-distance routes between every major city. In 1948, the French or British-owned rail lines were nationalized. These were privatized again during the '90s and nationalized once more in 2015. You can find necessary details about every train service in Argentina.

  Ferrobaires (www.ferrobaires.gba.gov.ar) is one of the biggest operators. Argentina also has a tourist service named "The Train to the Clouds" (El Tren a las Nubes: www.trenalasnubes.com.ar) that travels to the Northern area from Salta.

- **Bolivia**

Bolivia has several train services, run by western and eastern train companies. Visit www.fca.com.bo for the western network. This is more traveller-oriented, and consists of trains moving to Tupiza from Oruro. You can find two forms of train, the WaraWara and the expresso. 'Ejecutivo' is the best among these 3 or 4 classes. Train rides can be very cold, with travels in both directions made primarily at night. The primary rail line to Tupiza from Oruro runs about every day.

Visit www.fo.com.bo for the eastern network. In the Santa Cruz rail hub, trains move to the Argentine border in the South and to the Brazilian border in the East. There is a daily train to Puerto Suarez from Santa Cruz east. However, you can find a combination of services. Locals take a normal train that run for the maximum time. An express train is there as well. There is also an expensive and quick ferrobus, a sophisticated railcar.

- **Brazil**

Rail services are extremely limited in Brazil. An Intercity train service also runs to Belo Horizonte from Vitoria. This is a cheaper train that offers greater comfort than buses. It leaves every day from Vitoria at 07:00 and from Belo Horizonte at 07:30. You can arrive at your destination at about 19:30-20:00. There are two classes of this train. The 'Econômica' is the more affordable version while 'Executivo' is better with enough leg space, seats styled like that of aircrafts and AC. You can also find a restaurant car, although the quality of food is not reported to be very praiseworthy. In Brazil, it is run by the most successful and popular freight railway. You can enjoy a very picturesque trip, and will love to spend your day with this rail ride. The best area offering the greatest scenes is during the Belo Horizonte end of your travel. When you begin at the Belo Horizonte end, and make a trip to the direction of Vitoria, you can view much of these scenes in daytime. You can find details about the train at

www.vale.com/brasil/pt/business/logistics/r
ailways/trem-
passageiros/paginas/default.aspx (train details
are omitted in the English version and you
should choose the Portuguese option. Keep in
mind that 'horarios' stands for 'timetables' and
'preços' means prices).

- **Chile**

A few rail services ferry passengers in the nation's
south-central area, between Santiago and Chillán in
Ñuble, including the Talca to Constitución route in
the Maule area.

Most passengers use the website www.trencentral.cl
while www.efe.cl is the official website for the
Chilean state railways. Every day, multiple trains
from Terrasur connect the Alamada station of
Santiago with Chillan, Linares, Talca and Curico on
the main line powered by electricity. The trains are
preferente class consisting of a refreshment car and
standard class, and are air-conditioned. 3 such trains
can connect Chillan to Concepcion with a bus service
as well.

- **Colombia**

  The country has quite a few operational railways, following the bankruptcy of the State rail operator a few years back. However, Zipaquira (the site of a popular salt cathedral) is linked with Bogota by a practicable tourist train (www.turistren.com.co). The train starts a round trip every day from the La Sabana station present in Bogota at 08:30, and stops in Cajica and Zipaquira as well.

- **Ecuador**

  The place also has some exciting train services on offer. You can make wonderful trips through the Pacific Coast and Ecuadorian Andes areas. There are distinctive trains that offer a glimpse into the traditions, culture and customs of the place. The newest train travel packages include train trips to the Northern Andes, and include a mix of diverse cultures. You can get more information at www.ecuadorrail.net.

Hitchhiking in South America

In South America, Ecuador is regarded as the best nation for hitchhiking – given that the waiting time to be picked up is the shortest here. Chile is a nice place as well, to get fast rides in South America. Argentineans are known to be great hitchhikers, but hitchhiking in the country can be extremely slow, particularly in the north. It is more convenient in Patagonia. Bolivia is reported to the difficult to manage. However, if you clearly indicate that you are not a paying rider, you can get across places by hitchhiking. Both Colombia and Brazil are tough spots, and you will mostly be in gas stations in Brazil for the maximum time. Paraguay is a small nation. Peru is perfect for hitchhikers. Although hitchhiking is slow in Uruguay, the country is a nice place for meeting new people.

If you like warm climate, travel to South America during January - February. Make a trip during June – August if you like cold weather conditions. For the most part of the year, rain in the Amazon is common. In humid area, the sun shines very hot. Even where humidity is less, you can still feel very hot. You can visit South America at any time as a hitchhiker, as you can always find cars and other vehicles. Hitchhiking is eventually successful wherever there are roads. It is always a good idea to have patience.

South America Top Places to Visit

A large continent, South America provides travellers with an amazing variety in enjoyable experiences. This is a nation of delectable food, bustling streets and gorgeous natural parks.

Each traveller can find something gorgeous, from Medellin to Tierra del Fuego. Environmentalists and nature lovers love the well-maintained Pantanal in Brazil, whereas shoppers can pick between the colourful Andean village markets and elite boutiques in Rio de Janeiro and other major cities. You can gorge on delicious dishes, view picture-perfect sceneries and lost cities of old civilizations. There are plenty of choices in South America. Learn about a few of the best places to visit in South America below:

- **Rio de Janeiro**

  While visiting Rio de Janeiro, you should have to go for a class in samba, the most famous dance form in Rio. This cosmopolitan city, other than samba, is famous for the Copacabana Beach, the Bossa Nova and its Carnival. The statue of Christ the Redeemer, placed on top of the Corcovado Mountain, is the most popular landmark here. The 2016 Summer Olympics was hosted in Rio, although the locals love soccer a lot. One of the largest soccer stadiums on the planet, Maracana Stadium, is located here.

- **Punta del Este**

Punta del Este is a luxurious beach resort located on the Atlantic Coast of southeast Uruguay. It is frequently compared to the Saint-Tropez of South America, where young and pretty head-turners come by the yacht to flash some skin and splurge on swanky clubs and bars on the beachside. During summer, the beach turns into a wonderful place for watching people.

- **Machu Picchu**

The place beautifully represents the ancient Inca civilization before the coming of the Spaniards. It is comfortably positioned in the Peruvian Andes, and is a spot for the fortress and the emperor. This is a site where religious rituals were held, involving human sacrifices, to satisfy the gods. The place was left untouched by the Spaniards, and was deserted after the Spanish conquest. It was discovered only in the early 1900s by a professor from America. Machu Picchu was constructed from polished stones and it is a wonderful specimen of classical architecture from the Inca era. In Peru, it is the most visited destination for tourists with its amazing views.

- **Pantanal**

It can tough to travel to this place. It is mostly accessible by boat or plane, but the views are worth the trip. The place is mostly situated in Brazil (with some in Paraguay and other in Bolivia). It is the biggest tropical wetland in the world, and spreads over an area as large as the Washington State. Although it is not as popular as its counterpart in the Amazon, it is the best spot to view wildlife specimens, including capybaras and jaguars.

- **Montevideo**

This is a port city with a flourishing culture, and serves as the home and national capital of Uruguay and inhabits close to half of the population of the country. It has a rich history and consists of stunning and varied landmarks. You should make it a point to visit the 18th-century mansions and churches decorating the cobblestoned streets, and the partly Art Deco and partly Gothic Palacio Salvo.

- **Ushuaia**

  This should be on your priority list if you like to see remote places. It is the capital of Tierra del Fuego in Argentina, and is regarded as the southernmost city on Earth. The train to the End of the World ends in this place. This place is snuggled among mountains along a stunning bay. It is neither windy nor cloudy for most of the year, and is at its picturesque best. There is a museum in this colony, which served as a penal centre. You can see seals, penguins and orca whales here.

- **Tayrona National Park**

  This is located on Colombia's Caribbean coast, and is the second most visited park in the country. This protected marine reserve takes in sea as well as in land. It has an amazing biodiversity in flora and fauna. The assortment of wildlife here includes 70 types of bats, over 700 varied mammals and 300 bird species. It is known best for its amazing beaches, located in deep bays, having coconut palms offering shades and mountains as the backdrop. Most beaches are not good for swimming, due to the strong current.

- **Quito**

  This is the capital of Ecuador and is unique among global capital cities. The highest legal capital city in the world, it is most proximal to the equator. The Spaniards founded this old colourful town in 1534. It is still the largest and best-maintained site in entire America, and minimally changed as well. It is situated in the northern highlands of Ecuador and is surrounded by volcanoes, which can be viewed clearly on good-weather days. It is the only capital of the world always under threat from active volcanoes.

- **Cartagena**

  This major city on the Caribbean coast of Colombia witnesses a rich cultural scene, having art galleries and museums and festivals all through the year. In 1533, the Spaniards established this city. It was named after Cartagena in Spain. It served as the economic and political centre during the Spanish domination of South America. Although this is a modern city in present times, walled fortresses and historic centres still stand here.

- **Salvador**

This is also known as Salvador da Bahia. In 1548, the Portuguese established it. It is one of the most ancient American colonial cities. Its glorious past is evident in the historic centre Pelourinho where slaves were thrashed. This is the 3rd largest city in Brazil that also served as the first American slave port. Vestiges of its African heritage are still evident in the local cuisine and other cultural aspects. This party town also hosts the annual Carnival celebration, the largest party in the world.

- **Los Glaciares National Park**

The largest Argentine national park, it is the site of the largest ice cap outside Antarctica and Greenland. The ice cap nourishes 47 big glaciers. The Perito Moreno glacier is the most famous and unique of these, as it is moving ahead whereas the others are retreating. The largest Argentine lake, Lake Argentino, also stands in this park. The Patagonian Steppe and Magellan Subpolar forest, both well maintained, display the biodiversity and ecology of the park.

191

- **Colca Canyon**

  Its picturesque views make it the 3rd most visited tourist spot in Peru. Although not the deepest Peruvian canyon, it is one of the deepest canyons in the world. It is over 2 times deeper than the U.S Grand Canyon. You can see amazing sceneries, see the largest hummingbirds, view Andean condors and buy handicrafts from local villages.

- **Atacama Desert**

  This is the driest, and perhaps most unique, non-polar desert on Earth. It rains here just once every 4 years. It stretches along the Chilean coast for around 1,000 miles or 1,600 km, and is located between the Pacific Ocean and the Andes. The soil is similar to that on Mars, and thus it served as a location for some parts of Space Odyssey: Voyage to the Planets. It also stands out for its deep blue lagoons, expansive salt flats and active geysers.

- **Angel Falls**

  This is a stunner in the Guayana Highlands of Venezuela. The highest uninterrupted waterfall on Earth, it is 15 times higher than the Niagara Falls shared by the U.S and Canada. Water falls down into the Rio Kerepacupai Meru 3,200 feet (or 950 meters) from the Auyantepu Mountain. It owes its name to Jimmy Angel, an American who was the first pilot in 1937 to fly over the falls. Boat and plane rides are the most adventurous ways to get there.

- **Cusco**

  This is situated at a height of 11,000 feet or 3,400 meters in the Andes Mountains. Once the capital of the Inca civilization, it has a historic, colourful past. The Spanish conquered it during the 1500s, taking over control from the Incas. As per Peruvian constitution, it is the historical capital although not the national capital. You can find remnants of Inca sites in the adjoining region while the Old Town still contains traces of Spanish colonization.

- **Salar de Uyuni**

  This unique South American attraction is located about 12,000 feet or 3,700 meters above sea level in southwest Peru, it is the largest salt flat of the world. One of the flattest salt flats, it looks beyond earthly after rains and appears as a vast mirror. Flamingos love to breed here.

- **Lake Titicaca**

  It is the largest lake in South America, straddling the Peruvian and Bolivian borders. At a height of around 12,500 feet or 3,800 meters, it is regarded as the highest navigable lake on Earth, although some smaller lakes are located at higher elevation. It has 41 islands, many of which are inhabited. It has a vast number of water birds, and is home to 500 aquatic creatures.

- **Easter Island**

  This is known for the 900 wondrous statues known as Moai, estimated to have been carved a millennium back by the early residents of Polynesia from volcanic ash that had solidified. The closest people live around 1,300 miles away. The most remote peopled island on Earth, this Chilean territory involves very long trips to reach.

- **Amazon Rainforest**

  Consisting of a staggering 390 billion trees, it covers around three-fourths of the Amazon River Basin. The largest tropical rainforest in the world, it boasts amazing fauna and flora. 60% of this rainforest is situated in Brazil, with major parts in Colombia and Peru.

- **Torres del Paine National Park**

  One of the biggest and most visited national parks in Chile, it is situated in remote Chilean Patagonia. It offers amazing sceneries, including that of 3 peaks in the Paine Mountains landscape. The park, other than mountains, is line with steppe, forests, rivers and glaciers – which makes it a favourite of nature lovers. It also consists of endangered deer species.

- **Buenos Aires**

  The 4th most populated area in America, with 17 million individuals. It is situated on the Rio de la Plata, on the coast of Argentina. This cosmopolitan city is loved for its rich culture, lifestyle and architecture. The most visited South American city, it has the historic residential neighbourhood Recoleta. The most popular attraction in this district is the Recoleta Cemetery, the site of burial of Eva Peron, the second wife of Juan Peron, the famous Argentine President.

- **Galapagos Islands**

  Located around 900 km off the Ecuadorian coast, these offer an idea about the appearance of prehistoric animals, such as creepy iguanas and giant tortoises. The animals here inspired "On the Origin of Species", the controversial book of Charles Darwin from the 19th century. The archipelago consists of 18 prominent islands, developed due to volcanic activities.

- **Iguazu Falls**

  The largest waterfalls system of the world, consisting of 275 waterfalls of different sizes – with the biggest being Devil's Throat. This is one of the best tourist destinations in South America. The Iguazu River, for most of its course to the ocean, flows through Brazil. The majority of its falls are in Argentine territories.

Europe

A vast continent, Europe consists of the westernmost Eurasian region. Its south is bordered by the Mediterranean Sea, while its west is bordered by the Atlantic Ocean and the north is surrounded by the Arctic Ocean. You can expect a European trip to consist of costly coffee, uncooperative Frenchmen, boozy backpackers and wonderful sights, and your expectations can be true on most occasions.

This vast continent with diversity includes 51 nations, and contains fantastic galleries, scenic islands, crazy street parties, awesome music festivals, vibrant cities and memorable beach sunsets with free flow of cocktail.

For about $65 USD, you can pass a night in a castle in Bavaria, visit the Notre Dame in Paris and the Louvre Museum free of cost, cruise in Istanbul on the Bosporus for only $1 USD and gorge on full meals for lower than $12 USD in London. These days, tourists can visit Europe at cheap rates due to lower airfares prompted by a strong Dollar and very low-cost flights. Even after booking a European summer vacation, you can save money in many ways.

Europe Travel

Once you get the chance to travel around Europe, the land of cheese, wine and mouth-watering culinary delights, you are tempted to think about only one question: what is the ideal way to make a trip around Europe? Would you simply opt for a rail pass or make a trip by booking multiple low-cost flights? Is it better to buy bus passes that can help you travel through various nations? There are endless options. Read on and know about a few of the best options for travelling around this old continent.

Flying around Europe

These days, European travel has become a lot cheaper with the entry of many budget carriers into the picture. You can use websites such as Google Flights or Skyscanner to come across the best online deals. With advance booking, you can get many low-cost deals to fly from one destination to another. When you book early, airline companies like Norwegian, Transavia, Vueling, Easyjet and Ryanair, can offer you wonderful bang for your bucks. For only £14.99 GBP, you can board flights to Copenhagen from London Stansted. However, booking flights across Europe makes backpacking less unplanned. It is also often important to go through the fine print, as airline companies often have hidden fees to compensate for their low flight rates.

Flying around countries of Europe saves times as well as costs, and is the most practical option if you are short on time. You can get amazing deals if you make early bookings. If you manage to get low-cost flight rates, do not think twice and make bookings immediately. Flight costs quickly fluctuate, and you should make early bookings. You should also look at additional expenses, like check-in of your luggage.

Finding the Cheapest Flights around Europe

In case you do not consider a travel credit to be a perfect option, you need to look for ways to get the most low-cost flights. You can use the following tips to book your flights and get the best deals.

You can save a lot by travelling off-season. Going on trips during the summer season means you have to pay more. You can also find ways to save on your summer flight deals, although you can save the most during your off-season trips. It can also help you to be flexible with your choice of airports and dates. Travelling on weekdays and adjusting flight dates by some days can also allow you to save money.

Flying to various European airports can also help in saving on costs.

There are many low-cost airlines in Europe that will provide you with a good service for a very affordable price. Here is a list dividing each budget airline by country:

Austria

- Niki: www.flyniki.com

Azerbaijan

- AZALJet: www.azal.az

Czech Republic

- SmartWings: www.smartwings.com

France

- French Blue: www.frenchblue.com
- HOP!: www.hop.com
- Transavia France: www.transavia.com

Germany

- Eurowings: www.eurowings.com

Greece

- Aegean Air: www.aegeanair.com

Hungary

- Wizz Air: www.wizzair.com

Iceland

- WOW Air: www.wowair.com

Ireland

- Ryanair: www.ryanair.com

Italy

- Blue Panorama Airlines: www.blue-panorama.com

Latvia

- AirBaltic: www.airbaltic.com

Moldova

- FlyOne: www.flyone.md

Netherlands

- Transavia: www.transavia.com

Norway

- Norwegian Air Shuttle: www.norwegian.com

Romania

- Blue Air: www.blueairweb.com

Russia

- Pobeda: www.pobeda.aero

- Utair aviation: www.utair.ru

- Nordavia: www.nordavia.ru

Spain

- Iberia Express: www.iberiaexpress.com

- Level: www.flylevel.com

- Plus Ultra: plusultra.com

- Volotea: www.volotea.com

- Vueling: www.vueling.com

Turkey

- Pegasus Airlines: www.flypgs.com

United Kingdom

- EasyJet: www.easyjet.com
- Flybe: www.flybe.com
- Jet2.com: www.jet2.com
- Monarch Airlines: www.monarch.co.uk

Europe by Bus

You can also travel around Europe by bus. Once you arrive at a destination, buses can be a wonderful mode of travel for you. However, careful travellers can find buses that travel between major European cities as well. A bus usually costs less than a train, although the comfort factor is lower as well.

Eurolines (Eurolines.com)

Visit Eurolines (Eurolines.com), and you can find many bus passes that are valid in 29 countries of Europe and allows you to use its wide bus network. Pre-booking bus tickets for your first destination city will make you free to use their bus network for travelling for 30 days (265€) or 15 days (195€) between 51 cities in Europe. For a measly €9, you can also get point-to-point tickets from Eurolines.

It is best to ask your hostel staff about regional and local buses, unless you want a bus tour. There are regional as well as local bus stations, and even bus lines operating for long distances, in many cities. Bus passes with unlimited rides are also offered by some companies, just like rail passes. These can be helpful alternatives, or at least additions, to a rail pass. Learn about some of the major European bus companies below.

Busabout (www.busabout.com)

This is the largest bus pass operator in Europe that targets backpackers. The bus network consists of multiple pass options and runs every day from May to October. It covers 10 nations and 30 destinations, and you can hop on and off in your travel around Europe. Busabout, other than the bus network, also offers many European festival and adventure travel oriented packages.

Megabus (www.busabout.com)

This is used by many college students in the US, and it offers discount bus tickets to choicest international cities and all through the UK. For instance, you can pay about £15 GBP for a ticket to Amsterdam from London.

Lux Express Group (www.luxexpress.eu)

This is the biggest coach operator for international express routes in the Baltic area, and runs bus services in as many as 7 nations. Warsaw, Vilnius, Riga, Tallinn and St. Petersburg are some of the prime directions. Its network runs on Estonian domestic routes as well as in international routes. You can get bus services under Lux Express Special, Lux Express and Lux Express Lounge.

National Express (www.nationalexpress.com)

This is the best travel option around the UK. This multinational British public transport agency has its base in Birmingham and runs coach and bus services around the nation.

Europe Travel by Train

Train travel is a traditional favourite for Europe tours, and with good reason. The magic, the romance and the motivation are enormous. It can also be slightly mysterious for you, if you do not live in a nation where train is not a primary mode of travel. Europe has a very well-developed rail network and highly dependable train service. While European trains might not be ideal, most individuals regard these as the best travel option.

InterRail Vs Eurail

It is essential to know about your train travel options in Europe. First, you have to understand which rail pass option in Europe is applicable for you.

An InterRail (www.interrail.eu) pass is your option if you live in Europe. However, you can satisfy the eligibility criteria to get an Eurail (www.eurail.com) pass if you live outside Europe.

InterRail Pass

The pass is actually a train ticket that lets travellers ride on about any European train. You can use the pass to access 37 ferry and railway companies in 30 nations. You can just show your InterRail Pass to the staff to board most of the trains. You are expected to reserve an extra seat by a few train companies.

You have to be less than 28 years in age on the first day of the validity of a Youth InterRail pass, in order to qualify for the same. The age limit of youths has been raised to under-28 from under-26 from January 2017.

The passes offer freedom, flexibility and spontaneity. These can be your best option in case you do not wish to be stuck to particular dates and trains. With an InterRail (www.interrail.eu) pass, you can make a spontaneous, and not scheduled, exploration of Europe. You can stay in a city for shorter or longer duration based on your liking of the place, and change your travel plans while moving about as well.

It is a good idea to use the pass for Edinburgh to Athens travel and other trips that take very long, or for complex and long itineraries that can go haywire if you book low-cost, multiple point-to-point tickets and a train is cancelled due to a security alert, strike, flood or fire. You can get the flexibility to change your routes, dates and trains. Even when a pass comes at a slightly higher expense than a cheap ticket, it can be worthwhile to pay for the extra amount of flexibility.

With this pass, you can also get access to most trains in Europe. However, a few trains have to be reserved in advance. With a reservation, you can be assured of a seat on a particular train. You can make advance seat reservations as early as 3 months prior to the departure of a train. You can maximize your chances of getting a seat by making bookings as early as possible. You generally need a reservation for night trains and high-speed trains. You can be assured of a bed or a seat on the train with a timely reservation. Reservation fees are based on the accommodation type, class and train.

Eurail

Eurail (www.eurail.com) happens to be best option if you are looking for fun and comfortable train travel across Europe. With a single Eurail Pass, you can get access to broad rail networks as well as a few ferries in 28 European nations. You can get a Eurail Pass, whether you have a family with young kids, or you are an ace globetrotter or a first-time traveller. For a trip to savour for a whole lifetime, this is the only network that offers the broadest and most flexible coverage to those who would like to travel across entire Europe.

Whether you opt for low-cost advance-purchase tickets or use a Eurail pass, you can find train travel to be a comfortable and amazing way to travel to various major cities of Europe, and view many locations within a very short period. You can avail the passes at any age, irrespective of who you are. Millions of individuals have used Eurail to travel across Europe, since its launch in 1959.

The pass can be your one-stop train ticket to get access to multiple trains in more than one European nation. You can hop on or off at any time and any location that you want. You can get various rail passes from the Eurail website (www.eurail.com/en/eurail-passes), and plan a one-of-a-kind adventure according to your own preferences.

Only non-European citizens or residents can use this pass. Citizens in Europe can opt for an InterRail Pass (www.interrail.eu) as an alternative. In case you are not citizen of Europe but manage to prove yourself as a European resident, an InterRail Pass can be granted to you.

The pass can let you make back and forth trips between nations. You can visit the nations mentioned in your pass for as many times you need, and even use them to cross the borders as frequently as possible.

Train Travel Advantages in Europe

- **A Gigantic Network and Several Trains**

  Europe has a vast train network, and you can make train trips to even the smallest towns. There are several trains offered to most tourist spots every day. Generally, a train serves the most famous routes every hour, which helps raise the number of travel options.

- **No Baggage Limits or Fees**

  You do not have to pay additional fees for multiple luggage cases or for heavier luggage. Ensure that you can lift the luggage onto your train.

- **Possibility to Sleep On the Train and to Travel Longer**

  In the case of long-distance trips, opt for an overnight ride. Such trains consist of special sleeper cars with 2 or 6-bunk rooms. In a sleeper car, a bunk can cost around €20 to €50 more although no entire day would be lost in travel. Overnight trains come with normal seats, and no additional expenses are needed.

- **Disembark Right in the Centre of Your Destination**

  European rail stations, unlike airports, are situated straight in the middle of towns. As you are already in a city, there is no need to spend money or time to travel to the city. You can reach the city from airport at a cost of €8 to €35 within 20 to 60 minutes.

- **Bring whatever you want on a train**

  You may take everything along for a train ride, including alcohol. If you want, take a pack of beer or a wine bottle along. Sharing them with a few fellow passengers can make them your friends. Buy some cheap foods from the local grocery store for the trip.

- **No Need To Book ahead**

  You can skip booking ahead as most trains do not need a reservation. Turn up at the railway station before your train leaves and hop on.

- **Wonderful Views**

  The scenes of the countryside in Europe are amazing, and you can see some wonderful views during train rides.

- **Consistent and On Schedule**

  Over 90% of the time, trains are on schedule in Europe – partly because climate does not impact train services. Contrast this to flights being on schedule 65% of the time.

- **Peace and Quiet**

  You can find train rides very relaxing, sitting in silence at 145 MPH speed and watching the European countryside through the window.

Hitchhiking in Europe

It is exciting to hitchhike in Europe. You will love to hitch through many small nations. It is more or less safe to hitchhike here, and you will especially love to travel through motorways in the Western parts.

It can be quite convenient for you to hitch about in a few nations, such as Germany. For instance, you can travel large distances in just one lift. There is no limit on driving speed here, and you can drive very fast in this country. When it comes to hitchhiking, most nations are quite easy – such as in some countries in East Europe, Netherlands and Belgium - or at least average. Some other nations, such as Italy and Spain, are regarded as bad due to the long wait for a pickup. However, if you are patient, you can hitch a ride.

However, hitchhiking might not be the best transportation mode for a foreigner through Eastern Europe. Criminals view foreigners as profitable and easy prey. In case you want to hitchhike through any country in Central or Eastern Europe, you should take proper precautions and abide by useful safety tips and suggestions. Across the world, hitchhiking is increasingly turning out to be fraught with dangers. If you want to hitchhike in the eastern part of Europe, do so with utmost caution. Always follow your instincts in case you sense that not everything seems right. Transport facilities in Eastern Europe might not always be comfortable, clean or efficient.

Western Europe Travel

Western Europe is an old-world and romantic place, but interesting and vast as well, with many opportunities. The beauty of Europe is of course in London and Paris, but it is more evident in the off-beat routes. You can view some amazing tourist destinations in Western Europe.

The Countries of Western Europe including the Scandinavia region are: Andorra, Austria, Belgium, Denmark, Finland, France, Germany, Gibraltar, Greece, Iceland, Italy, Ireland, Liechtenstein, Luxembourg, Malta, Monaco, Norway, Netherlands, Portugal, San Marino, Spain, Sweden, Switzerland, United Kingdom. These nations are the most popular and in-demand travel destinations on Earth. Western Europe, with its diverse geography, mouth-watering cuisines, fantastic music, exciting history stunning architecture and rich culture, should be on the itinerary of every tourist.

Here are some destinations in Europe that you must visit, irrespective of the time of the year:

- **Brussels**

    The friendliest European city, it has been influenced by every major culture in Europe. For NATO, EU,

Benelux and other international agencies, it is a big centre. Most people speak Dutch and French here, with the Belgian capital being heavily impacted by these two cultures – as evident in its social, cultural and political life. Manneken Pis, Grand Palace and the Guinness record holder Delirium Café are the must-see places. Savour tasteful delights like Belgian chocolates, Brussels waffle and many varieties of beers.

- **Copenhagen**

One of the happiest and safest European places. If you want to get the feel of Europe, take a relaxing stroll on Copenhagen's cobbled streets. This wonderful travel destination in Europe is a paradise for tourists, and you can find friendly individuals, various cafes and historical buildings across the city and spots close to the capital. Shop at the Stroget and visit the Tivoli gardens and The Little Mermaid statue. Food lovers can gorge on Danish pastries, Smorrebrod and other Danish culinary delights.

- **Berlin**

This powerful capital of Germany has a long, rich history. This European spot is a wonderful mix of art, culture and science. It annually attracts many travellers who come to the place to personally experience its nightlife, orchestras and museums. You should not miss the Reichstag, the Berlin Wall and the Holocaust Memorial. The city gives stiff competition to traditional heavyweights. Do not miss popular local cuisines like Doner kebabs, Spanferkel and Currywurst.

- **Paris**

This is Europe proper, and the rich city has many imitations around the globe that can hardly match its beauty. It stands for modern lifestyle. There are attractions like the Champs-Élysées, the Notre Dame and the Eiffel Tower. It has the biggest assemblage of art at museums like Pompidou, Orsay and Louvre. Stroll along the Seine, shop down the squares and grand boulevards and sit at a bistro or café to get the real feel of Paris.

- **Dublin**

This is a city for fun lovers who want to enjoy a good time. The Dublin culture is incomplete without its pubs and the popular Guinness beer presented by the Irish people. It has popular attractions like fish & chips, Colcannon and Irish stew.

- **Rome**

  This vast city is famous for its Vatican and the wonderful architecture and art objects. It contains Pantheon, Colosseum and various other things to remind of its ancient beauty and status as an empire. The Capitoline Museums and the Borghese Gallery are architectural and historical marvels. You can check out the popular gelato, espresso and long lunches there, and walk down cobbled squares and alleyways to get a feel for the place.

- **Edinburgh**

  This Scottish capital is a much-loved destination for arts and education. The city still has its medieval heritage structures intact, along with modern-day buildings and rising standards of education. The Scottish National Gallery, The Scott Monument and Edinburgh castle are some popular places to visit. Do not miss the globally renowned Scotch or Scottish Whiskey and the famous Haggis during a trip there.

- **London**

  The European capital is the richest and largest city of the continent. It is known for cultural impact and diversity, and you can see as well as experience new things here. There are landmarks such as the Tower of London, the Big Ben, Westminster Abbey, Buckingham Palace, all-year exhibitions in the National Gallery, British Museum and Tate Modern and modern icons such as The Shard – the highest building in Europe – and the Gherkin skyscraper. This is also a popular shopping destination.

- **Vienna**

  Known as "The City of Music", it consists of classical European architecture set amidst nature. The city teems with theatres, museums, restaurants, cafes etc., and the green meadows on its outskirts transport you to The Sound of Music. You should visit places like the Vienna Opera House, Viennese Cafes, Freud Museum, Schonbrunn Palace and St. Stephen's Cathedral. You should also try Viennese culinary delights like Sachertorte, Apfelstrudel, Croissant and Wiener Schnitzel.

- **Florence**

  It serves the perfect combination of the Renaissance period of World History and the greatest time from European history. The artistic city can look like an open-air museum for you, with the many historic destinations situated so near to each other. You should not leave without seeing the Uffizi, consisting of the masterpieces by Michelangelo, Raphael, Leonardo da Vinci etc. The romantic city has lovely piazzas that show the amazing sculpture and architectural wonders. Walk to the top of the magnificent Duomo to view the fantastic heritage structures.

- **Amsterdam**

  The city museums have enough art objects to remind you of the golden age of Europe, The Dutch Golden Age. There are Rembrandt masterpieces in the Rijksmuseum, Van Gogh's artistic wonders in a dedicated museum, Holocaust memorabilia in the Anne Frank House remind us of the darkest hour in human history and more. The Dutch capital is made more inviting and beautiful by the canals that line its well-preserved buildings.

- **Athens**

  Some vacationers feel slightly disappointed when they find a modern metropolis in Athens. But a trip to the Acropolis and the old Plaka neighbourhood satisfies them, where they can see the birthplace of democracy and view a few ancient wonders that still manage to amaze. The Acropolis Museum with its incredible art assemblage, the Parthenon and the National Archaeological Museum with its important ancient Grecian artefacts draw huge appreciation from tourists.

- **Barcelona**

  The place symbolizes modern Europe, and is a wonderful combination of the past and the future. The city itself deserves a second look for its liberated spirit. It is home to some of the most unique 20th century architecture, including the Sagrada Familia, which is still under construction and promises to be an eternal monument. The Parc Güell feels like a land of imagination. Walk down the Passeig de Gracia to view some of the most innovative pieces of architecture. This is a place where Gaudi co-exists with Picasso. A museum stands here, dedicated to the earliest art objects of Picasso. Other amazing attractions include modern marvels like Frank Gehry's fish sculpture and the Agbar Tower, the Palau Nacional's medieval art objects and the Miró Foundation's wonderful collections.

- **Lisbon**

  The Atlantic capital mostly enjoys a sunny climate the year round. It was the first global capital and served as the entry point for people from the East to Europe. The rich history of Lisbon is evident through its collections in the Maritime, Ancient Art and Orient museums, and reflected on the Jeronimos Monastery, the Tower of Belem and other marvellous sculptures of the Age of Discovery. The unique Tile Museum in Lisbon is where you can see the tile painting art, and admire it. You can witness it at various other monuments located around the city. The hilltop terraces in the city offer exciting, beautiful scenes.

- **Seville**

  It is the fourth largest Spanish city, and serves as a perfect blend of modern technology from the 20th century and medieval Spanish beauty. A hot favourite destination for tourists, it has many attractions that can engross and excite tourists. There are places like Plaza de Espana, The Alcazar and Seville cathedral that are must-visit places on a European itinerary. Do not miss out on popular cuisines such as tortas de aceite, Jamon iberico and serranito.

- **Madrid**

  This destination is a must for every art lover. Other than the amazing Prado collection consisting of Velazquez and Goyas, you can find more Spanish Golden Age masters being featured in the Thyssen-Bornemisza, the Reina Sofia and various other internationally famous museums. You can view amazing masterpieces by Miró, Salvador Dali and Picasso in the Reina Sofia. The Thyssen-Bornemisza has fantastic art objects from all major European art periods, with artists like Monet, Rubens and Dürer being featured. However, if you really want to get a feel for life in Madrid, walk down the streets of Chueca, dine at a tapas restaurant, stride down the majestic Gran Via, savour the nightlife in the city, sip on an espresso at any outdoor café on a plaza or visit the Plaza Mayor and other plazas. Experience Madrid like a native.

- **Venice**

  Stand in the St. Mark's Square, the hub of the once richest city of the world and global trade capital, and you will love the views. Take a trip on the Gondola, the unique boats, past the majestic palazzos and the most beautiful private residences in the city. Sail down the romantic canals. Take a look at some of the most exquisite and expensive art objects of the world at the Accademia Gallery. You can enjoy the fantastic combination of Baroque, Gothic, Byzantine and Renaissance architecture and art, and should also devote some time to the modern creative art in the Peggy Guggenheim Museum.

- **Zurich**

  One of the most prominent cities and the largest financial centre in the world, it is home to many financial institutions and banks. It has a history of over 2,000 years and there are various heritage structures around the city that bear testimony to its glorious past. The city boasts of a unique combination of society and culture, and is known for its active nightlife. Make sure that you do not miss traditional local delicacies like Tirggel and Zurcher Geschnetzeltes, and visit local attractions like Uetliberg, Lindenhof and Lake Promenade as well.

Eastern Europe Travel

The region of Eastern Europe embraces many varied histories, languages, ethnicities and cultures. Eastern Europe, South-eastern Europe/Balkans, The Baltics and East Central Europe are some of the most well-known sub-regions of this region.

The Eastern Europe countries include: Russia, Czech Republic, Poland, Croatia, Slovakia, Hungary, Romania, Moldova, Serbia, Lithuania, Latvia, Estonia, Slovenia,

Bulgaria, Ukraine, Belarus, Montenegro, Bosnia, Herzegovina, Albania, Kosovo, and Macedonia.

It sees a confluence of cultural activities, and you can take part in folk singing, fine arts and many other activities. There are elegant cities like St Petersburg, Prague, and Budapest that are home to wonderful collections of art objects in palatial ambiences. Some of the places are just like open-air museums, such as the art-nouveau architecture spread across Riga, the vast Red Square in Moscow and the Main Market Square or the Kraków's Rynek Główny.

It is impossible to ignore the charms of this amazing place, and you will surely be excited by the stunning, luscious charms of Eastern Europe.

Awesome Destinations in Eastern Europe

Eastern Europe is weaning away many travellers who are perpetually looking for trips to exotic destinations. The place has the glamour of Italy, UK or France and comes with a lot of grandeur, cultural riches and stunning medieval architecture. The place is witnessing steady growth in the number of tourists.

- **Budapest**

  This is a beautiful place that is divided by the long Danube River that meanders through it. It is a site of historical wonders and hills. Flat plains on the East bank have made modern clubs and cafes. There are many tourist attractions in Budapest, including The Royal Palace, The Great Synagogue and the Memento Park. You can go on night cruises on the river, under the beautiful Szechenyi Chain Bridge and past the majestic Parliament Building – both of which are stunning during the night.

- **Istanbul**

  Istanbul is one of the largest global cities and certainly the largest in Turkey. It is the capital of the Byzantine and Ottoman Empires. It stretches across a strait of narrow shape connecting Europe and Asia, which makes it the sole city on the planet to span two continents. It is one of the best tourist destinations in Turkey, with its exotic ambience, amazing nightlife, shopping, dining, historic sites and amazing architecture. You can find the most stunning historic sites in Istanbul in The Old City, comprising of Topkapi Palace, Hagia Sophia and Blue Mosque.

- **St. Petersburg**

This is a diverse city with various colourful areas. The authorities try their best to preserve the unique beauty of the place. Due to this reason, each newly developed project is coordinated with care. Public opinion plays a vital role in this case.

It is often considered to be the most forward-looking city of European style in Russia, and serves as a fantastic tourist spot – particularly for culture and history lovers. Over 80 theatres, 2000 libraries and 220 museums constitute the cultural landscape of the city. The innovativeness of St. Petersburg is displayed in the wonderful hostels with minimalist interior designs of Scandinavian style, noisy underground clubs, bohemian cafes and uptight art galleries.

- **Bucharest**

Bucharest is a modern, dynamic city with an exciting history. It serves as the capital of Romania. In the early 20th century, it got the nickname "Little Paris". The place boasts historic as well as sophisticated architecture, wonderful boulevards lined by trees and modern cafes. It has plenty of attractions, with the huge Parliament Palace being the most impressive landmark in the city. The huge and expansive structure is beaten only by the Pentagon in size.

The architectural and cultural wonders of the place include the circular domed building named the Romanian Athenaeum that also serves as the main concert hall of the city, the National History Museum and the Bucharest University.

- **Bratislava**

The Slovakian capital, this city has a lot of charm. This small old town boasts of medieval grandeur, and the magnificent hilltop castle presents a magnificent view of the city. There are fantastic bars and restaurants lining its narrow streets, where you can drink, eat and relish the local culture. Check the Slavin Memorial and the Bratislava Castle for the best views of the city. Come here during Christmas and visit the main square located in the middle of the city to shop in the traditional Market. There are authentic local holiday specialties, which include savoury mulled wine - a beverage that you must not miss for the world.

- **Nida**

  The beautiful Nida is where the main settlement happened on the Curonian Spit on the side of Lithuania. The Curonian Spit is a curved sand dune located between the Baltic Sea and the Curonian Lagoon. Lithuania and Russia share this UNESCO World Heritage Site, where Nida is a popular tourist attraction. The ancient relics remind the tale of a primitive fishing village. Its beauty is enhanced by vibrant boats in its harbour and colourful wooden cottages.

  From Nida, you have to take a hike through a pine forest for a short distance to get to white sand beaches. To the south of the village, you can find the Parnidis Dune – the most impressive and vast dune. Walk up to its elevated summit and you can find wide views of the rippling, pristine dunes. Go for a tour and explore the Curonian National Park. Both experiences will make you understand why this fantastic place draws so many visitors.

- **Skopje**

  Skopje is among the most compelling and diverse capital cities in Europe. It is a perfect combination of Islamic and Christian cultures. The combination has resulted in a colourful, lively society. The city has an infectious social vibe, with local people gathering in the parks and playing chess or going to bars and cafes for conservation and music. The city comes into its element at night. You can go to the Carsija neighbourhood and enjoy the best museums and historic structures of Skopje. The Plostad Makedonija Square, along with its Triumphal Arch, is dedicated in memory of its national heroes.

- **Dubrovnik**

  Dubrovnik, a landmark in Croatia, has earned the nickname "Pearl of the Adriatic". In Eastern Europe, it is one of the loveliest towns. In 1979, UNESCO designated it as a World Heritage Site. The place boasts impressive sculptures, museums, churches and architecture. Go for a walk along the wall of the city to complete your trip. This vantage point offers you breath-taking views of the Adriatic and the city.

- **Split**

  It is the second largest Croatia city. This amazing city is located on the Adriatic's Eastern shores, and it is centered on the majestic Roman monument Diocletian's Palace, now designated as a World

Heritage Site by UNESCO. Mountains along the coast serve as a beautiful backdrop to Split, and serve to make the city gorgeous. The city has its activity centre in the palace, a beautiful maze of streets consisting of shops, bars, restaurants and people. You can see every highlight within walking distance of the palace. In the summer, Split offers a vibrant beach scene. You can enjoy plenty of games and scenes of the sea in the famous Bacvice Beach.

- **Mljet Island**

  Mljet is the greenest and one of the loveliest islands in Croatia. The island is mostly covered in dense Mediterranean woods, with small villages, vineyards and farms in a peaceful ambience. The Mljet National Park makes up its north half. Its dense, wonderful vegetation and clear salt-water lakes give it an unspoiled charm. You should go to Polace to view the amazing Roman Palace that dates back to the 1st to 5th century. Go to one of the best Polace restaurants, Konoba Ankora, to enjoy foods by the sea.

- **Old Orhei**

  Moldova is the site of the Oreil Vechi Monastery, a cave monastery that is sculpted in a majestic limestone cliff. It is possibly the most haunting spot in Moldova. The other attractions consist of caves newly opened across the valley, an ethnographic museum in Butuncei located close by and wonderful views from the headquarters of the monastery.

- **Belgrade**

  Belgrade is a beautiful city and the capital of Serbia. Its ancient relics and nouveau masterpieces apart, it is the site of the Kalemegden Citadel - a majestic citadel with a bloody past still recalled despite its funfairs and vibrant cafes. Go for an underground tour to get a better feel of Belgrade and its turbulent past.

- **Ljubljana**

  Ljubljana is the capital city of Slovenia. The city is culturally rich and consists of some of the best hotels, museums and restaurants in the nation. The beautiful square Presernov Trg is located in the middle of the city, and serves as a favourite meeting spot for locals and tourists. The site makes up the

Ljubljana River banks, with the river flowing through its middle. The area sees restricted car traffic, although you can take a bike ride or a stroll freely. There are terrace cafes along this river, which offer a party vibe to the street. The National and University Library and the Ljubljana Castle are two instances of superb architecture, and you should visit these to get a feel for the city's baroque beauty.

- **Warsaw**

A complex city, Warsaw has a lot of spunk. During the Second World War, the Polish capital was heavily destroyed. However, it fought back to rebuild itself and regain much of its lost glory. The city is today associated with terrific optimism and tons of energy. The persistence of the city can be witnessed through its booming music sector and gala art openings.

You can get a hang of its history through a tour to the Old Town that consists of beautiful buildings or go to the Warsaw Rising Museum with its epic memorabilia. Try the Warsaw Powisle Station Bar to knows its modern status. The place sees a confluence of cultures, and boasts of fantastic music and an eclectic mix of drinks and foods.

- **Krakow**

  Krakow is a former Royal capital and one of the oldest Poland cities. According to legend, the city was developed after conquering a dragon. The place has a dramatic, long history. UNESCO has designated the Historic Center of Krakow as a World Heritage Site. The Old Town is the largest market square in Europe and consists of stunning churches and palaces and ancient homes. You can walk through the city to learn more about it. The place is known for its stone Adalbert Church and the Wawel Royal Castle. Its new Schindler's Museum reminds of the emotional tale of Schindler and the Nazi occupation in Krakow. The Museum is situated in the old factory of Oscar Schindler, and offers an unparalleled experience.

- **Moscow**

  The city is located in the hub of Soviet mystique, and represents both modern and old Russia. This is a very inspiring city and serves as a home to some amazing performing arts as well as the famous Museum of Russian art. You should visit the Red Square and Kremlin, the Tretyakov Museum with the most important Russian art collection and the St.

Basil's Cathedral – an iconic emblem of Russia. You should also visit this Eastern European city for the globally famous Bolshoi Theatre and the Gorky Park.

- **Riga**

  The Latvian capital serves as a foundation for cosmopolitan Baltic region. It has the most important and biggest display of Art Nouveau architecture in Europe. The Old Town looks just like a fantasyland with its fearsome gargoyles and trim gingerbread homes. The majestic Riga Castle, the vast and ancient Central Market and The Riga Art Nouveau Center are some other places that attempt to unravel the fantasies behind the wonderful facades.

- **Sophia**

  Sophia, the capital city of Bulgaria, stands out due to its wonderful blend of architecture of Communist and European style. This is where you can find many stone civic buildings of Soviet style as well as decorative Orthodox churches. There are huge manicured parks in this city, which lie very near to the huge Mt. Vitosh and offer a chance for hikes and skiing. You can get a refreshing experience from the busy streets of the city. Sophia boasts of the Manastirska Manernitsa restaurant where you can gorge on mouth-watering Bulgarian foods, Park Borisova Gradina and The Nevski Church, which is the loveliest park in Sophia.

- **Tallinn**

  Tallinn seems like a place straight out of fairy tales with its medieval architecture and cobbled streets that are preserved very well. This is a historic centre with two tiers and stands as one of the most beautiful walled cities in Estonia and Europe. You should check out the Oleviste Church, the main landmark of Tallinn and the most ancient Gothic town hall that is located in north-eastern Europe. The observation

  deck of the Church offers the most amazing view of the Old Town. The Gloria Wine Cellar further adds to the attraction of this seemingly fantastical place. The place looks beyond a wine store with its subterranean spots and flickering candles.

- **Vilnius**

  Vilnius, the capital of Lithuania, happens to be stunning as well as strange with its complex combination of Gothic and Baroque architecture. You cannot miss the attractive Baroque beauty of the place. The Gate of Dawn is the most famous landmark of this city and serves as a symbol of the new identity of Vilnius, a break from its ancient past. The present and past blend in this place, and provide tourists with an infectious mix of warmth, fabulous cuisine and spirited nightlife. You can go for a walking tour of this ancient place to view all its major attractions. The place has a turbulent history with many tragic incidents dotting its past. You should walk into the Museum of Genocide to learn and appreciate how far Vilnius has come from its torrid past.

- **Kotor**

Kotor is a fortified town on Montenegro's Adriatic coast. Its Bay is known for Old Kotor that has a lot of intrigue and adventure, and was built like a maze to offer protection to its citizens. Even local people lose their way while moving through its narrow streets. You should take a tour of the city to view all its attractions and experience all its beauty. The city has the deepest bay depths in the Mediterranean Sea. The landscape adjoining the place consists of very steep mountains that dip straight to the edge of the water. It offers stunning sceneries to feast your eyes on.

- **Sarajevo**

  Sarajevo (Bosnia and Hercegovina) suffered heavy destruction during the conflicts of 1990, but rose like a phoenix from its own ashes and has turned into one of the most fascinating places in Eastern Europe. Its rich religious and cultural diversity makes it more appealing. You should visit Biban to fully admire the culture of Sarajevo and enjoy appetizing local cuisines and magnificent views of the city. The Tunnel Museum is another place you should not miss. It offers a throwback to the horrors and hope that inspired the creation of this manually-dug tunnel.

- **Prague**

  Prague (Czech Republic) is a city renowned for its hidden courtyards, historic architecture and a huge labyrinth of cobblestoned streets. The skyline of this fantastic city is lined with thousands of towers, spires and domes. It is home to many awesome museums and theatres, wonderful gardens and parks and a sophisticated café culture that offer enough reasons for vacationers to throng here. The Letna Beer Garden, The Prague Castle and Veletrzni Palac Museum are some of the best spots to visit in this city. The fascinating city demands that you take a tour to visit all its major attractions.

- **Olomouc**

  Olomouc is a hidden Czech Republic gem. According to legend, Julius Cesar was the founder of this city. The historic architecture and culture of the place has strong influence of the Romans. It is a quiet blend of young energy and historical, rich beauty that make it as much of an interesting destination as Prague. It is home to the Archdiocesan Museum, Premysl Palace, 6 decorative Baroque fountains and Horni Namesti.

- **Berat**

  Berat is a one-of-a-kind mountain town with a laidback, friendly aura. It is one of the most beautiful places in Albania and is referred to as, "The city of a thousand windows". From Mt. Tomorri to its majestic castle, Ottoman houses are stacked up similar to stairs. The place has wonderful cafés visited by many locals after sunset who like to enjoy a drink and talk to each other.

You should check out the Kalasa neighbourhood, lying beyond the walls of the castle. You can get the best sights and scenes from the castle. Go for a tour of the city with an expert guide or visit the Onufri Museum to learn more about the art and culture of the place.

Africa

Travel around Africa

Africa, in terms of population as well as area, is the second-largest continent. This is almost completely a separate landmass, with just a small-sized land bridge in the North East that connects Western Asia with the continent. The entire continent of Africa has an area of around 30,244,000 km^2, which includes the surrounding lands that it encompasses. The total area constitutes of around 20% of the entire land area of Earth. The Mainland Africa area is shared by 6 island nations and 48 countries.

The continent is a traveller's delight, and has amazing sights on offer. There are savannas filled with wildlife specimens as well as high sand dunes. Africa has numerous wonders that can be personally experienced on trips to Morocco, Rwanda, Botswana, South Africa, Tanzania and more. You can feast your eyes on the sight of wildebeests annually migrating while in a safari in Serengeti. You can capture photos of the sun-swept Moroccan cities. You can go on thrilling safaris with your entire family, and spot giraffes, elephants, lions and many other creatures in Tanzania.

Going on a safari is the most famous reason why people intend to visit Africa. South Africa, Kenya and Tanzania are among the most famous countries to see wildlife specimens. The Masai Mara National Park in Kenya is the cheapest safari option, although based on which season you are travelling in; you might find it better to visit the Kruger National Park, South Africa or Serengeti, Tanzania. The sights and sounds of wild animals migrating is an experience of a lifetime, and you should not miss the opportunity in order to save some bucks. Although these are the most famous nations for safari purposes, you can find many wonderful options in nations situated in slightly off-beat locations.

A lot of people travel to Africa to experience the local culture and get the chance to enjoy tribal experiences. Even today, some areas of Africa are untouched by 21st-century progresses in science and technology. You can visit parts of West Africa to see how women line up for wells to collect water for daily use. You can go to Ethiopia, where many traditions and ceremonies are still intact despite changes in the rest of the world, and get an idea about primitive life. Once you venture in off-beat locations, you might often need a hired car and a guide. You can share the cost by planning ahead and finding other travellers to ride with.

This can be a win-win situation for every member of your travel group.

There are world-famous beaches in some African nations. Although a beach holiday is far from what you imagine when you first think about a holiday in Africa, it is a wonderful way to let your hair down during adventure trips in the 'dark continent'. If you belong to an elite crowd, Cape Town in South Africa can be appealing for you. If you want backpacking trips, Tanzania and a few other nations can be the best places to visit. You can dive off the Ivory Coast in Africa, and stay in some wonderful beachfront resorts in various African countries that boast of a coastline. Whether you wish to enjoy drinks while swinging on a hammock or wish to relax in full style, you can find a suitable African beach for your purpose.

You can climb the highest African peak, Mount Kilimanjaro. Climbing this famous African Mountain is a dream for many people. Going on this fantastic trek requires you to have lots of patience and preparation, but the actual experience makes it all worthwhile. You can also trek to Mount Kenya, and some other lesser-known African peaks. These trekking paths are often slightly less challenging but the experiences are nearly as enjoyable.

If you want an exotic adventure, you can go off the beaten track and go on a camel trek to view the African landscape. You can get a first-hand idea about the unique culture of the Bedouins. You can finally get the chance to sleep under stars and ride with some wonderful people from different parts of the world. Whether you take a ride in Egypt or Morocco, the experience will be truly one-of-a-kind for you.

Flying in Budget Airlines Around Africa

Budget carriers are becoming increasingly popular across Africa, and serve routes taken by the growing African middle-class section. The journey has not been easy for low-cost airlines. African countries signed an agreement in 1988 for "open skies", just like the one cleared in Europe that paved the way for low-cost airlines companies like EasyJet and Ryanair. Most nations are yet to enforce the agreement in actuality.

However, with potential travellers growing in number, the new budget carriers are convincing governments gradually about the advantages of increased travel by air. You can also try Flydubai (Flydubai.com) for flying around Africa. Although the airline is not based in Africa, it connects 12 cities on the African continent with a layover for passengers in Dubai.

African Low-cost Airlines List:

Egypt

Air Arabia: www.airarabia.com

Air Cairo: www.flyaircairo.com

Kenya

Jambojet: www.jambojet.com

Fly540: www.fly540.com

Morocco

Air Arabia Maroc: www.airarabia.com/en/air-arabia-maroc

Nigeria

Dana Airlines: www.flydanaair.com

South Africa

FlySafair: www.flysafair.co.za

Kulula.com: www.kulula.com

Mango: www.flymango.com

Tanzania

Fastjet Tanzania: www.fastjet.com

Zimbabwe

Fastjet Zimbabwe: www.fastjet.com

Travel Africa by Bus

This is the method of travel where a proper sealed road network exists. Across Africa, international bus services are highly common. In the richer states of the continent, you can choose from 'luxury' air-conditioned buses - although the movies are of the trashy Hollywood or Bollywood variety - and old, rough European rejected buses with sub-par construction and non-operable air conditioning system. Some African nations offer you the second variety. In the poorer states, sealed roads are few or non-existing. The buses are primitive and always heavily crowded with goods, people and livestock. The buses frequently stop, either due to something being broken or due to passengers. Here are some popular bus services in Africa:

- **ABC Transport (www.abctransport.com):** Operates in many West African nations. ABC Transport, based in Nigeria, has the most sophisticated coach service operating in the sub-region in West Africa. This is a good service, ideal for tourists, travellers and businesspersons.

- **Intercape (www.intercape.co.za):** The biggest intercity bus network running along Southern Africa, with coaches running in Mozambique, Malawi, Zambia, Zimbabwe, Botswana, Namibia and South Africa.

- **Baz Bus (www.bazbus.com):** A perfect option that offers hop-off and hop-on bus service to backpackers. Users can avail door-to-door service to come across interesting individuals. It is a fun and safe way for South African travel, and is a perfect substitute for car hire services.

- **Greyhound (www.greyhound.co.za):** Covers every major South African city as well as Maputo in Mozambique, Bulawayo in Zimbabwe and Harare. This is a luxury coach operator and offers intercity transport in South Africa. The service always focuses on comfort and safety at reasonable fares.

- **Easy Coach (www.easycoach.co.ke):** In East Africa, it aims to be recognized as the Best Road Passenger Transport Company. Registered in the Republic of Kenya, this is a courier and passenger transport service provider with a vast branch network in the provinces of Nyanza and Western areas. It offers a comfortable and dependable scheduled transport service to night as well as day passengers.

Others bus companies in Africa to consider are:

Swaziland

- TransMagnific: www.goswaziland.co.sz
- Zulu khaya Lami: www.zktours.co.za

Morocco

- Citybus Transport Groupe: www.citybustransport.ma

Angola

- Macon: www.macontransp.com

Minibus

In many transport systems in Africa, the small minibuses bear the brunt. They often travel at very high speeds and are loaded with around 30 passengers, while they have 18-person capacity at best with room for a conductor or tout. Although the front seat offers the most comfort, it is known as the 'death seat' due to the high incidence of head-on crashes in the continent.

In Africa, these minibuses are referred to by various names like poda-podas in Sierra Leone, tro-tros in Ghana, dalla-dallas in Tanzania and matatus in Kenya. The same names can be used in bush taxis and shared taxis. Minibuses generally take off only when they are filled to capacity, a process that can take many hours, and frequently stop to pick passengers up and drop them at their chosen destinations. These buses are also often stopped by roadblock police who love to unload every traveller and engage in long discussions with them about documents and penalties that might need to be paid.

Hitchhiking trips in Africa

In Africa, it is common for travellers to hitch for rides, although you can be expected to pay for a driver's services.

In Africa, safety in road is not up to the mark, given that passengers do not always fasten seatbelts. This can be a problem when you are stranded in remote locations. In some nations, speaking English, Portuguese and French can be a benefit.

You can only depend on trucks in many places out of the course. Although these are mainly used to transport goods, truck drivers are always eager to make some extra money by ferrying passengers who pay. Most passengers have to ride atop cargo, although better 'seats' can be frequently availed for a higher fee.

It can be quite an experience to sit atop a truck making its way through African roads, riding completely exposed. However, you should bring along a cushion or mat to keep your butt more comfortable on the cargo or the car engine and use a wrap as a protection against dust and sunlight during hours of travel. Keep in mind also that truck rides take more time than bus travel.

You can usually wave to stop a truck on many routes. However, on the night prior to departure you may often arrange lifts at the 'truck park' – a dust patch or compound you can find in around every major town in Africa.

The 'fares' are more or less fixed, and you should expect to pay slightly lower than bus fare for a ride for the same distance. Before hopping aboard, ensure that the charges suit your budget. Take your own water and food along if you intend to travel for more than 1 day or 1 night.

Overland Low-cost Travel In Africa

Given that most trippers like to travel to south from north, at times overland truck agencies drive empty trucks back from South Africa's Cape Town, Harare and Victoria Falls. Sometimes, travellers are ferried back to Nairobi (Kenya) or Arusha (Tanzania) for rates that you can negotiate. Sometimes, you can stop for 2 days by Lake Malawi. In towns for departure, ask around to learn about hangouts for backpackers to get tips on when the trucks are expected to leave.

Train Travel in Africa

You can of course travel by train around Africa. There are especially fantastic train travel options in Southern Africa. Although train travel is neither the most efficient nor the most popular way for travelling in Africa, it can appeal to you if you love travelling slowly and traditionally. Although you can travel faster from Point A to B, these African train rides can reiterate to you that the journey is often all that matters, and not the destination.

- **Desert Express in Namibia (www.namibiareservations.com/dx.html):** This tourist train operates between Walvis Bay, Windhoek and Swakopmund, and allows excursions at times to the Etosha National Park in the north. You can find on-board dining rooms, sleeping cars for trips for many days, conference facilities and more. The Desert Express, while not as luxurious as a few other African trains, is convenient and sophisticated enough.

- **Jambo Kenya Deluxe (www.kenyatraintravel.com):** Runs between Nairobi and Mombasa and the route is well-travelled on. People who wish to reach their destination very fast - by a noisy plane or by a hot, crowded motor vehicle - most frequently use it. Train travel is the third option that allows passengers to travel to coast from capital in a relaxed way. You can travel with comfort aboard Jambo Kenya Deluxe and feast your eyes on the savanna with zebras, ostriches and giraffes while relishing gourmet foods and fine wine in its dining car. Sleeping berths consist of basic facilities but offer comfortable travel, although faucets, lights and other things do not often work as properly as expected.

- A passenger train in **Benin, Train d'Ebene** was conceived by a French expat named Guy Catherine who owns many properties around Benin. The innkeeper purchased some carriages dating back to the colonial times around 2005, repaired them and used them to offer rides to hotel guests for varied distances. The Train d'Ebene travels between Parakou's inland capital and Cotonou's coastal town on a narrow-gauge railway track. You can stop overnight in spots like Somba country, W National Park, Dassa and Abomey, and learn about the history and culture of Beninese, stretch your legs and explore the area.

- **Blue Train (www.bluetrain.co.za):** This is a famous and awesome train travel option in South Africa. It is possibly the most popular African train, and owes its name to the rich indigo colour it is always painted in. The train is known as the 5-star "hotel on wheels," and provides travellers with the best accommodation, wine, food and sights. This Pretoria to Cape Town journey is 994 miles (1600km) and is 27 hours long. You might have a stopover at a pioneer town or at a diamond mine. You can also find a Pretoria – Durban service every year for around 2 times. Although the route sees other trains, not all of them come with the sights of wild animals running across the savanna, top African chefs serving up award-winning dishes, bathrooms with gold fittings or bed linens at their silkiest best.

- **Shosholoza Meyl (www.shosholozameyl.co.za):** Another train service in South Africa, this is a cost-effective substitute for the Blue Train and offers intercity journeys over long distances across South Africa – mainly between various major cities and Johannesburg. The name of this train means "a pleasant journey" and charges lower than $95 to take you past the same beautiful sceneries. Although not elegant, the trains offer decent comfort. You do not have to travel by car or board a flight from Johannesburg to Cape Town.

- **The Kilimanjaro (www.tazarasite.com)** and the Mukuba Express refer to two passenger trains running on the bi-national railway named Tazara that covers the 1,860km long journey between New

Kapiri-Mposhi, Zambia and Dar Es Salaam, Tanzania. Trains set off 2 times every week, and the trip takes 2 nights and 2 days for straight trips. While punctual or luxury-loving travellers might dislike the route, adventurous travellers will love it. These trains are seldom punctual and are not very comfortable either, but the stunning experience and sceneries make the rides worthwhile.

- **The Lezard Rouge (www.lezard-rouge.com)** is an old train for tourists in Tunisia. Its name stands for "red lizard." The train runs every day to the Atlas mountain foothills in southern Tunisia, close to Tozeur. The train makes winding trips to Redeyef from Metlaoui and passes through the Selja Gorges while stopping for periodic views. This is a 1-hour trip in each direction.

Driving around Africa

Some African nations might need you to get an International Driving License. Check with your car rental agency or the embassy in your nation to ensure that you satisfy all the requirements. While crossing borders, make sure that the authorities stamp your passport. Otherwise, while trying to leave the country, you will face major issues.

Driving at night in Africa can be highly risky, and you should try to avoid it. The roads are frequently dim-lit and in an inferior state. Some drivers also tend to drive without keeping their lights on. The roads are frequently in bad shape in many nations, and especially in rural regions. You can find cattle, sheep and big domestic animals on the roads.

A vast continent, Africa has very few cops – especially in remote regions. You can often encounter drunk drivers. Be cautious about drunken pedestrians. Make sure that you are aware of every legal requirement for driving in the African nation you intend to drive in. Laws tend to vary across African nations. Some nations expect drivers to wear seat belts, have their bumper featuring a white sticker or reflector or drive with hazard triangles. Others do not require these things.

During motor rides through Africa, you are sure to face a roadblock. Not following the laws will require you to pay a big fine. You cannot hope to be excused due to your ignorance of the laws. If you have to stop at a roadblock, respond to the cops with courtesy and answer their questions with politeness. Turn your internal car light on at night. Ensure that you are actually talking to an official and demand to see his identity card. If he fails to show it, pay no fines and challenge him to take you to the local police station. Avoid night travels in places of unrest and instability.

Travel Around African Territories

Touring Africa can be slightly overwhelming for many first-timer travellers to the continent. Inferior hotels with high rates, lack of proper infrastructure and sub-par public transport facilities often frustrate even hardened travellers. Many tourists prefer to travel to the continent as a part of an overland journey. Many agencies offer packaged tours that target backpacker crowds. However, you do not need them if you are adventurous and have a flexible travelling schedule. It can also be very essential for you to choose an appropriate area, as the sizeable continent has plenty of differences across its regions.

Places to visit in Northern Africa

It can be very satisfying and exciting to go on a Northern Africa trip. You can get plenty of things to see, and it can be tricky for you to plan an itinerary. As a traveller, you should consider visiting the ski slopes of Morocco or the underwater reefs of Egypt. Travel to the Sahara Desert for spectacular sceneries and Egypt for its ancient wonders that can excite any history lover. The wonderful combination of French colonial influence - as in Mediterranean promenades, and Arab charm - as seen in the Medinas bustling with worshippers – is unparalleled here. The Arabian culture is usually predominant although Egypt, Tunisia, Algeria and Morocco have major French influences. In areas like Niger, Mali and Chad, the official language still happens to be French. Some amazing places to visit in Northern Africa are:

- **Tunis**

  The capital of Tunisia has many attractions. The old medina of Tunis is comparable to the Moroccan medinas in Fes and Marrakech. The Bardo National Museum, one of the best North Africa museums, is located in this city. It stands in a wonderful spot and consists of treasures gathered from many ancient sites lying across Tunisia. The ancient Carthage ruins are located here. The city has a light rail system. It has many hotels.

- **Casablanca**

  Casablanca is a very popular city located in northern Africa. This top Morocco holiday spot has an exciting background, and the movie "Casablanca" shows only some of it. You can visit the famous Rick's Café and take a walk in the streets and alleyways of the city infested by many vendors. Following independence, Casablanca has embraced new influences along with the old ones. The old streets are lined by many top hotels.

- **Ras Mohammed National Park**

  Some of the best scuba diving activities in the world can be expected in the Red Sea. If you are a certified diver, you can swim past the shipwrecks from World War II, discover stunning white coral reefs and even dive alongside sharks and dolphins. Visit the Ras Mohammed National Park, one of the most popular diving destinations in the Red Sea. The oldest national park in entire Egypt, it is famous for its diverse marine life and pristine coral reefs. More than a thousand types of fish species reside here. The Yolanda Reef and the Shark Reef, visited by the Napoleon wrasse and grey reef sharks, are the two top diving sites.

- **Sahara Desert**

  The desert crosses each North Africa nation, although the most amazing sights are in the section running through Tunisia. The Matmata region is surrounded by many singular troglodyte dwellings, which were seen as Tatooine residences in the Star Wars flicks. The fortified granaries and the stone forts dating back centuries in these desert hills are also stunning to look at. The Ksar Ouled Soltaine fort is especially amazing. The Tunisian Sahara is loved for its salt lakes, lovely dunes and the chance to camp at a tented hotel under the starlit sky.

- **Atlas Mountains**

  Trekking is a main activity in the Atlas Mountains in Morocco, and you can find trekking routes for trekkers with various levels of capacity. The highest peak in North Africa is Jebel Toubkal, measuring 4,167 meters or 13,667 feet, located in the High Atlas Mountains. Trekking to the summit can be challenging but worthwhile due to the amazing views. You can trek to the summit and return to the Imlil town in just one day, but you are advised to take a minimum of 3 days to get used to the weather and enjoy the sights. Snowboarding and skiing enthusiasts should visit the Oukaïmeden ski resort during the winter season.

- **Marrakesh**

  Marrakesh is a metropolis bustling with activities, and is located at the base of the Atlas Mountains. It is one of the 4 imperial cities of Morocco. It is not for people who are solace seekers, and you can be overwhelmed with the sights, smells, sounds, and hawkers wooing you for a bargain. One of the most exciting North African cities, it is a treasure trove for visitors with its historic sites like El Badi Palace or Saadian Tombs. Gorge on true Moroccan dishes in Djemma El-Fna, the central square, experience refreshment at the local hammams and make trips to the old medina.

- **Pyramids of Giza**

  The Pyramids of Giza consist of 3 varied pyramid complexes, and these are situated immediately outside Cairo. These are possibly the most iconic ancient wonders of Egypt. It is one of the ancient Seven Wonders of the World, and possibly the oldest and still existing one. Its 3 main pyramids are the tombs of Menkaure, Khufu and Khafre, three popular pharaohs. The pyramid of Khufu, referred to as the Great Pyramid of Giza, happens to be the largest of these. It was constructed around 4,500 years back. The feline Great Sphinx lies before the pyramids and is known as "the Father of Terror" in Arabic. It is constructed out of just one stone block.

- **Luxor**

  Luxor was the richest city in ancient Egypt and it was constructed around Thebes, an ancient site, which still draws tourists. The city still has its stunning temple and many wonderful museums. The old site Karnak is located near Luxor. It served as the most important worship site for Egyptians of ancient times. It comprises of many stunning obelisks, pylons, kiosks and sanctuaries, dedicated to the gods of Thebes. The Valley of the Queens and The Valley of the Kings, the royal burial grounds, lie across the River Nile from Luxor. You can also find the tomb of Tutankhamun located here.

- **Fes**

  For over 400 years, Fes served as the capital of Morocco. Today, it is regarded as the cultural and religious centre of the nation. It is the most complete medieval Arabian city. This strange city is an attractive combination of modern world sophistication and Middle Age beauty. You would do well to take a walking tour of the city and view its tanneries and other attractions such as the Jewish Quarter, the Mellah, the Royal Palace and the Merenid Tombs. The city has a more authentic vibe than Marrakesh.

- **Siwa Oasis**

  Siwa Oasis is situated near the Libyan border, in the Western Desert of Egypt. It is the remotest oasis town of Egypt and consists of many palm groves and olive trees. It has a unique culture, courtesy of its residents. The town has its small airport and wonderful road to thank for placing it on the map, although it is an offbeat travel destination. It is popular for its hot springs, beautiful landscape, and Fatnas island that offer a chance for desert safari. Alexander the Great came here to see the Oracle of Amun.

Eastern Africa Top Destinations

The eastern part of Africa is visited by many travellers. You can easily get an international flight to Nairobi, and go to Mount Kilimanjaro in Tanzania in the south or go for a safari in Masai Mara. Malawi is an inviting and friendly nation, and you will love to rest here for some time before moving to South Africa.

East Africa has become a favourite destination for tourists, with places like Uganda, Tanzania, Rwanda, Kenya and Burundi. These regions attract tourists with wildlife, friendly people, stunning sceneries and vibrant culture. While planning a trip to East Africa, ensure that you are aware about the local political situation, given that the affairs can quickly worsen here. You can visit the place at any time, although dry and rainy seasons can pose some problems. Every destination has its own advantages, such as the Serengeti / Masai Mara where the migration of wildebeests happens during specific seasons.

- **Mount Kilimanjaro**

  This is one of the most popular Tanzania attractions, and happens to be the tallest mountain peak in Africa. Unlike other northern Tanzania parks, Mount Kilimanjaro National Park should not just be visited for its wildlife. The park offers a magnificent view of the lofty, snow-clad peak and the opportunity for many people to scale it. You can climb the peak at any time, although the dry season from late June to October is the best period.

Mount Kilimanjaro is a World Heritage site and was developed due to volcanic activities along the Rift Valley more than 1 million years back. It has 3 points that were formed around 750,000 years back, Mawenzi, Shira and Kibo. The Uhuru Peak on Kibo, one of the Seven Summits on the planet, is the highest point. The peak arises from the farmland to the rainforest, the slopes of which have eland, elephants, monkeys, leopards and buffaloes. You can find many preying birds in the alpine zone.

- **Maasai Mara**

This is one of the most gorgeous game reserves in the world. The Masai Mara is Serengiti's northern extension and borders Tanzania. It acts as a corridor of wildlife between the nations. It owes its name to the Masai tribals who wear red cloaks and stay in the park, grazing on animals as they have been doing for hundreds of years.

265

The Masai Mara park is popular for the Great Migration that sees Thomson's gazelle, zebra and many wildebeests travelling from and to the Serengeti in the July – October period. Many crocodiles and hippos have their home in the Mara River. You can spot many predators in this park, including quite large populations of leopard, lion and cheetah, particularly in the dry December – February period. The park is located high enough, which ensures gentle climatic conditions throughout the year.

- **Pemba and Zanzibar islands**

These two islands are in the Zanzibar archipelago. Zanzibar, a big holiday destination famous for its spectacular beaches, is also known as Unjuga. The islands boast some of the most fantastic beaches on the planet, with different surfing experiences based on which side of the island tourists are present on. Travellers can relish the sight of white, soft sand and sail on shallow, transparent water with traditional boats. You can visit Stone Town, situated in the centre of Zanzibar, and boasting a busy port, narrow alleyways and old Arabian townhouses.

- **Lake Nakuru National Park**

It is located in Central Kenya, and was founded in 1961. It is known for its pink flamingos, living here in huge flocks. It is home to over 450 different species of birds and many other wild creatures. These birds jam Lake Nakuru, which is one of the lakes of the Rift Valley constituting around 1/3 of the total area of the park. Other than birds, you can see white rhinos, pythons, waterbucks, warthogs, leopards, lions and various other animals in this park. There is woodland, sweeping grasslands and rocky cliffs surrounding the lake. The largest African euphorbia candelabrum forest is in this park as well. The tall, indigenous succulent plants of this area make the arid landscapes look more interesting.

- **Serengeti National Park**

Thousands of tourists come to the Serengeti National Park (www.serengeti.org) every year. This is a vast plain devoid of trees, with millions of wild animals coming here in search of fresh grasslands. It is the largest Tanzanian national park, and draws thousands of tourists every year. The December – June period is the best time to view wildlife specimens here.

Wildebeests and zebras annually migrate in large numbers in May – early June period. Millions of wildebeests and zebras migrate here every year in May – early June. One of the most spectacular natural events, the migration is a major attraction for tourists from across the globe. The Serengeti National Park is home to jackal, hunting dogs, foxes with bat ear, hyena, cheetah, leopard, lion and vast herds of antelope. The park also has around 500 species of birds, as reported. Many birds love the swamp region. In the Masai language, 'Serengiti' stands for an 'extended place'.

- **Nairobi**

This is the largest city and capital of Kenya, and is famous for its rich colonial heritage. At one time, it served as the British capital in East Africa – and attracted settlers to its tea and coffee industries. Modern Nairobi has wonderful wildlife attractions and popular historic sites to attract tourists. You can explore the contemporary art, culture, nature and history of Kenya in The Nairobi National Museum. The botanical garden on the museum grounds is a delight for nature lovers. The Karen Blixen Museum is another famous tourist attraction. It is the restored house of Isak Diensen, the famous Danish writer who penned the book, "Out of Africa". You can visit Nairobi National Park to see wildlife specimens, including the black rhinos that have been given a sanctuary here. There are other safari favourites, such as cheetahs, wildebeest, zebras, buffaloes, leopards and lions. The David Sheldrick Wildlife Trust, located within this park, offers opportunities to have close meetings with orphan elephants. The Giraffe Centre, located closed to the popular Giraffe Manor, should not be missed for anything.

- **Seychelles**

This lies close to the equator, East of Kenya. This is a virgin, spectacular area with countless tropical island attractions. Seychelles is home to many flourishing coral reefs, virgin jungles, nature reserves listed with UNESCO, stunning beaches strewn with boulders and more. The 115 granite and coral islands of this archipelago are the peaks of an expansive underwater plateau.

Around 50% of the land area in Seychelles is protected. Many atolls and islands are located in its marine sanctuaries. Tourists can go for a hike on the mountain rails, go rock climbing, gorge on savoury

Créole culinary delights, capture unique photos of the flora and fauna and relish relaxing on the stunning beaches. You can participate in water activities in the clear blue waters. Seychelles has some of the best fishing grounds on the planet, and has top class sailing, surfing and snorkelling activities.

- **Volcanoes National Park**

The Volcanoes National Park is located in Rwanda, about a couple of hours driving distance away from its capital Kigali, and is home to the majestic and scary mountain gorillas. This is the place where popular American zoologist Dian Fossey set up the Karaoke Research Center and proceeded with her campaign on gorilla conservation. The park, other than mountain gorillas, serves also as a sanctuary for over 170 bird species, black-fronted duiker, bushbuck, elephants, golden monkeys, buffaloes and spotted hyenas. Lots of vacationers spend time here to scale Mount Bisoke, volcanoes and Karisimbi.

- **Morne Seychellois National Park**

  In Seychelles, it is the largest national park and covers over 20% of the Mahé region. The mountain chain Morne Seychellois, which lies within its lush green borders, overlooks Victoria and is 905 m tall. You can hike from the Danzil village to this park, pass tea plantations. From the mountain slopes, you can relish in amazing views of Mahé's southwest coast. You can walk to the Baie Ternay and Port Launay Marine Parks by walking westwards through this park. The lonely Anse Major beach and the Bel Ombre hamlet lie to the north-west of the park.

- **Bujumbura**

  Many people refer to it as Buji, and this is a comparatively small city. It has not witnessed major development in the last few decades due to continuing socio-political conflict. It has maintained other features from its French colony period, such as amazing nightlife, beverages and foods with French influence. Many restaurants serve French cuisine here, in various qualities and prices. The city has various important sites, such as the university in Burundi, one of the best African museums - The

Living Museum – displaying modern and ancient Burundi crafts, and the Independence Monument that reminds of the German, French and Belgian colonization.

- **Mohéli**

This is generally regarded as the biggest attraction of the Comoros Islands. Although the smallest of the islands, it is the most interesting one. The island is fully wild and undeveloped, and has very few people living here. It is slightly out of sync with modernity. The Parc Marin de Mohéli is the only national park in this nation. The island is lined by craggy islets that can be a heaven for any nature lover. It is referred to as Moili or Mwali by the locals, and is a fantastic habitat for marine creatures like dolphins, sea turtles and whales. The virgin beauty of this place compensates for the lack of sophisticated amenities for many visitors.

- **Kampala**

This serves as the capital of modern Uganda, just as it was the capital city during the times of the Buganda kingdom.

It boasts fantastic flair and charm for an African city. The Kasubi Tombs still contains some thatched relics from the ancient times. The bustling mosque minarets, the largest Central-east Africa market – the Owino market, Central Kampala with its sun-cracked streets and the Nakasero Hill - which is home to the villas of the expats and elite.

Western Africa Top Destinations

Independent travel in this part of Africa comes with challenges, but can be very satisfying. Visitors can have much to see in the Cape Verde archipelago. The coastline of Senegal is lovely and consists of wonderful villages. There are friendly locals in The Gambia. Ghana is a more comfortable and relaxing place that other West Africa nations and you will love to start and end your African trip from here. West Africa is a large territory with many states and millions of residents. Although it has a tragic past, the hospitality of its residents and its bright prospects do not give any idea about it. In Western Africa, some of the best tourist destinations include:

- **Agadez**

  Agadez in Niger has a rich heritage with centres of culture and trade – just like Timbuktu. It is a fantastic town and serves as the entryway to the stunning Tenere Desert and Air Mountains. It is home to top spots like the Grande Mosque and Palais du Sultan. The ancient Agadez quarter comes with narrow streets dotted with old-style mud homes. The town has the most energetic town spot in the Grande Marche. You can see Fulani with big Chinese hats, Hausa merchants dressed in colourful, long robes and Tuareg nomads who make a living selling livestock and camels.

- **Cape Verde**

  The Cape Verde archipelago spans the Africa continent in the Atlantic Ocean. There is more western influence in this country, as compared to the other parts of Africa. There are more, and generally better, traveller facilities in this place. However, the feel of the nation is similar to a destination in Africa. The bustling markets and the fantastic music in every city of Cape Verde offer the feel of a nation within African coast.

It is quite tough to spot Cape Verde on a world map or even on the African map, given that the nation has plenty of attractions. Every island comes with various attractions. Cape Verde has a vibrant, loud music scene, and a great place for nightlife lovers. It has a spectacular terrain for water sports or hiking activities, although you can just relax on its golden sandy beaches if you just want to have a relaxing time on the black sand beach by the picturesque city.

- **Accra**

  Accra is the capital and the largest city in the state of Ghana. It is friendly and has a wonderful character, consisting of more than 2 million residents. This is a comfortable destination for any type of tourist, a family vacationer, a solo traveller, a business tourist or an annual vacationer.

  There are many beaches around the city, loved by vacationers, especially the Labadi Beach. The wonderful National Museum is located here, and consists of many historical treasures of the country. The city is also home to the W.E.B. Dubois Centre, Independence Square, the Kwame Nkrumah memorial, International Trade Fair and the National

Theatre. The place has much traffic, amazing music, mouth-watering foods and vibrant markets.

- **Abidjan**

  It consists of the Parc du Banco, located on the city outskirts, where travellers can see the flora and fauna of the rainforest. The largest open-air self-service laundry is located close to the park's entrance. The Hotel Ivoire is located within the Abidjan city. It was once a glamorous spot, although it is in shambles now. Another worthwhile spot to visit in Abidjan is St Paul's Cathedral. Indeed, the Ivory Coast has many fantastic sightseeing destinations.

- **Sine-Saloum Delta**

  This is located in south-western Senegal. This vast area consists of rivers, islands, lagoons and mangrove forests. This is a wonderful place to go on a boat ride, explore the wonderful fishing villages and to see pelicans and flamingos. One of the ecological jewels of West Africa, the Sine Saloum Delta was designated in 2011 as a World Heritage Site by UNESCO.

The area has constantly shifting dunes, sand islands, mangrove swamps, fantastic beaches and a one-of-a-kind estuarine ambience. It is an area of wonderful diversity, with its delta offering honey, fresh water, oysters, wood and fish to the local communities. It is developed from two rivers that converge on the Atlantic, the Sine and Saloum. Mangroves cover 60% of the entire delta.

- **Coastal Forts**

  The Atlantic Coast in Ghana is dotted with old castles from the 1600s, constructed by different European rulers. The forts were initially used for storing goods, such as spices, gold and ivory, to export. This slave trade later transformed many of these castles into dungeons and prisons. European rulers got involved in internal conflict to get forts under their control. In the next few centuries, the control of these forts changed many hands.

  You should not miss the Cape Coast Castle and Museum and St George's Castle in Elmina, the two forts loved by many tourists. The forts were the British headquarters for close to 200 years. Some forts here have been transformed into guesthouses that offer just basic accommodation.

- **Saltinho Waterfalls**

  A popular waterfall in Guinea-Bissau, the Saltinho Waterfall is a tourist landmark. The place can be reached by a vehicle. First-timers are recommended to go with a tourist guide. You need to travel south from the Bissau-Buba road for less than 1 hour. Once the Geba River and the Corubal River merges together, the Saltinho waterfalls and rapids develop. It has a bridge that lets people stay together and relish the view. The immediate village offers many other tourist attractions, and other tourists can check in at the hotel located close by. The place has many handmade musical instruments, made by the Tabato natives, on offer.

- **Togo**

  The nugget of Africa, Togo is famous for its virgin northern hinterland, white sandy beaches and voodoo shrines. The tall mud homes in the villages of Koutammakou, inhabited by the Batammariba natives, serve as the national symbol of Togo. This small but wonderful country has its capital in Lome, situated on the coast, comprising of clubs and bars in every corner and the best nightlife in West Africa. Travellers can also relish the experience of Loma's markets, the traditional and voodoo ones. You can meet with interesting locals who come to the markets to shop and talk. Like them, you can gorge on pounded white yams or spicy fufu, an extremely popular West African fast food, consumed with various sauces – those with the taste can delight in smoked fish or even spicy sauces with peppers and tomatoes.

- **Dakar**

  Dakar is a beautiful city spread across the Cap-Vert peninsula in towns that were formerly colonized by the French. The place owes its beauty to the ambience and the people, and not just from the architecture. Its desolate, hot and dusty streets are made lively by locals moving about in crisp suits and fabrics in vibrant hues. Roads are frequently congested with traffic. You can be overwhelmed with smells and sounds in Medina and the markets. The pop music of Senegal, with the influence of jazz, fills the air.

  You can visit Iles De la Madeline, the sole roosting spot for African tropical birds with red bills. Travellers can also come across authentic Lake Retba or Pink Lake, which owes its pink color to the cyanobacteria present in the water. Lake Retba is a famous spot for salt harvesting, and many tourists take home salt from this site as a souvenir. The city is a fantastic combination of Arabic and colonial architecture, and is known for amazing sites like Dakar Grand Mosque, Dakar Cathedral and IFAN Museum of African Arts.

- **Gbarnga**

It might look like one more of those broken-down cities sprouting from the inland Liberia forests and sweeping mud plains. However, the Bong County regional capital is more than its heritage and history than many other cities. This town boasts of the century-old Cuttington University, which is one of the most esteemed universities in the nation. It is more interesting than the more famous coastal spots due to the fantastic earthy guesthouses and waterfalls.

- **Jacqueville**

The small Jacqueville is known for its sun-swept beaches with ivory sands, and its large pineapple grove swathes can satisfy beach lovers easily. There are many colonial buildings and ancient Parisian arcades, which stand desolate under palm tree shades. The thatched beach huts along the shore are complemented by timber longboats that are painted. This is a fantastic place where you can come and get an idea about the beautiful seaside personality of this nation.

- **The Gambia**

  This is referred to as the 'Smiling Coast of Africa', as it has some of the friendliest people of the world. Almost every native living close to the coastline speaks English. The nation has a vibrant ambience, an infectious culture, golden sandy beaches and first-class bird watching experience. Even as one of the smallest African nations, The Gambia has many attractions on offer. As a first-timer, you will love the place for some of the most exciting, diverse destinations in Africa. Over the last decade or so, the place has turned into one of the most popular tourist destinations in the world.

- **Sal Island**

  This is referred to as the sunniest island of Cape Verde. Although the island has about 20,000 people and a growing population, and has an international airport, it is quite a virgin tourist destination. The island has a very dry and hot climate, and has many miles of relaxing sandy beaches that make it a wonderful tropical paradise.

- **Mole National Park**

  The Mole National Park has vast expanses of savannah in saffron colour, and offers the most cost-effective African safaris. It has around 90 species of mammal, such as warthogs, baboons, buffaloes, kob antelopes and African elephants, and more than 300 species of birds. Elephant sightings are common in the December – April period, and you can also see other mammals round the year.

  The headquarters of this park offers wonderful driving and walking safaris. You are not permitted to explore this park alone, and you can arrange an armed ranger to accompany you in your 4WD. If you want a change from spotting elephants, you can go to the Mognori Eco Village located on the park borders for an ecotourism venture, know about the local culture, take village tours or go on canoe safaris.

Southern Africa Top Destinations

Southern Africa is considered a centre for many international flights, and South Africa offers a very convenient point of entry. You can visit Namibia, Botswana and South Africa when you are in the southern part of Africa. In some regions, the transport facilities are good enough. However, you might like to hire a driver and a private car for remote places. This will reduce some hassles and let you view more destinations.

- **Madagascar**

Madagascar is located on the south-eastern coast of Africa. An unmatched tourist destination, it has numerous attractions such as awesome culture, unique wildlife and picturesque nature. This big island country consists of varied rainforests, animals, plants, landscapes, reefs and beaches. It has a fantastic history, home to many species of plants and animals, it has unique flora & fauna. There are many varieties of chameleons and around 70 varied species of lemurs. Madagascar and its adjoining islands come with 5 families of primates, 5 families of birds and 8 plant families that are unique to this region. It is home to endemic wildlife, and include flat tailed gecko and various types of chameleons, Aye-Aye, comet moths, dancing lemurs, tomato frogs etc. Some of the stunning parks you must visit include: Masoala, Kirindy, Ranomafana, Ankarana Montagne d'Ambre, Berenty and Andasibe-Mantadia.

- **Lake Malawi**

This is the 3rd largest African lake, and this spectacular freshwater lake is big enough to make you feel like you are standing before an ocean. It makes up for around 1/3rd of the total area of Malawi. You can take part in many water sports activities such as scuba diving, swimming, kayaking, sailing and powerboat cruises, go to the rustic fishing villages and relax on the golden beaches. There is a minimum of 700 species of wonderful cichlid fishes, and 4 of these are endemic.

- **Botswana**

The nation has an amazing array of wild animals, and the place has a huge advantage due to its wildlife. There are many endangered animals, like rhinos and wild dogs, and many birds live in the region.

It has impressive natural landscapes, including the serene and sublime Okavango Delta and the expansive Kalahari Desert. It has an empty, vast terrain with some areas being beautiful and others being dense. Its landscape is uniquely African and can satisfy all your expectations of the trip. Such natural attractions are expensive to visit. At present, Botswana happens to be one of the costliest African destinations. Here, some luxury accommodations are quite expensive and can only be afforded by the super-rich during honeymoons and other once-in-a-lifetime visits. However, there are cost-effective self-drive tours for travellers on a tight budget, and these are frequently more amazing ways to explore the spectacular sights of Botswana.

- **Island of Mozambique**

One of the major attractions of entire Mozambique, The Island of Mozambique is a tourist's delight. It is named as one of the UNESCO World Heritage sites and can teach you much about the culture and history of Mozambique from the 1600s and 1700s. During the 10th – late 15th century, Arab merchants used the natural harbour of Mozambique and its island as a centre for maritime trading. In 1498, the famous Portuguese explorer Vasco da Gama came to the island and declared it as a Portuguese colony. He came 4 years later with Portuguese settlers, and St. Gabriel – the first Portuguese fortress was constructed. St. Gabriel (1507 – 08) does not stand here any longer. If you have a thing for beach holidays, the Mozambique Island is one of the best beach destinations in Africa. It is a traveller's paradise due to the vast beaches, warm climate and sunshine.

- **Chobe National Park**

  The park is in the Okavango Delta of Botswana, and has four distinct eco-systems. You will love to visit the Savuti Marsh, which especially boasts of one of the highest wildlife concentrations in Africa throughout the year. The park has close to 120,000 elephants and its vast herds should ideally be viewed from a river cruise during sundown. The park should best be visited in the May – September period when the climate is cooler and drier. During this time, the place sees a congregation of Wildebeest, Giraffe, Buffalo, Eland and Zebra. The place has various types of accommodations to suit various budgets. You may also get a houseboat on hire. It is more cost-effective than some of the other parks of Botswana and is accessible by car. The park inhabits elephants of all sizes. You can find more than 450 bird species, wild dogs, lechwe, kudu, crocodiles, pods of huge hippos and the Big Five: Black or white rhinos, Cape buffalo, African leopard, African lion, and the esteemed African elephant.

There are amazing views of sunset in the Chobe River, and many wild beasts come down to the Chobe River banks during the sundown. The various activities and its proximity to the Victoria Falls are other great advantages of Chobe.

- **Quirimbas archipelago**

The archipelago is situated south of the Tanzanian border, and it consists of over 30 islands and islets. Among these, Medjumbe, Ibo, and Vamizi are the most popular. The Quirimbas served as the most vital trading spot in the past, for spice traders and for Arab slaves at first and then for the Portuguese settlers of Mozambique. These days, the island inhabits mostly rural fishermen who survive on the bounty that the adjoining areas have on offer. The archipelago is internationally known best for its tranquil beaches and the Quirimbas National Park which boasts of fantastic diving sites.

Quirimbas is known best for its stunning dive sites, and you can explore many of these all around Situ. A few of these are famous in the local area, and there are plunging reef walls that can be viewed through the crystal-clear water. The reefs are known for lovely coral cover, shimmering fluorescent fishes moving in shoals and spectacular underwater photography. Others are slightly rarer diving spots, but you can get the joy of discovery and adventure while exploring them.

- **Cape Town**

  One of the loveliest cities on the planet, Cape Town is located at the foot of the legendary Table Mountain of South Africa. The most common tourist destination in entire Africa, it is situated at the southwest tip of the Western Cape Province of South Africa. The metro has a gentle Mediterranean weather, a stunning natural backdrop and a proper infrastructure.

  The centre of Cape Town is situated in a comparatively small region between Table Bay and

Table Mountain. Cape Town is a home base for tourists to explore the local attractions, which includes the Wineland valleys and rolling hills and the numerous diverse beaches of the area.

The adjoining region has soaring mountains, fantastic beaches and tranquil vineyards. Culture reigns supreme in the city centre. You can find designer shopping malls and first-class restaurants here, along with beautiful museums and rustic markets. The city also comprises of many historic sites, which include Robben Island, District Six and Bo-Kaap. The Robben Island is the place where Nelson Mandela was kept incarcerated for the most time.

- **South Luangwa National Park**

One of the best African safari destinations, South Luangwa National Park is located in Zambia and has one of the highest wildlife concentrations in the continent around the Luangwa River. There are hundreds of hippo pods, more than 400 bird species, one-of-a-kind giraffe and zebra species, African wild dogs, elephant, leopard and lions. This is a wonderful park that is a must-visit destination during a southern Africa trip. South Luangwa is popular for its huge pods of hippos, and the big animals live well in the Luangwa River as well as its lagoons. There are many leopards and lions, and many buffalo herds. One of the few African national parks to permit nocturnal drives, it is the spot where you can see a leopard most easily. The Cookson's wildebeest, the Crawshay's zebra and the Thornicroft giraffe in the Luangwa Valley are unique to the place. The valley is also home to the African Wild Dog, a highly endangered species.

- **Victoria Falls**

The world's largest waterfall as far as height and width are concerned, the Victoria Falls was discovered in 1855 by David Livingstone. 108 m (355 feet) in height, it is situated on the border of Zambia and Zimbabwe. It was developed by the Zambezi River, which falls down into a deep chasm measuring 100 meters. The boom of this waterfall is audible even 40 km away. It boasts of a wonderful assortment of flora and fauna. You can see many varieties of fishes and numerous birds here. Designated a World Heritage Site by UNESCO, the Victoria Falls is mainly popular for the "Devil's Pool" that is situated next to a cliff and offers a place to view many wonderful things and go swimming in.

- **Etosha National Park**

  This popular park in Namibia owes its name to the shimmering, gigantic Etosha Pan expanse. This salt pan stretches to around 1/5th of the entire area of the park. The pan turns into a giant lake during the rainy season, and becomes a home for pale pink flamingos. The dry season sees water evaporating from the spot and shape-shifting mirages taking its place. The remaining part of the park, around the edges of the pan, is similarly arid. Although the entire park is in the throes of drought, the animals are drawn to its waterholes due to their water requirement for survival. You can have a wonderful time in this park, and choose from various camps. Namutoni, Halali and Okuakuejo are three most famous camps, which intersperse at regular intervals. You can avail camping accommodation and chalet in all the camps, and various facilities such as gas station, pool, shop and restaurant.

- **Fish River Canyon**

  The second largest canyon on Earth and the largest canyon in Africa, the Fish River Canyon is up to 550m deep and 160km long, 27km wide in a few spots. It is the 2nd most famous attraction in Namibia for tourists due to its rugged beauty. You should make it a point not to miss the Fish River Canyon during a Namibia trip. You may go to the canyon for a fantastic adventure or spend an entire day taking a hike along the rim. Go on a trek along the Fish River Canyon Hiking Trail, the most famous southern Africa hiking trails, for a real adventure. The trail is 90km long and includes a 5-day hike. You will not find any amenities or any mobile phone network in this canyon. The trail has just a couple of emergency stations, which makes it unsuitable for beginners.

- **Lesotho**

  This landlocked, exotic nation is nestled in high mountains, and is the only country on the planet with an elevation of more than 1,000 m. A friendly nation, Lesotho boasts of stunning sceneries. The country is known for its prehistoric rock art, the Thaba-Bosiu plateau-fortress, first-class

Maletsunyane Falls and amazing horseshoe waterfalls. The country is encompassed by the famous lands of South Africa and cannot be reached very easily. With dust-filled sandstone plateaus and dense stark rock mountains, it cannot easily be navigated. However, the views of Lesotho are worth the effort.

The wild and primeval backcountry has vast grassy plains that are occasionally broken by thatched San villages. Huge mountain dams have only tamed the giant mountain rivers to some extent. Hikers report that the trekking is amazing, with stunning valley scenes and beautiful cascading waterfalls around each corner.

Middle East

A cultural place, the Middle East is mainly situated in western Asia, as well as in some sections of south-eastern Europe and northern Africa. The Middle East has its western border surrounded by the Mediterranean Sea, with Syria, Lebanon and Israel resting on it. In Africa, Egypt is bordered by the Mediterranean and is often regarded as a section of the Middle East. Cyprus and Turkey physically connect Asia and Europe and are often called Middle Eastern and European.

Just to the north-east of Turkey, you will find Georgia, Armenia and Azerbaijan being situated. At times, these can work as isolated areas or are related with Asia, Europe and the Middle East. The Arabian and the Red Seas are located to the south of the Mediterranean Sea and adjoin the southern section of the Middle East. The waters are bordered by Oman, Yemen and Saudi Arabia, while Jordan and Iraq joins them to the western part of the area. The Persian Gulf rests at the middle area of the Middle East and gives the area a shape similar to a hook. Iran, Kuwait, Bahrain, Qatar and the United Arab Emirates are some nations located along the Persian Gulf.

Middle East Characteristics

Most of the area of the Middle East has warm, desert weather and physical condition. The place has very high temperatures, which can reach peak levels during the summer season. In parts of Iran and Iraq, temperatures are found to climb as high as 71 ° Celsius or 160 ° Fahrenheit. During the summer months, the average temperatures are generally about 49 ° Celsius or 120 ° Fahrenheit. The weather conditions are slightly milder during the winter months. The climate sees an extremely small amount of rainfall, which explains why large areas here are deserts. Some regions of the Middle East surround Lebanon and Israel and other Mediterranean countries, and have a warm Mediterranean climate just like sections of Italy and Greece. The territory of Turkey stretches over different types of continental and arid climate. The northern areas such as Iran in the Middle East, Central Asia and Afghanistan have a type of weather that is similar to a steppe climate. Although winters here are colder, there is very small amount of rainfall in the area.

The Middle East, due to its arid weather condition, has quite a few of the largest deserts in the world. The Syrian Desert in the region stretches to Saudi Arabia, Jordan and Iraq as well, and is a perfect combination steppe geography as well as traditional desert. The Arabian desert around the Persian Gulf, Iraq, Jordan, Oman and Yemen is the place where you can find more of the rolling sand dunes that frequently recall desert imagery. The Empty Quarter or the Rub 'al-Khali, located in the middle area of the Arabian Desert, happens to the largest sandy desert in the world that gets annual rainfall as low as 30 mm or 1.2 inches. The Sahara Desert is possibly the most popular desert on Earth, and it stretches all across north Africa and through Egypt to reach into the Middle East.

The entire Middle East landmass measures around 3.82 million square miles. In this area, the largest nations include:

- Pakistan (340 thousand square miles)
- Egypt (384 thousand square miles)
- Iran (580 thousand square miles)
- Saudi Arabia (800 thousand square miles)

Qatar (4,473 square miles), Lebanon (3,950 square miles), Cyprus (3,568 square miles) and Bahrain (295 square miles) are the smallest nations in the Middle East.

Flying around Middle East

The Middle East is regarded as a lofty, ancient and mysterious place. It boasts of many attractions for tourists, whether sun-swept beaches in stunning Dubai, the unique streets of Jerusalem, the ancient Petra ruins or camels trekking through vast expanses of sandy deserts, which can satisfy any tourist. In the last 10 years, airline companies in the Middle East have become major players from almost nobodies in the industry.

The airlines have ideal locations, between Europe, Africa and Asia. Other than the geographical benefit, major investment on infrastructure and the highly sophisticated fleets have transformed these air terminals into international airports. The air hubs operate flights 24/7, attract talent from foreign nations, offer salaries almost tax-fee, very inexpensive oil and no nosy unions. All these factors make them very successful.

Whether you wish to travel to Dubai or Oman, you can have a nicer and an inexpensive journey although with a Middle East stopover. The flight space is becoming increasingly competitive, with carriers like Saudia, Oman Air or Fly Dubai competing for market share. The three carriers – Etihad, Qatar Airways and Emirates - stand head and shoulders above the others in offering superior services and connecting almost all cities on the planet. These carriers are the biggest among all airline companies here, and sponsor football clubs, give flights away and are endorsed by Hollywood celebrities as well. The companies are constantly carrying a larger number of passengers and adding new tourist destinations.

However, if while travelling the Middle East you are intent on saving money, you can find many budget carriers that offer a satisfactory air travel experience to tourists at quite low prices. You can find low-cost flights around Amman, Muscat, Abu Dhabi or Dubai fairly easily. With the larger number of tourists being interested in budget travel, there has been a spurt in the number of cheap airline companies serving the Middle East and the adjoining regions at present.

Middle East Low-Cost Airlines:

Israel

Up: www.flyup.com

Jordan

Air Arabia Jordan: www.revamp.airarabia.com

Kuwait

Jazeera Airways: www.jazeeraairways.com

Oman

Salam Air: www.salamair.com

Saudi Arabia

Flynas: www.flynas.com

Flyadeal: www.flyadeal.com

United Arab Emirates

Air Arabia: www.airarabia.com

Flydubai: www.flydubai.com

Yemen

Felix Airways: www.felixairways.com

Bus Travel through Middle East

In the Middle East, buses are the most dependable machines. These are possibly the only option to travel from point A to B in most spots. Most buses offer comfortable and trustable services.

The quality of comfort and expense of bus travel significantly varies through the entire area. In most buses, both local passengers and drivers love loud videos and that make sleep almost out of the question. The 'non-smoking bus' policy is not maintained in most buses either.

A bus service or minibus service operates in most towns and cities. They are run on regular fixed routes, fast services, low fares and fixed stops (in some cases). However, if you are less familiar with a town, it can be tough to become accustomed to it. Few buses display the destinations, and even most of those that do actually display in languages other than English and are extremely crowded.

Without a local who speaks in your language, it is best that you stand along a footpath – best at a bus stop – of a main road standing in the direction that you wish to travel and call out the name of the destination aloud to slow down a driver who would like to pick you up. It is best that you call SAPTCO (www.saptco.com.sa), a good bus operator, while making bus tours around the Middle East. It runs direct international services to:

- ✓ Jordan

- ✓ Egypt

- ✓ Kuwait

- ✓ Qatar

- ✓ Bahrain

- ✓ UAE

SAPTCO also services to Sudan and Egypt through connecting ferries.

Oman

MWASALAT: www.mwasalat.om

Israel

Egged Bus Company: www.egged.co.il

Saudi Arabia

SAPTCO: www.saptco.com.sa

Jordan

Jett Bus Company: www.jett.com.jo

Train Travel in the Middle East

Train networks are available in Turkey, Iran, Israel, Egypt and the Palestinian Territories, and some routes have the best option for transport, as between Luxor and the capital of Egypt. The comfort level varies across nations, and many of the trains in Egypt are in dire need of being renovated. While the trains in Iran are alright, Turkey and Israel use new trains on a few routes. Trains usually ply less often, and these run slower when compared to buses. Many stations are slightly far from the town centres that they cater to. You can only buy train tickets at the station. It is either highly advisable or mandatory that you make reservations.

- **Trains in Egypt**

  A fascinating country, Egypt has many attractions. Cairo, its capital, is one of the most beautiful cities on the planet. You can easily travel independently around Egypt, and you do not have to book any tour. You can rely on Egyptian Railways to provide you with the most comfortable travel option between

Suez, Port Said, Alexandria, Aswan, Luxor and Cairo. You can relish amazing sights from the train, particularly along the River Nile among the palm trees and fields on the routes of Cairo-Alexandria and Cairo-Luxor-Aswan. Train trips often offer you an insight into the nation. The two main Egypt train operators are the Sleeper Trains Cairo-Luxor-Aswan (www.wataniasleepingtrains.com) and the Egyptian National Railways (Enr.gov.eg).

- **Trains in Israel**

  When you are in Israel, you can move around easily on a low-cost and efficient rail network that is supervised by Israel Railways (www.rail.co.il). You can make trips between Be'er Sheva, Akko, Haifa, Jerusalem, central Tel Aviv and Ben Gurion Airport. Generally, trains run after every 30, 60 or 120 minutes to or from Jerusalem. However, it can be difficult to reach Israel by sea or land, due to a lack of ferries in the Eastern Mediterranean area and the war in Syria.

- **Trains in Iran**

  In Iran, the IRR Iranian Islamic Republic Railways (www.raja.ir) is the train operator. You can check www.iranrail.net, an amazingly useful unofficial website in English language with fares and timings for trains plying in Iran.

- **Trains in Turkey**

  Any travel guide for Turkey will inform that you that the country has a quality bus network, with buses being faster and better than trains. However, it is important to consider whether you would like to travel in a bus for 12 hours when you can travel in a low-cost AC train, with a comfortable Pullman seat allowing enough leg space or a bed in a comfortable private sleeper. The amazing sceneries are not affected due to ongoing development on the roadside. Travellers gush about the train experience in Turkey. The best trains in Turkey are now modern, AC-equipped and run by TCDD (www.tcddtasimacilik.gov.tr). Those who travel smart board a train for long-distance trips and then board a bus for short trips to go to places that are located off the train network – such as in the Cappadocia.

Driving in the Middle East

It can be more liberating to drive your own car in the Middle East, although it can be tiring and expensive. It is tough to find a Middle East route that would justify the hassle and expense.

Always ensure that the hire price includes insurance. Become familiar with the policy. Unless your car is insured for potential mishaps, do not hire a car. Insurance is compulsory as well as highly advisable in most countries of the Middle East. It is strongly advised that you opt for fully comprehensive insurance for any vehicle, whether one on hire or your own.

Ensure that you are insured for off-piste trips and trips between Middle Eastern nations in case you intend to go on cross-border trips. In case of any accident, you have to submit your accident report as quickly to your insurance provider as possible or to your car-hire agency before having your vehicle repaired.

The environment across the Middle East tends to vary a lot, although it can be worse than what most travellers experience back home. Typically, the main roads are good or fair at least, although the sub roads are not okay in many places. Generally, the international roads are crowded and narrow. The Palestinian Territories, Israel, Turkey and Jordan possibly have the best roads while those in Syria, Lebanon and Iran can be better or worse than your expectations. While some of the roads in Egypt are okay, you would do well to avoid the others.

Top Places to Visit in the Middle East

The Middle East, despite its social and religious strife, is one of the most beautiful places on Earth. You can view some of the most amazing wonders and places.

A vast territory, the Middle East is often ignored in its totality. It is generally regarded as only the land with the best and most wonderful deserts, the friendly and warm Bedouins and the endless number of spice bazaars.

Sadly, in most cases the international media focuses only on the bad events and occurrences in the Middle East. This has significantly distorted the perception of people and most travellers feel that the Middle East is like a single nation and it is too dangerous to visit the place.

In actuality, the Middle East is very different. It comprises 14 varied nations that significantly differ from one another. These include: Iran, Saudi Arabia, Kuwait, Iraq, Israel and the Palestinian territories, Egypt, Syria, Lebanon, Jordan, Yemen, Oman, Bahrain, Qatar, United Arab Emirates. These have shared borders and boundaries with each other.

Some of the best destinations to visit In the Middle East include:

- **Jerusalem**

  In Israel, Jerusalem is the most famous city and one of the oldest traveller favourites. It has kept attracting tourists for more than 2,000 years. You are likely to be surprised to know that even in the Middle Ages, there were dedicated travel books offered regularly for the reference of European pilgrims. These included information about the most important shrines and saints to visit while travelling to the Holy Land. Jerusalem continues to be a bucket-list destination, and offers a powerful spiritual experience. You can visit some of the most sacred spots of Islam, Christianity and Judaism. The Biblical landscapes and the ancient bazaars and old streets of the ancient city transport you to a very different and unique world that you have probably grown up reading about in Biblical tales, adventure stories or fairy tales.

- **Riyadh**

  The largest city and the capital in Saudi Arabia, Riyadh is also the business and cultural centre of the nation. It is an expansive and huge place with plenty of interesting activities and spectacular sights. It is a large megalopolis that blended Arab traditions with western influences. If you like desert adventure, camping, camels, bowling, shopping activities and history, Riyadh is the place that you should visit.

- **Abu Dhabi**

  One of the famous Middle East tourist destinations, and many travellers regard it as a wonderful city. This is a city with rich heritage and culture and has good restaurants and luxury hotels. It boasts some of the most attractions, like: Heritage Village, Sheikh Zayed Mosque, The Souks, and Khalifa Park. People love to visit this fascinating emirate to explore the city, enjoy a nice holiday, view state-of-the-art infrastructure, personally experience its fantastic history and participate in its wonderful pleasures.

- **Beirut**

  The capital and the most important city of Lebanon, Beirut is situated on a small-sized isthmus that spreads to the Mediterranean Sea from the shoreline. Although Beirut has been ravaged by wars, it has restored itself and turned into one of the main Middle Eastern cultural cities. The traditions of old times are still upheld by this city. Beirut is recognized as a city of traditions, history and wonderful culture, and has different types of ancient architecture and monuments. Alongside its ancient wonders, the city also boasts modern amenities such as nice restaurants, sophisticated clubs and bars, plush hotels and a lovely beach ambience. It has many various modern attractions.

- **Petra**

  You will love to visit Petra in Jordan, which is a spectacular ancient wonder with pre-historic sites and unmatched sights. This rock-carved city woos visitors with marvellous primeval structures and red-coloured charm. This is a fantastic attraction for travellers and tourists who like ancient adventures, with plenty of magnificent architectures and a rich history to explore. The UNESCO has designated Petra as a World Heritage Site, and it is a wonderful holiday destination.

- **Doha**

  The capital of Qatar and its largest city, Doha boasts of some of the loveliest attractions. For sophisticated 21st-century people, there are various attractions such as thrilling activities on the desert, golfing activities and shopping trips at the souks. There are many modern shopping malls in Doha, which stand as a contrast to the spectacular views of the sea and the virgin sandy beaches.

- **Dubai**

  A vacation paradise, Dubai stands as a famous travel destination. The city is filled with many tourist attractions such as the tallest buildings of the world, souks or open-air Arab markets, modern shopping malls, timeless deserts, plenty of fun activities and beautiful beaches. One of the richest cities, Dubai has many amazing nightclubs, modern bars, elite restaurants, fancy hotels and more.

- **Tel Aviv**

  In Israel, it happens to be the second largest city. This vibrant place is one of the most remarkable cities on the planet, dating back to times as old as civilization itself. It varies from the largest Israel city, Jerusalem, and consists of many holy sites and sacred wonders. This cosmopolitan metropolis boasts exciting beach activities, holiday approach and fabulous nightlife. This is a sophisticated city that offers all the attractions imaginable.

- **Manama**

  Manama is the capital of Bahrain, a fascinating Middle East nation with a culture and history similar to other destinations in the Middle East. A cultural place, Manama has many amazing natural features, fabulous attractions, architecture and sophisticated substructure.

  The name of the city stands for "Sleeping Place," but this capital of Bahrain is ever energetic. The city sleeps only a little, with visitors flocking to the place every weekend for late-night shopping, fine dining and drinking after work time. It always remains active and consists of many parks, museums and religious sites that can be explored all through the day.

- **Cappadocia**

  In central Turkey, this semi-arid area boasts of prominent "fairy chimneys" with conical and tall rock structures gathered together in Göreme, Monks Valley and other places. There are other prominent sites, including homes that date back to the Bronze Age and were carved by cave dwellers (troglodytes) into the walls of the valley. Later, these were used by early Christians as shelters. There are many rock-faced churches in the Ihlara Canyon that are 100m in depth.

- **Eilat**

  The only Red Sea resort in Israel, Eilat is located on the tiny Red Sea coastline stretch, and is between Egypt and Jordan. The popular diving spot in Red Sea is a major draw here. There is a wonderful underwater Coral Beach Reserve that is located to the town's southern section. If you like land more than the sea, you will love to remain on the beaches. The Timna Park, an awe-inspiring sculpted natural world, is located to the north of this town. It is one of the most surreal and beautiful sites in Israel. The place, with its incredible landscapes and rocks with strange shapes, can be a major attraction for visitors.

Oriental Asia

Oriental Asia or East Asia, the eastern sub area of Asia, is a vast area of around 4,600,000 sq. mi. It comprises around 28% of the Asian continent. Geopolitically as well as geographically, the area involves China as well as Taiwan, Japan, South Korea, North Korea, Mongolia, Macau, and Hong Kong.

The entire region of East Asia consists of over 1.5 billion individuals. 22% or more than 1/5th of people on the planet and 38% of the Asian population stay in East Asia. The riparian and the coastal sections of East Asia form one of the places on Earth with the biggest population. The population in Western China and Mongolia is low, with the areas being distributed in a very sparse way. For any sovereign state, the population density in Mongolia is the lowest. East Asia has an unparalleled combination of fascinating culture, rich history, wonderful cities and great sceneries. Whether it comes to Hong Kong harbour, serene Mongolia, the ever-active Tokyo or the legendary Great Wall of China, there are many attractions. The region of Asia is diverse and extremely large. Even if you set out of home for travelling long term, you will possibly visit only a few Asian nations.

You can find numerous travel routes across the area, and every one of these has a wonderful ambience and culture.

Extremely popular with tourists, Asia has many fantastic nations where you can find many beautiful spots. Tourists from various continents across the globe can come to East Asia for a rich mix of history and culture, religion, animals, exotic foods, scenic islands and fantastic cities. It is highly likely that you will spend less on Asia trips, than on tours in any other part of the world.

Flying Around Oriental Asia with Low-Cost Airlines

Small East Asian airlines are constantly opening up the routes for travel across Asia and the whole world. There are more low-cost carriers crossing the Asian skies than any other continent. In the last few years, the Skytrax series of the low-cost airlines have flown the most in Asia. If you want to make the best choice this year, the following table will reveal the list of the budget. This will make it more convenient for tourists to access the website for every airline and book cheap flights.

China

- 9 Air: www.9air.com

- China United Airlines: www.flycua.com

- Jiangxi Air: www.airjiangxi.com

- Ruili Airlines: www.rlair.net

- Spring Airlines: www.ch.com

- Urumqi Air: www.urumqi-air.com

- West Air: www.westair.cn

Japan

- AirAsia Japan: www.airasia.com/jp

- Jetstar Japan: www.jetstar.com/jp

- Peach: www.flypeach.com

- Skymark Airlines: www.skymark.co.jp/en

- Solaseed Air: www.solaseedair.jp

- Spring Airlines Japan: jp.ch.com

- StarFlyer: www.starflyer.jp

- Vanilla Air: www.vanilla-air.com

Hong Kong

- HK Express: www.hkexpress.com

South Korea

- Air Busan: www.airbusan.com

- Air Seoul: flyairseoul.com

- Eastar Jet: www.eastarjet.com

- Jeju Air: www.jejuair.net

- Jin Air: www.jinair.com

- T'way Air: www.twayair.com

Taiwan

- Tigerair Taiwan: www.tigerairtw.com

Travel by Bus in Oriental Asia

- **Bus travel in China**

  As far as travelling in China is concerned, most travellers like to board a train or flight given that trains are cost-effective while flights are fast modes of travel. However, there can be times when the vast intercity bus system in China can be the ideal option for you. This could be due to the trains being overcrowded or flights being over-expensive. It could also be as you might like to save some money or go to a spot that is not served by a railway station or airport.

The online purchase of bus tickets has not become a viable option yet. This leaves you with just two options – you can purchase a ticket at the nearest bus station or use an alternative source to buy it from. At present, China has a "real name ticket system" that needs you to have a passport or an official proof of ID to buy bus tickets. Keep in mind that you cannot transfer a purchased ticket to any other person without first returning the same and purchasing a new ticket. You can also try an alternative. Go for www.chinabusguide.com, or a similar service, and buy tickets. Although the service can be used easily, some Chinese cities are excluded.

- **Bus Travel In Mongolia**

For most of the destinations, you have to purchase the tickets a minimum of 1 day in advance. Buy your ticket early in the morning to get a seat for the next day. If possible, buy tickets at least 2 days in advance during the Summer Sports Festival (Naadam) and the Lunar New Year (Tsagaan Sar).

If you wish to travel Mongolia by bus, you need to reach Ulaanbaatar – the capital of Mongolia. There are two prominent bus stations in this city, dedicated to domestic trips.

- Dragon Tuv – Buses travelling to the west operate from this station.

- Bayanzurkh Tovchoo – Every bus going to the east starts from here.

- **Bus Travel in South Korea**

  Reliable and quick bus services run across South Korea on the expressways, and connect just about every minor and major point. South Korea has two types of express buses – deluxe express buses and regular express buses. Long-distance buses connect each part of the country, and these run between towns and major cities at 15-minute intervals. You can find a bus at least every hour for small towns, temples, villages, provincial and national parks.

When buses are not filled to capacity, locals pay no heed to reserved seating arrangements and take whatever seat they prefer. You can check schedules and book bus tickets in South Korea in two handy websites - www.hticket.co.kr and www.kobus.co.kr.

- **Bus Travel in Taiwan**

  As a tourist to Taiwan, you will not experience any dearth in the number of buses. If you are looking for the most cost-effective travel in Taiwan option, buses are what you need. These are low-cost and are very frequent. Most of these are very comfortable and the seats are thick, styled like armchairs. You can board these to go to any spot on the island. You can visit the website www.taiwanbus.tw to learn about the bus companies and routes to tour around Taiwan. Kuo Kuang and UBus are two of the major bus service providers.

- **Bus Travel of Japan**

  For medium as well as long-distance travel around Japan, you will find highway buses to be a low-cost alternative. Many highway buses offer overnight travel on longer routes. Buses are typically quite cheaper, although these run slower than express trains. Discount fares have reduced a lot, particularly on competitive routes. You can also avail the Japan Bus Pass, which permits bus tours at very low costs. You can check the willerexpress.com official homepage to get further details about this travel pass.

Every area in Japan has prominent attractions, such as cuisine, culture, history and natural sceneries. There are many bus lines across Japan, and you can use these to make direct travel to over 1,000 locations, safely arrive at your preferred destination and enjoy sights of the landscape along your trip. There are two useful websites, Japan Bus Online (japanbusonline.com) and Japan Bus Lines (japanbuslines.com), which let tourists book tickets for bus in Japan.

Travel by Train Through Oriental Asia

- **Train Travelling Around China**

  China boasts one of the busiest and largest train networks on the planet, with trains linking almost every city and town. Trains in China are a low-cost, safe and comfortable way to travel throughout the country. A train trip in China is nothing short of an experience, when compared to the less eco-friendly and less trustable internal flights. Keep in mind that you can only book a train ticket 20 days prior to your trip, meaning you cannot purchase a ticket too early beforehand.

The peak seasons in China include the Summer Holidays (July - August), National Day (October 1), May Day (May 1) and Spring Festival (January or February). If you intend to travel anytime during the peak seasons, you need to purchase train tickets as quickly as possible or risk all the tickets being sold out. You can check out the website www.china-diy-travel.com to get train times for Chinese Railways in the English language. Some of the reputed websites for agencies selling train tickets for China include:

- www.chinahighlights.com
- www.ctrip.com
- www.china-diy-travel.com

The Kowloon-Canton Railway Corporation (www.mtr.com.hk) offers connecting trains for Beijing, Hong Kong and Shanghai as well as local trains in Hong Kong.

- **Train Travelling In Mongolia**

  You can avail general travel information for trains at rail.cc/en/Mongolia. You have to purchase your train ticket locally at any railway station in Mongolia, if you wish to travel by train. You can find train connections in Mongolia from Ulaanbaatar to Zamyn-Üüd, Sükhbaatar, Sainshand, Darkhan, Erdenet and Choir. There is the Trans-Mongolian Railway that crosses the nation from Ulan-Ude (Russia) and Moscow to Beijing (China).

- **Train Travelling in South Korea**

  If you wish to travel out of Seoul and visit various other places around South Korea, it is possibly best that you make a train trip. In Korea, the on-board amenities and the speed are the two factors based on which trains are categorized. Usually, the trains are classified in 7 different ways. The ticket rates in Korea are based on the distance travelled and the classification of the train. The Honam Line and the Gyeongbu Line are the two prime railway lines here. Jeolla and Gyeongjeon Line, reaching Changwon on the South Coast and Yeosu, are the other railway lines. The KORAIL Pass is an exclusive railway pass that allows foreign visitors to have an affordable vacation across Korea. You can use it unlimited on any train – even on KTX express trains – for a specific number of days. For further information, please check the link www.letskorail.com.

- **Train Travel in Taiwan**

  If you want to travel around the island of Taiwan, you will find train trips to be an easy option. Train services cover many towns and cities. The Taiwan Railway Administration comes with an extensive system that runs along the west as well as the east coasts. Other than the tourism branch lines, the Central Mountains are not covered by any services. You can find clean, reliable, safe and comfortable trains with minimal delays. You can reserve seats, and have snacks and foods served. Trains connect all the major cities here. Visit the Taiwan Government Railway website TRA website (www.railway.gov.tw) for timetables and fares.

- **Train Travel in Japan**

  One of the best railways in the world, Japanese rail services are frequent, comfortable, fast and clean. Japan Railways (jr-central.co.jp), also referred to as 'JR', is the main operator. A cluster of distinguishable railway systems, it offers a single linked service all through the nation. JR operates the bullet train Shinkansen routes in Japan. Much like the KORAIL pass in Korea, the JR Pass or Japan Rail Pass is an extremely low-cost rail pass that allows long-distance train trips in Japan. Only foreign tourists can use it. The pass can be used for unlimited times in Japanese railway trains for 1, 2 or 3 weeks at an unimaginable cost for Japanese residents. The pass is available in 2 types – First Class Cars and Ordinary Cars. The First Class cars, also known as Green cars, have more room than the Ordinary cars. The JR pass is valid on about all trains in the JR network that operates across the nation including local trains, rapid trains, limited express and Shinkansen express. You can look at a map that shows all the main train lines that you can use with the pass. The network is very economical due to the different rail pass schemes available. For further details, check www.japan-rail-pass.com and www.jrailpass.com. There is a vast network of private railways other than JR services. Generally, every major city and its adjoining areas are served by a minimum of one private rail line. It connects the city to other proximal cities.

Driving around Oriental Asia

- **Driving Around China**

  You will require an International Driving Permit to drive in Macau and Hong Kong. If you are a foreigner, but happen to be a Chinese resident and possess an official motorcycle license in China, you can be allowed to drive motorcycles. As a first-time rider, you may find Chinese roads to be complex, the costs of driving to be higher in China and other dangers, and it is more sensible to use the taxis and the metro system. Both options are efficient and cost-effective in Shanghai and Beijing.

- **Driving In Mongolia**

  The driving standards in Mongolia vary a lot, and have not maintained pace with the significant growth in the total number of vehicles. The maintenance of vehicles can be poor here, even for rental cars. It is advised that you avoid driving during the night and wear seatbelts whenever you can. If you can, it is suggested that you use the services of a professional driver with plenty of experience and familiarity with driving conditions in the country. It is hazardous to go driving in Ulaanbaatar, given that traffic congestion is heavier on the roads. There are few signposts and plenty of accidents. You will require an International Driving Permit if you wish to go driving in Mongolia.

- **Driving in South Korea**

Unfortunately, you cannot drive in Korea with a foreigner's driving licenses, as these are not valid in the country. However, before your arrival in Korea, you can opt for an International Driving License with a validity of up to a year. As a foreign traveller, you need to obtain your IDP (International Driver's Permit) is the same nation where you received your driving license from. Always carry along your driving license with you, given that the IDP is valid only when it is used with a valid driving license. Remember that the full name on your IDP and your passport must be the same.

- **Driving in Taiwan**

Although you can find driving to be enjoyable in Taiwan, it is sometimes stressful as well. Driving is indeed the best way to check out more areas that are generally inaccessible, such as Taitung, Hualien and Nantou. However, while visiting Taipei, it is best to choose only public transportation systems given that both driving and parking in this city can be an issue. The properly positioned speed traps cameras along the sides of the Taiwanese roads are infamous. You can easily view the cameras, and there are plenty of well-marked signs and warning times in Chinese language as well. Spotting the cameras can be fun for riders. Traffic in Taiwan resembles that of the U.S. in that it is cantered on the right side of the streets. Travellers from Thailand, Hong Kong, Australia, U.K. and Singapore need to be cautious, given that it is on the opposite side of the road that the traffic moves along. If you wish to legally drive in Taiwan, apply for an IDP in your native country first. An IDP is enough in most cases for driving a vehicle in this country.

- **Driving in Japan**

  Driving is more enjoyable in rural Japan than in the urban areas, although the rural roads are much narrower. Some of the tunnels are not properly illuminated, as you should be careful while driving through them. It can be impossible for you to pass the mountain roads during winters due to the snow.

The signposts are in Japanese outside of the cities, and not being conversant with the language can be tough. You should always have a proper map with you. It can also be useful to have satellite navigation systems, and you can plug the phone numbers of the areas that you wish to access as coordinates. Many modern rental Japanese cars also come with GPS, as many homes are numbered in the order of their construction and many streets are unnamed. In order to drive in Japan, you should possess an international driver's license with one-year validity.

Top Destinations to Visit in Oriental Asia

- **Beijing**

Beijing, the main option for international tourists, is the Chinese capital for more than 855 years. It is an ideal blend of modernity and elegance, and is the best tourist destination that offers well-rounded knowledge of China. You may take a walk along the crisscrossing hutongs or stroll around the red Forbidden City to get a feel for everyday life in

China. The Badaling Great Wall, located to the north of downtown Beijing, happens to be the most well-maintained area. You must visit the destination. The mega Olympic venues, top-class museums, vibrant shopping streets and growing skyscrapers can give you a true feel of the sophisticated capital.

- **Hong Kong**

Hong Kong, a vibrant Asia metropolis, is known as one of the 'Four Asian Tigers' due to its fantastical economic state. The city is known as the Pearl of the Orient, and is the 3rd most important financial hub on Earth, after NY and London. The city is also reputed as a Shoppers' Paradise.

The colonial history of Hong Kong allows the combination of different cultures. The colourful lights make the cityscape look shining under the nocturnal sky. Explore the night in the city by taking a tram to Victoria Peak, enjoying wine in Lan Kwai Fong in Central or having a magnificent view of the Victoria Bay that offers 'the night scene worth millions of dollars'. The wonderful night sky is also visible from an evening cruise in the Hong Kong harbour.

- **Busan**

It is a famous destination for South Korea visitors, and is renowned for its wonderful historic buildings, beaches and city life. The 2nd largest city in South Korea, Busan is situated on the mainland's south-eastern corner. Foreign visitors as well as Koreans all over the nation love to visit the Haeundae Beach, although it can be overcrowded. The beaches in Songdo or Daedepo are the quieter ones. Busan is fashionable, sophisticated and cosmopolitan. The city boasts of traditional markets side by side with sophisticated restaurants and the largest department store of the world.

- **Shanghai**

Shanghai varies from Beijing, with its vast heritage, and has a very metropolitan ambience for its visitors. In the list of 'Top 10 Cities to Visit in China', it comes in 2nd position. It is regarded as the centre of fortune and commerce of the nation, and is regarded as the 'shoppers' paradise'. The city has a distinctive landscape and a colonial backdrop. It has the Huangpu River, referred to as its mother river, with the Bund, which is the biggest waterfront sightseeing belt. Many classical architectures of western-style can be seen here. The Lujiazui Financial Zone across the river presents a completely varied sight. The Jin Mao Tower, World Financial Center and the soaring Oriental Pearl TV Tower form a part of one of the most fantastic skylines of the world. Shanghai presents a wonderful nocturnal view, with numerous elegant streetlights, constantly moving headlights and flashing neon lights.

- **Seoul**

  This is a modern, vibrant city, and offers the actual '24-hour party' experience that other cities only promise to visitors. With aesthetic design, stunning city parks and cultural landmarks, the city is trying to make itself over beautifully. You can find amazing spots for relaxation, shopping, drinking and eating, whether in Apgujeong's stylish boutiques and chic restaurants and bars in Hongdae. If you love to shop for souvenirs, antiques, arts, crafts or jewellery, you should go to the shops and fascinating markets of Insa Dong.

- **Ulaanbaatar**

  There are many Soviet-style blocks and neighbourhoods, with skyscrapers and sprawling concrete roads. There is Ulaanbaatar, which is just the opposite of Mongolia. This is a vast, loud, bold and brash place, and consists of many sophisticated shopping malls and designer outlets.

Beneath its bright lights, the city also has a traditional charm with the Genghis Kahn's great monument, the wide squares having chatty local people, the attractive National Museum of Mongolia or the 19th-century Bogd Khaan palace constructed by the Mongolian masters.

- **Taipei**

Taipei is the capital city of Taiwan, and is located in the Northern area. In Taiwan, it is the fourth largest administrative region consisting of 12 districts having limitless travel attractions. This is also the sole Taiwanese city where travellers can reside in during their entire period of stay. However, they can still come across enough attractions on offer in Taiwan. In Taiwan, Taipei is regarded as a "must-visit" city, due to its museums, historic architecture, religious and cultural sites, beverages, foods, entertainment and shopping destinations. The main tourist attractions in the city are Raohe night market, National Palace Museum, Ximending shopping district, National Chiang Kai-shek Memorial Hall, Taipei 101, Shilin night market.

- **Kagoshima**

This is a sister city to Naples due to its lush green vegetation, outgoing local people and warm weather conditions. Kagoshima is an attractive place and the capital city of Kagoshima Prefecture. In Japan, it is one of the southernmost cities of Kyushu. It has many beautiful flowers, wide streets and palm trees. The stunning bay of the city overlooks the active volcano Sakurajima that seems to rise from the sea off the coast. In the July to August period, you can see spectacular views – such as when there is display of fireworks every evening over the bay. The frequent eruptions of the volcano often envelop the town in a unique white ash coat.

- **Tokyo**

If you love to meet new people, Tokyo will be closer to your heart. The metropolitan region of this capital of Japan is the most populated on the planet. Whether the fish market at Tuskiji or the traditional gardens with their spring cherry blossoms, there is more than enough to see here. From karaoke bars to shrines, the city combines the modern with the ancient. It can be very energizing to walk the streets of this bustling city. When the very intense speed of Tokyo gets too much for you to bear, you can visit the lovely Shinjuku Gyoen National Garden and relax there. It is the title-holder of the costliest city in world to live and the easiest city to move around due to its wonderful subway and rail networks. Tokyo is popular for its cultural side due to its Sumo Wrestling and other long-established Japanese activities, baseball, football (soccer), and professional sports clubs as well as worldwide famous cuisine, theatres, festivals, several museums and more. Tokyo is known for its theatre and music, along with many venues that cover rock and pop concerts, symphony orchestras, modern and Japanese dramas and more.

- **Kyoto**

This serves as the capital of just Kyoto prefecture, although it was once Japan's imperial capital for over a millennium. The city is situated on central Honshu Island, and is popular as the City of 10,000 Shrines due to thousands of Shinto shrines, which include the Buddhist temples and the highest rated

Fushimi Inari Shrine. The city inhabits 1.5 million individuals. The place is also renowned for the July celebration, the Gion Matsuri festival, regarded as one of the best Japanese festal occasions. One of the largest cities of Japan, Kyoto is western Japan's educational centre having higher academic establishments and various universities. It is one of the biggest tourist destinations of Japan and it has preserved much of its past environment being the only major Japanese city to have avoided destruction during the WWII. It is popular as the home of the Japanese emperor. It is the most important cultural centre for roughly 1,100 years in Japan. Today, the city is a top draw for its sculptures, paintings and many other art forms in numerous galleries and museums.

- **Nara**

This city has long been celebrated as the core of Japanese culture. It is situated in central Honshu, south of Lake Biwa. It has a pleasant backdrop consisting of farms, tall hills and thick forests. The city is rich in artistic treasures and historical buildings, and draws over a million tourists every year. This makes it one of the most popular cities in

Japan. Any trip to the city should include a walk to its several old buildings and many captivating streets, each of which are placed in a picturesque backdrop that can be viewed easily from the Mount Mikasayama that is located close by. The city has preserved its rural community atmosphere, and has turned into a sort of cultural destination. It is one of the prominent craft centres of Japan, and is popular for its lacquerware (Nara-shikki), ceramics (Akahada-yaki), fans (Nara-uchiwa) and carved wooden dolls (Nara-ningyo).

- **Nagoya**

This has become the country's busiest port due to its convenient position that makes it open to the Pacific. For a long time, it has been a prominent manufacturing destination for ceramics, textiles and other established industries. In the 12th century, the ceramics industry was set up here. Due to its many factory tours and many workshops, it has turned into a tourist attraction. You can still see many of the historic sites of the city, including the 16th-century castle that was reconstructed much like its city centre after the WWII destruction. This vast city, in the modern times, is a joy to visit due to its amazing network of modern art galleries, streets, museums and historic temples.

Southern Asia

South Asia as a term is used to indicate Asia's southern area, consisting of the SAARC countries of the sub-Himalayan region. South Asia, for some authorities, also includes adjoining nations to the east and the west. South Asia is formed from the present territories of Afghanistan, Bhutan, India, Sri Lanka, Bangladesh, Nepal, Maldives, Pakistan. An economic cooperation organization in South Asia, The South Asian Association for Regional Cooperation (SAARC) was set up in 1985. It consists of as many as 8 countries, which includes South Asia.

The region is spread over around 1.9 million mi2, which means 3.4% of the world's land surface or 11.51% of the Asian continent. Around 1.749 billion of the inhabitants of South Asia make up around 1/4th of the global population, which makes it the most densely populated and the most populous geographical area on the planet. It overall makes up around 39.49% of Asia's population. It inhabits people from many cultures, and accounts for more 24% of the world's population.

The place enjoys a tropical climate, other than the Himalaya. It has a dry winter and receives monsoons in summer. However, it is natural here to experience extremes of weather. Monsoons are more or less absent in Western Pakistan, while lasting for 6 months in Southern India. There are two monsoons in Sri Lanka, one falling between October and November and another in May.

In every place, you can see historical Indian culture influences. The 4 big religions of the world originated in South Asia - Hinduism, Buddhism, Sikhism, and Jainism. It was only later, about the 7th century, when Muslim invaders introduced Islam and the religion became prominent during the Mughal Empire. The different cultures of South Asia were unified during the British culture influences, and particularly due to the growing and frequent usage of the English language. This happen before India's Independence in 1947, during the days of the British Empire when India was referred to as the "Jewel in the Crown".

Flying with Low-Cost Airlines in South Asia

The rise of budget carriers makes it possible for you to travel cheaply across South Asia. Low-cost airlines are very useful, and these can allow affordable travels, at times costing less than train or bus tickets.

Cost-effective carriers have brought even the blue-collar population together. These are designed to help travellers make trips affordably and enjoy faster travelling opportunities without splurging pots of money.

It can be quite cheap to fly in South Asia, particularly if you purchase tickets well in advance. Some of the famous budget carriers serving the area include:

Kyrgyzstan

- Air Manas: www.airmanas.com

Pakistan

- Airblue: www.airblue.com

India

- Air India Express: www.airindiaexpress.in
- AirAsia India: www.airasia.com/in
- GoAir: www.goair.in
- IndiGo: www.goindigo.in
- SpiceJet: www.spicejet.com

Nepal

- Himalaya Airlines: www.himalaya-airlines.com

Travel By Bus in South Asia

Bangladesh

The country has a wide variety of vehicles, and you can find cars, buses, CNGs, rickshaws, scooters, motorbikes, tractors with people on trays, bicycles with 4 people and many other transportation facilities.

The year 2016 saw a major connectivity between Bangladesh and India, when two bus services began. These connect Dhaka-Shillong-Guwahati and Kolkata-Dhaka-Agartala and link West Bengal to 3 of the north-eastern states in India through the capital Dhaka. It is possible for you to book tickets online from websites like www.shyamoliparibahan-bd.com and www.shyamoliparibahan.com.

Bhutan

Only Indian tourists on a budget, residents and locals are likely to use buses for travel, given that public buses are overcrowded. The winding roads of Bhutan make bus rides even less enjoyable. At least once daily, you can find buses running from the capital Thimphu to Paro, Phuentsholing, Haa and Punakha. The long-distance buses ply between 1 to 3 times each week from Thimphu to places like Zhemgang, Phobjika, Samtse, Trashigang, Mongar, Trashi Yangtse. The fares are low, and you can visit www.bhutanpost.bt to find fares, routes and timetables to be easily accessible.

India

Most people in India use buses for transportation. Every state or region has a bus system of its own, and these run long-distance and intercity. Buses can be overcrowded. However, these run more frequently than trains and even quicker at times – which makes them more advantageous. Each bus has a fare collector and he makes his way through the bus for fare collection. In some cases, you can purchase a ticket right at the bus station. In India, buses run just about anywhere. In many mountainous cities and towns, these are the sole ways for travel. These are the cheapest travel options, with services being frequent and fast.

On curvy or mountainous roads, the terrain can be dangerous. It is often that drivers operate buses carelessly, and there are always risks of accidents. Unless you have no other option, try to avoid buses at night. With drivers often being fatigued or drunken, driving conditions are frequently risky here. During long-distance trips, every bus makes toilet or snack stops, offering a break, although this lengthens the time of the journey. You can book most deluxe buses in advance at travel agencies or bus stations or even online at the websites of bus companies, such as Makemytrip (www.makemytrip.com), Redbus (www.redbus.in) and Cleartrip (www.cleartrip.com).

Nepal

In Nepal, buses are the primary form of public transportation and these are very cheap. However, the cheapness often reflects on the quality of rides and internal ambience. Buses stop for any individual and run to almost any place, although you can find it more convenient to find a seat when you board a bus at the station instead of somewhere along the road. It is better that you book buses for long distance trips around 2 days in advance. In lowland Nepal, most towns can be accessed from Pokhara or Kathmandu by bus. However, most buses in Nepal are very uncomfortable, slow and noisy, and you can be almost certain about breakdowns – even where 'deluxe' buses are concerned. Services, luckily, are quite frequent. Even if your first bus breaks down during the middle of your journey, you can board another bus. You can visit busnepal.com and www.bussewa.com to access bus schedules and tickets.

Pakistan

The country has well-established bus services between cities and in urban areas, with both private and public sectors running services. Bus services such as Royal Express (royalsexpress.com), Daewoo Express (www.daewoo.com.pk) and Niazi Express (www.niaziexpress.com) have set up sophisticated intercity services that connect to most Pakistani cities and run throughout the day. The Intercity buses are well maintained and more sophisticated. You can book bus tickets online from the bookme.pk/bus website.

Sri Lanka

Buses are the most cost-effective way to travel in Sri Lanka. There is a vast network throughout the country, and buses ply to each small corner here. Bus travel is especially convenient when you travel to lesser-known travel destinations. If you wish to book online bus tickets, visit the website busseat.lk.

Travel by Train around South Asia

- **Bangladesh**

  The country has a vast rail network built by the British, which links most of the important cities and towns, such as Dhaka and Chittagong. This network has two halves, eastern and western, divided by rivers flowing throughout the nation. The eastern network is mainly meter gauge and the western network is mainly broad gauge. Unfortunately, the connections between the two networks are not often very good. You can visit www.railway.gov.bd to find a railway route schedule and map, and buy tickets online at Bangladesh Railway Esheba (www.esheba.cnsbd.com).

- **India**

  Riding on an Indian express train offers the safest and most comfortable travel option. The Indian passenger rail network consists of 6,800 stations and 63,000 km of rail routes, and is the third largest on the planet after Russia and China. When it comes to passenger kilometres, it is the largest in the world. Indian Railways have more than 1.5 million employees, and stands as the biggest employer in the world. In India, trains run to just about any place. You can find train fares and times on www.indianrailways.gov.in and access information about train fares and times on www.indianrail.gov.in.

- **Nepal**

In Nepal, rail transport includes just 2 railway lines. On the Nepalese side, Nepal Railways operate both railway lines. You can purchase tickets in local train stations.

- **Pakistan**

Pakistan Railways is the main railway line in the nation, and handles passenger traffic as well as serves all the needs for large-scale goods transportation. It contributes to national integration as well as economic growth in Pakistan. In summer 2009, it was reported that Pakistan is not permitting westerners on its trains to prevent embarrassment in case of possible death of western tourists in potential terrorist attacks. You can visit www.pakrail.com to access more information about Pakistan Railway Corporation.

- **Sri Lanka**

  This is a remarkably stress-free, safe and friendly place for travelling about. It is an excellent and low-priced way to get around. Train trips offer actual experiences of the local culture, and you can view picturesque scenes during train rides from Colombo to Dutch colonial Galle, up to the Tea Country and from Colombo to Kandy. If you are travelling for over 80km, you can stop your trip at any station, before the destination for 24 hours without fine. It is important to make fresh seat reservations on the next phase. Many intercity trains allow you to reserve seats in First or Second Class. You can make reservations at many train stations up to a month before departure. Visit www.railway.gov.lk, the Sri Lanka Government Railways website as well as the site slr.malindaprasad.com that offers information about train services and schedules.

Top Destinations to Visit in South Asia

- **Goa**

  This has long been known in India as the best beach holiday destination. Goa has over 60 miles of gorgeous seashore and consists of many fantastic beaches of the world, each having its own specific beauty. However, it is only in the last two decades that westerners have 'discovered' the beautiful western coastline that overlooks the Arabian Sea. Visit the isolated Agonda Beach for tranquillity, and go to the Calangute Beach that is the most crowded and commercial space. If you love spa vacations, yoga getaways and posh resorts, visit the Morjim, Mandrem and Ashwem beaches that are loved by Westerners and rich Indians. You can also visit Palolem, which has a lovely backdrop.

- **Delhi**

The Indian capital is popular for being the seat of the judiciary, legislative and executive Government branches. However, Delhi is also a major metropolis and cultural centre with activities related to arts and culture. It is the gastronomy and fashion hub as well. Tourists throng the place for wonderful nightlife and dining experiences. You can also view the city for its stunning forts, temples, mosques etc., including the Baha'i Lotus Temple, Jama Masjid and Red Fort.

- **Mumbai**

  Mumbai is the economic capital of India, and is situated along the sea. It was built in 1911. Once officially referred to as Bombay, this famous multinational metropolis of India is also the largest city of India. It is India's commercial capital and one of its major port cities. The city has an eclectic culture, with the presence of Bollywood, and a huge TV industry that employs thousands of local people and foreigners. A gorgeous city, Mumbai has never-ending sights of interest - including the Gateway of India, an iconic symbol of the city.

- **Cox's Bazar**

  One of the longest sea beaches on the globe, sprawling for a 75-mile long area. It is the most popular beach resort in Bangladesh and can be compared to Cancun due to its major constructions and hotels that mainly serve the elite of the city. It is unlike any other beach vacation that you might have experienced. In Bangladesh, it is regarded as one of the most widely visited tourist spots. One of the main tourist attractions in Cox's Bazar is Aggmeda Khyang, a majestic Buddhist monastery.

- **Dhaka**

A visit to Bangladesh is nothing without a visit to its capital city. This is also the largest city in Bangladesh. It is the cultural, economic and academic hub of the country. Over 18 million people live here.

Dhaka is the hub of almost all activities in Bangladesh. It houses fantastic tourist attractions like the National Memorial, Bangabandhu Memorial Museum, Ramna Park, Baldha Gardens, Ahsan Manzil, Pink Palace, Dharmajika Buddhist Monastery, Lalbag Fort, Shahid Minar, National Parliament House, Maynamati American Church of the Holy Resurrection, Liberation War Museum and the Hatir Jheel (Lake). It is the main city in Bangladesh, and has many 3, 4 and 5 star hotels along with numerous restaurants, hotels and guesthouses.

- **Agra**

This is most popular for its highly famous and beautiful architectural symbol of love, the Mughal mausoleum Taj Mahal. This spectacular marble structure has a lovely white dome. It is one of the Seven Wonders of the World and is a must-visit spot for anyone who visits Agra. Agra, other than the Taj Mahal, boasts of Agra Fort and Fatehpur Sikri - two other UNESCO World Heritage sites. It is undoubtedly the most visited Indian city.

- **Khumbu**

Thousands of tourists annually to trek to the Mount Everest's summit to visit Khumbu, the area of Everest that falls in north-eastern Nepal. Every year, the trip starts at the Lukla airstrip from which hikers walk to the Everest Base Camp through a two-lane, clear trail. Khumbu is mainly situated in the Sagarmatha National Park, and constitutes the Sherpa village of Namche Bazaar that serves as the stage for most expeditions to the peaks. The Tengboche Monastery, the main Buddhist centre of India, is also located here. The monastery has various comfortable accommodations, and many of these offer amazing views of Everest, the tallest mountain peak on Earth.

- **Kathmandu**

This is the cultural capital of the country, and the stage where most of the Nepal adventures start from. Kathmandu is where most overseas flights land. This is a highly populated metropolis with over 1 million residents, and has many artisan workshops, trekking agencies, religious sites, tourist shops, restaurants and hotels. The Durbar Square, a popular spot in the city, is still going through restoration after the devastating Nepal earthquakes that happened some years ago. There are plenty of other sites that should be explored as well. The age-old Buddhist complex of Swayambhunath is located on top of a forested hill and is a must-visit spot that offers magnificent sights of the Kathmandu Valley.

- **Thimphu**

Thimphu is one of the must-visit destinations in Bhutan. This charming city is the Bhutanese capital, located in the Himalayas and offering wonderful views of the Chuu River that flows through it. It is surprisingly the only city on Earth without any traffic lights. The city has preserved its old-world charm and culture. Modern construction is monitored closely, with the Government allowing construction of new buildings to a certain height and only in Bhutanese style. Travel to Bhutan for the Last Shangrila Tour and view the best Bhutanese capital landmarks. For visitors, the National Memorial

Chorten, Motithang Takin Preserve and Tashichho Dzong are the main attractions in Thimphu.

- **Maldives**

  The Maldives comprises some of the most gorgeous islands of the world. However, the sea is what makes the islands actually beautiful. The lucent aquamarine waters are crystal clear and the impressive white shores peek barely over the Indian Ocean. It includes new local guesthouses and 26 natural atolls, and the rolling waves have started changing the Maldives from a popular honeymoon hotspot to a destination for backpacking, surfing and adventure. It is now a paradise that everybody can visit. Peek under the fantastic waters to see coral reefs prosper. The reefs attract divers and snorkelers from across the globe. Many surfers flock to this place for solitary breaks.

- **Sigiriya**

  Archaeologists and tourists must place this ancient city on the list of places to visit during a Sri Lanka trip. This old city is situated over a steep slope, and topped by an around 600-feet-high plateau. Also known as Lion's Rock, the plateau oversees the jungles lying below. You can access the place through the rooms and staircases emerging from the mouth of the lion. You can also view fountains, gardens and ponds. It is the eighth wonder of the world according to the locals. The primitive rock fortress was once a monastery and is from the 3rd century BC. Recently, it has transformed into a royal residence.

- **Mirissa**

If you want to spend a wonderful vacation in a tropical paradise, Mirissa is your place. The landscape does not have any luxury resorts to spoil its beauty and travellers can spend the entire day in perfect tranquillity, enjoying magnificent views of the beach. During the night, there is more activity in the place. The biggest fishing port located on the southern coast of Sri Lanka, Mirissa is a perfect destination for tourists to go whale and dolphin watching. With swaying coconut palms, gorgeous golden sand beaches and options for spending days relaxing in a hammock, it is what every visitor dreams. The crescent-like spot, known for its amazing sunsets and sunrises in Sri Lanka, will make you agree that it is almost impossible to get better than this.

Southeast Asia

Southeast Asia consists of eleven countries that reach from eastern India to China, and is generally divided into "mainland" and "island" zones. The mainland (Myanmar, Cambodia, Laos, Thailand, and Vietnam) is actually an expansion of the Asian continent. Maritime or island Southeast Asia includes Brunei, Indonesia, Malaysia, the Philippines, Singapore, and the new nation of East Timor (formerly part of Indonesia).

Virtually all of Southeast Asia lies between the tropics, and so there are similarities in climate as well as plant and animal life throughout the region. Temperatures are generally warm, although it is cooler in highland areas. Many sea and jungle products are unique to the region, and were therefore much desired by international traders in early times.

For example, several small islands in eastern Indonesia were once the world's only source of cloves, mace, and nutmeg. The entire region is affected by the monsoon winds, which blow regularly from the northwest and then reverse to blow from the southeast. These wind systems bring fairly predictable rainy seasons, and before steamships were invented, these wind systems also enabled traders from outside of the region to arrive and leave at regular intervals. Because of this reliable wind pattern, Southeast Asia became a meeting place for trade involving China and India, the two great markets of early Asia.

Southeast Asia Travel

For a long time Southeast Asia has been a most wanted corner of the world for backpackers, known for its perfect beaches, low prices, tasty cuisine, and good air connections.

The countries of Southeast Asia represent a totally different culture for Western travellers. Instead of cathedrals, they normally find temples. Instead of cold temperatures and snow in the winter, for the most part they would be bathed in tropical weather. They may find simple accommodations in remote fishing villages but also luxurious five-star hotels in the bigger cities and on the more popular islands.

Southeast Asia will appeal to active, exciting travellers, who want to trek through steamy jungles, dive in some of the world's best coral reefs, camp or go white-water rafting on new rivers. But the region also offers the less active travellers something, who, after a day of visiting temples and other cultural sites, just want to relax in the comfort in a luxury hotel.

Flying Low Cost in Southeast Asia

Southeast Asia's population as well as tourists are making low-cost airlines in the continent become more predominant, due to the necessity of travelling fast without spending too much money. Budget airlines are successfully expanding all over the world, and have been growing heavily in Southeast Asia as well as changing the way that people perceive air travel. As the air travel industry has developed, travellers' opinions have also changed.

Population are travelling much more, spending less money and exploring new locations. Travelling across Southeast Asia can be pleasantly economical, especially if tickets are bought early. Here is a list of trendy low-cost airlines operating in Southeast Asia and their websites to access in order to find the cheapest fares.

A popular budget airline in Southeast Asia, AirAsia (www.airasia.com) offers users the option to explore the best destination in the continent using the AirAsia Asean Pass, a travel pass that permits travellers to discover the splendour of the region using fixed credits. AirAsia is the largest low-cost airline in Asia and flies to a large number of destinations, connecting almost every corner in the continent.

Low Cost Airlines in Southeast Asia

Indonesia

Citilink: www.citilink.co.id

Lion Air: lionair.co.id

Indonesia AirAsia: www.airasia.com

Batik Air: www.batikair.com

Singapore

Scoot: http: www.flyscoot.com

Philippines

Cebgo and Cebu Pacific: www.cebupacificair.com

PAL Express: www.philippineairlines.com/en

Philippines AirAsia: www.airasia.com/ot/en

Malaysia

AirAsia and AirAsia X: www.airasia.com

Malindo Air: www.malindoair.com

Travel By Bus in Southeast Asia

There are two popular companies providing hop-on hop-off bus services in Southeast Asia. Travellers desiring to discover new places, travel around, as well as meet other backpackers and have an amazing time doing it must consider these bus services available in Southeast Asia. The two main companies providing hop-on hop-off bus travel around Cambodia, Laos, Myanmar, Thailand and Vietnam are Stray (www.straytravel.asia) and Bamba Experience (www.bambaexperience.com).

There are also local bus companies operating in each country in Southeast Asia:

- **Myanmar**

  Travelling by bus is the easiest way to get around Myanmar when travelling on a budget and it is the only way to get to certain areas. Bus routes are run by a range of different private companies, serving nearly all parts of the county. Almost continuously cheaper and faster than trains, Myanmar buses range from less luxurious but nice buses (without air-con), local buses to mini 32-seaters, and luxury air-conditioned express buses. Two good websites to check prices and schedules are

myanmarbusticket.com   and
www.starticket.com.mm.

- **Cambodia**

  The range of road transport is extensive in
  Cambodia. On sealed roads, the large air-
  conditioned buses and speedy express minivans are
  the most popular choices. Elsewhere in the country,
  a shared taxi, local minibus or pickup truck is the
  way to go. All major cities are now well-linked by
  bus to Phnom Penh along sealed roads, but if you're
  travelling from one end of the country to the other
  you may have to change buses in Phnom Penh or
  another hub. Two excellent bus-ticket booking
  websites   in   Cambodia,   Bookmebus
  (www.bookmebus.com)   and   Cambo   Ticket
  (www.camboticket.com)   are   popular   among
  travellers in the region.

- **Laos**

  Land transport is the easiest way to discover Laos. It
  has beautiful nature, colourful villages inhabited
  with dozens of different ethnicities with their own
  language, tradition, social structure and way of life.
  Laos has no train system, apart from the cross-

border train from Nong Khai, Thailand to Tha Naleng station in Vientiane, so buses are the main form of public transportation and tickets can be purchased in local bus stations.

- **Thailand**

Buses are a practical mode of transportation to travel around Thailand. The fares are affordable and buses run more frequently than trains. Ordinary and many air-con buses are run by Baw Khaw Saw (BKS), the government controlled transport company, despite the fact that privately owned, licensed air-con buses, some of which operate from Baw Khaw Saw terminals, also supply the most popular long-distance routes. There are various websites allowing travellers to book tickets and check schedules online; www.thaibusbooking.com and www.thaiticketmajor.com are very popular among travellers.

- **Vietnam**

Bus travelling is the cheapest and most convenient method of transportation for foreign travellers In Vietnam, given that the bus system has been well-developed and covers almost every part of the country. Contemporary air-conditioned buses operate between the main cities. Deluxe class services are available and travellers have allocated seat and enough space. Some offer relaxing reclining seats, others have padded flat beds for really long trips. These sleeper buses can be a good alternative to trains, and costs are similar, tickets and schedules are available at Mai Linh Express (www.mailinhexpress.vn) and The Sinh Tourist (www.thesinhtourist.vn).

- **Indonesia**

Buses are economical, simple to book, and leave generally on time in Indonesia. The average long-distance bus has padded seats but little leg room or headroom; it is thus worth choosing a luxury bus if offered, which costs twice as much but would offer reclining seats. In popular destinations such as Bali, a more enjoyable option is tourist shuttle buses despite the fact that is far more expensive than local services; these will take travellers between places as quickly as possible. The traditional company operating on Bali and Lombok is Perama (www.peramatour.com).

- **Malaysia**

  Malaysia's national bus network is comprehensive and easy to use, with regular express coaches between all major cities and town. Most intercity buses are comfy, with air conditioning and curtains to screen out the blazing tropical sun, though seats can be tightly packed together. A handful of well-established bus companies give reliable service in Peninsular Malaysia. The largest is Transnasional (transnasional.com.my), whose services have the entire Peninsula pretty well covered. Alternatives include Konsortium Bas Ekspres (www.kbes.com.my) and Plusliner (plusliner.com.my).

- **Philippines**

  Bus transport Philippines is centred in the capital, Manila. No matter where you want to go or how you want to get there, you need to start in Manila. All transportation, be it planes, buses or ferries, start here.

  There is a bus service that will take you from Manila to just about anywhere in the Philippine Islands. Some will even transport you on ferries where required. A good website to book bus tickets and check schedules is PH BUS (www.phbus.com).

- **Singapore**

   Singapore's bus system has an extensive network of routes covering most places in Singapore and is the most economical way to get around, as well as being one of the most scenic. There are also many express bus services from Singapore to Kuala Lumpur. Among them, few of the famous and popular express bus operators like Aeroline (www.aeroline.com.sg), Grassland (www.grasslandsg.com), along with First Coach (www.firstcoach.com.my) offer almost hourly trips between Singapore and Kuala Lumpur.

Travel by Train in Southeast Asia

- **Myanmar**

   Travelling by train can be one of the most interesting ways to explore Myanmar, as railway journeys often afford picturesque views and chances to mix with locals that are often not possible otherwise. In overnight sleeper carriages and upper class, a more comfortable journey is possible than on buses sometimes, even though with a notably bouncier ride than you will be used to on trains in a different place. Further information about train travel in Myanmar is available at www.go-myanmar.com.

- **Cambodia**

  Even though plans are in the works for a nationwide network, the train service is currently limited to four destinations, running from Phnom Penh through Takeo and Kampot, finishing at Sihanoukville.

  Two trains alternate on the tracks, the Blue Train and the Yellow Train. The seating arrangement is slightly different with sideways or front-facing seat, but both trains are air-conditioned and tickets are the same price. Given that the trains are restored from the 1960s, the experience is more modern than you might expect. The Government of Cambodia's Royal Railway website (www.royal-railway.com) provides train schedules and online booking options.

- **Laos**

  At the present time Laos has merely 3km of railway line linking Nong Khai to Vientiane Prefecture via the Friendship Bridge. Plans are underway to extend this line to central Vientiane, and eventually connect with a Chinese-funded railway line from Kunming to Vientiane via Luang Prabang, which is currently under construction. State Railways of Thailand (www.railway.co.th) runs trains across the Friendship Bridge to Thanaleng in Laos, near Vientiane.

- **Thailand**

Thailand has one of the greatest metre-gauge rail systems in the world and train travel is easily the best way to get around and see the country. It is comfortable, cheap, safe, and environmentally friendly. Unlike flying, it's a genuine Thai experience, which makes the journey as much a part of your trip as the destination. The SRT (State Railways of Thailand) operates passenger trains in three classes – 1st, 2nd and 3rd – but each class varies considerably depending on whether you're on an ordinary, rapid or express train. In 2016, SRT announced the purchase of 115 modern train carriages with seat-mounted TV screens and more comfortable bathrooms that will be used on the northern train route. Train is the best way to travel between Chiang Mai and Bangkok and a train+bus or train+ferry combo is the best way from Bangkok to Krabi or Phuket or Bangkok to Ko Samui. State Railways of Thailand (www.railway.co.th) runs trains from corner to corner around the country.

- **Philippines**

The Philippine National Railways resumed daily long-distance passenger trains between Manila and Naga City in 2011, in the past discontinued for years due to typhoon damage. The Bicol Express train is a comfortable and safe way to travel between Manila and Naga, overnight with comfortable air-conditioned sleepers bought second-hand from Japanese Railways. However, train services are 'temporarily' suspended after hurricane damage; these trains were suspended in late 2012 and are still suspended in 2017. It is not clear when or if train services will be reinstated. Please check the Philippine National Railways (www.pnr.gov.ph) to find out the latest information.

- **Vietnam**

Operated by Vietnam Railways (www.vr.com.vn), the national carrier railway system is an ageing but pretty reliable service, and offers a relaxing way to get around the nation. Travelling in an air-con sleeping berth provides tourists with some spectacular scenery to enjoy along the journey. The train journeys are a true Vietnamese experience, an important ingredient of a holiday around Vietnam. Travel by train possibly will even enable travellers to meet some Vietnamese people, and understand a bit more about their culture. It is possible to book tickets online using the travel agency Bao Lau (www.baolau.vn), which has an efficient website, details seat and sleeper-berth availability, and accepts international cards. E-tickets are emailed to buyers and there is a commission charged per ticket.

- **Indonesia**

Train travel in Indonesia is limited to Java and Sumatra. In Java, trains are one of the most comfortable, fastest and easiest ways to travel. In the east, the railway service links up with the ferry to Bali, and in the west with the ferry to Sumatra. The easiest way to check times and fares on Java is at the agency site www.tiket.com, which has an English version. The official Indonesian Railways site is www.kereta-api.co.id, but this is currently only in Indonesian, nevertheless travellers can click

"Reservasi" and use the journey planner to check train times and fares, with little or no knowledge of Indonesian necessary. Google's Chrome browser would be an excellent tool to translate anything if necessary. Booking opens 90 days ahead and tickets can be bought online until 2 days before the date of travel. Passport numbers and contact numbers for each passenger are necessary to book tickets online.

- **Malaysia**

  Malaysia has national railway companies that run a modern, comfortable and economical railway service, although there are basically only two lines and for the most part services are slow. One of the main lines runs up the west coast from Singapore, through Kuala Lumpur, Butterworth and on into Thailand. There are two main types of rail services in Malaysia: Express and local trains. Express trains are air-conditioned and have 1st class (premier), 2nd class (superior) and occasionally 3rd class (economy) seats and, depending on the service there are also sleeping cabins. Local trains are usually economy class only, but some have superior seats.

  Express trains stop only at main stations, while local services, which operate mostly on the east-coast line, stop everywhere, including the middle of the jungle, to let passengers and their goods on and off. As a result, local services take more than twice as long as the express trains and run to unpredictable schedules, but if travellers have time availability, local trains provide a vibrant experience and are good for short journeys. Train schedules are reviewed a few times a year, so check the Keretapi Tanah Melayu website www.ktmb.com.my, where you can buy tickets.

- **Singapore**

Rail transport in Singapore mainly consists of a passenger urban rail transit system spanning the entire city-state: a rapid transit system collectively known as the Mass Rapid Transit (MRT) system operated by the two biggest public transport operators SMRT Trains and SBS Transit, as well as several Light Rail Transit lines also operated by both companies. The Land Transport Authority of Singapore (www.lta.gov.sg) can be accessed for further information. One of the easiest, cheapest, most comfortable way to get from Singapore to Kuala Lumpur is by train. The trip last about 6 to 7 hours, and is cheaper than a 4-to-5-hour bus ride which costs about $25 USD and is definitely cheaper than the cheapest air ticket available. In addition, train travel usually comes with wonderful scenery of the countryside, eating train station food, or perhaps a pleasant, effective, and economical sleep with an overnight train. The best way to buy the ticket is to just book from www.ktmb.com.my, on which you can pay by credit card and print out tickets online.

Driving around Southeast Asia

Self-drive holidays are ideal for those looking for more independence and autonomy, but many travellers would avoid it in South East Asia. Is self-driving in this region really safe? Yes, if travellers use common-sense and follow each country rules respecting local lows.

In the countries where an International Driver's Permit is accepted, it allows travellers to drive or ride the same class of vehicle covered by their home country license. If travellers are qualified simply to drive a car at home, they are not allowed to ride a scooter or motorcycle just because of an international permit. Similarly, if the motorcycle license restricts travellers to a particular engine size, drivers cannot jump on a pimped-up scooter with a throbbing engine. It is up to the travellers to make sure they are licensed for the type of motorbike or scooter they hire.

In South East Asia, the main vehicle hire options are either a motorcycle or a car. Since the majority of locals use motorcycles to get around, they make a great option for tourists and offer more freedom when driving off the beaten track. However, if travellers prefer to feel really safe, hiring a car is the best option. Just bear in mind that car journeys can be a little slower due to traffic congestion. Another important fact is that tourists should be aware of scams when renting vehicles and never leave passports as a deposit for the vehicle hired, or they may not get their passport back. Before setting off from the hire place, it is recommended to ensure the vehicle runs properly and give it a thorough check for scratches, nicks, and dents. It is also recommended to take pictures of any imperfections, as this will improve your chances of getting your deposit back when the vehicle is returned.

While planning a self-drive holiday anywhere in Southeast Asia or anywhere in the world, is very important to have insurance. Before leaving home, is essential to talk to the insurance provider to ensure coverage for any type of accident whilst driving. Drivers may also need to upgrade their policy to include third-party damage and vehicle breakdown coverage as well. Reputable car rental agencies should also offer additional insurance when hiring a vehicle; please remember to read the small print.

Hitchhiking in Southeast Asia

Hitchhiking in South East Asia is usually extremely easy, particularly when compared with Western Europe, and for the most part very safe. There are however a few factors to consider that can make life on the road a lot easier; certain elements are similar to hitchhiking in Europe, but also there are quite a few differentiation when hitchhiking in South East Asia.

Southeast Asia is a very tropic region where temperatures can easily surpass 35 Celsius during the day. Also, there are monsoon seasons that can affect travellers' hitchhiking plans. It is necessary to take enough water and food along and a hat or rain cover in case of getting up on the back of a truck in the outside. Wear proper shoes and ensure bags are packed tight, always carrying valuables on the body within internal pockets or using a small bag.

It is necessary to be patient. There are times where travellers might wait for hours to get a ride depending on their spot. Rides might also take forever as the drivers do not care about getting to a place as fast as possible. Anyhow, just know that journeys might take a bit longer than expected. On average, though, hitchhiking rides can be even faster at times than taking buses or trains.

It is essential to find the right spot. A day before leaving a place, travellers must have already looked for the best spots to take a hitch in order to avoid long waiting time. In general, when located in a city, travellers have to get out of it and position themselves along the main road leading to their destination. Never take a hitch within the city; it is tiring and annoying and it will never lead to a good ride. Make sure to get out of town and stand along a street so that there is no option but to go straight ahead.

Top Destinations to Visit in Southeast Asia

- **Yangon**

  A big but yet not modernized city, Yangon, with Victorian buildings, tree-lined avenues, lakes and parks and a bustling city centre of friendly vendors, colourful stalls and people going about in their daily chores dressed traditionally in their Longyi and flip-flap sandals. The Bogyoke Aung San market (also known as Scott's Market) is a must for every visitor and so is the magnificent Shwedagon Pagoda, the well-known landmark of Myanmar. The first fundament of the Shwedagon is believed to have been built more than 2000 years ago, and the pagoda is revered by Buddhist and non-Buddhists alike.

- **Phnom Penh**

Cambodia's capital is the frenetic heartbeat of the nation. Phnom Penh is a city of confused streets with motorbikes and car horns that can frazzle at first glance. Deserted completely during the Khmer Rouge madness and left to wither and decay, Phnom Penh has bounced back to become one of Southeast Asia's most lively cities. For visitors, this is Cambodia's most cosmopolitan destination, with a café and restaurant scene unequalled in the rest of the country. It's also home to a scattering of important historic sites that help find an answer for both Cambodia's ancient and modern history. The National Museum is home to swag of Khmer sculpture that traces the nation's history from the pre-Angkorian age right through to the phenomenal majesty of the god-Kings of Angkor. The Royal Palace provides gorgeous examples of traditional artistry, while Tuol Sleng Museum and the killing fields of Choeung Ek speak of the horror and brutality the people of this country suffered under Khmer Rouge rule.

- **Sihanoukville Beaches**

  Located in Kompong Som Province, Sihanoukville is a tale of two halves, with a bustling but drab central district and its shoreline area home to a vibrant beach resort. The beaches here are Cambodia's top destination for sand and sun holidays and are popular with both foreign and local tourists. There's something for every kind of beach-goer there. Independence Beach and Sokha Beach boast luxury hotels. Serendipity Beach and the Brash Ochheuteal Beach area are the most popular sandy strips and in recent years have emerged as one of Southeast Asia's backpacker party areas. For a much quieter scene, just to the south is Otres Beach with beach huts huddled directly on the sand, a sprinkling of classy boutique hotels, and a number of up-and-coming restaurants.

- **Luang Prabang**

  The most popular place to visit in Laos, Luang Prabang is an historic city that once served as the capital of the Kingdom of Laos. Located at the convergence of the Mekong and Nam Khan rivers, the city has numerous monasteries and Buddhist temples, with monks walking through the city collecting alms in the morning. There are several waterfalls nearby, some of which offer elephant rides to visitors. A night market at the end of the town's main street is a good place to buy souvenirs. Venturesome eaters might want to try fried Mekong River moss, which is a local delicacy.

- **Bangkok**

This city is everything travellers would expect from the capital of Thailand: it is noisy, crowded, colourful, exciting, infuriating, and smile inducing. There are ancient sites to be visited and modern shopping malls that have a kitschy yet high-end ambience. Bangkok can be overwhelming as its life-force smacks visitors in their face, but it is an interesting city that represents Southeast Asia's tension between the developed and developing worlds. Bangkok also serves as a gateway to many other parts of Thailand. From here, travellers are able to hop on a short flight to Koh Samui, Phuket, Chiang Mai, and other popular places. It is also possible to board a train or hop on a bus for little money, and visit national treasures such as Lopburi, Ayutthaya, and many other gems of the country.

- **Singapore**

This is a city-state, formerly a British colony. It is one of the most prosperous cities in the world and has the world's busiest sea port. The downtown area is ultra-modern, boasting some of the greatest building achievements on the planet, including the wonderful triple towers of the Marina Bay. The old parts of the city show a Malay, Chinese and India influence that presents a delightful mix of styles, all working in perfect harmony. Sitting on an island as it does has given it a feel all of its own. It is the second most densely populated city on earth, after Monaco, yet has more than 50% of its area covered by greenery, fifty major parks and four nature reserves.

- **Phuket**

From elephant trekking through the incredible rainforest to exploring sea caves to bungee jumping and zip-lining over a lake, there is so much to explore and experience in Phuket. It is the largest island in Thailand, and is a beautiful tourist destination that offers plenty of interesting things to see and do.

With stunning beaches laden with white sand, lush green tropical forests, the nightlife at Patong and exciting boat tours, Phuket is truly an irresistible spot for those who love nature. While some the attractions in the island are not worth your time, there are certain places that you must definitely visit, if you are planning a trip to this beautiful island. Phang Nga Bay, Karon View Point, the Big Buddha, and Wat Chalong temple are among the must-visit places in Phuket.

- **Lombok**

In spite of the fact that Lombok is situated close to the stunning island of Bali, it hasn't gained as much popularity as its neighbour. Even though Bali attracts millions of tourists every year, many places on Lombok remain still untouched, due to which mass tourism is yet to be popular in this island.

Although Lombok has the reputation of being a rather difficult place to explore in Indonesia, you will be sure to see and experience some amazing things while you are there. Other than its eye-catching beauty, Lombok holds plenty of other attractions including superb beaches, lush forests, impressive hiking trails and Indonesia's second largest volcano.

- **Bali**

  The profoundly religious and unequalled culture of Bali, the famous island in Indonesia with a picturesque backdrop of sandy beaches, rugged coastlines, desolate volcanic hillsides, abundant rice terraces, valleys, lakes and stunning hills and mountains have earned it the name "The Island of the Gods". Bali offers something for everyone - from lazing away on the beach to top-quality surfing to exploring the historical, cultural and archaeological attractions, visitors can have a great time in Bali. Surrounded with stunning natural beauty, Bali is indeed a special place to visit. To soak in all the things Bali has to offer, travellers would need to be on an endless vacation.

- **Ha Long Bay**

  With over 2000 islands, aqua-green water and a cluster of lush limestone karsts, Ha Long evokes a fantasy look and feeling. This magnificent bay is often in the list of top 5 best destinations in Vietnam.

Be ready to get on a junk boat and sail to the sea for a most breath-taking trip. Spending overnight on the ocean, feeling the tranquil beauty of the sea at night and enjoying a sunset on the bay are some of the extraordinary experiences that on-land tours just cannot offer. Do not hesitate to be a bit adventurous and take a kayak among the hundreds of karst outcrops or cruise around the jungle-covered islands. Travellers can explore lakes, caves, and grottoes in this glorious area and visitors might find their own little gem there.

- **Ho Chi Minh City**

What makes Saigon so irresistible is its essential vitality. As the biggest commercial hub of Vietnam, Ho Chi Minh City has a special vibe that pulsates and refuses to rest. Thanks to its complex blend of different cultures, historical traits and Western influences, the city offers a mix of culture, architecture, and street life that will at times fascinate and at other times thrill. While in Saigon, make sure you explore the Vietnamese coffee culture and experience the exciting nightlife, with plenty of street restaurants where you can have barbeque, ice-cream, fruit and hotpot, all late at night when the local Vietnamese finish their work and populate the lively streets.

- **Hoi-An**

Gorgeous Hoi An is the most atmospheric city in Vietnam, with bags of surviving historic architecture. The old town quarter is a joy to explore, packed to the brim with well-preserved merchant houses that hark back to Hoi An's trading centre heyday of the 15th century, when the town was a major meeting point for Chinese and Japanese merchants who flocked the city for the local silks. Plenty of the old merchant houses have been opened to the public, tourists can easily get a taste of these times. The best is the 17th-century Tan Ky House, with fascinating architectural and decorative elements.

- **Krabi**

A beach town on the southwest coast of Thailand, Krabi is a beautiful city that tourists love visiting. Crystal-clear waters, pristine beaches, and impressive seaside cliffs attract kayakers, rock climbers, snorkelers, scuba divers, and boaters alike. Nearby temples and waterfalls make for a one-of-a-kind place; and visitors absolutely must head to nearby Railay Beach that is only accessible by boat for what is undeniably the best sunset in the country.

- **Langkawi**

  Located off Malaysia's north-western coast in the Andaman Sea, Langkawi is an archipelago of 99 islands boasting charming rainforest, beaches, forest-clad mountains and mangroves. In recent years, resorts, hotels, restaurants and other tourist facilities have developed in Langkawi, offering visitors the opportunity to experience the archipelago's extraordinary natural beauty.

- **Perhentian Islands**

  Located off the coast of north-eastern Malaysia not far from the Thai border. The Perhentian Islands are the must-go place in Malaysia for budget travellers. The two main islands are Perhentian Kecil and Perhentian Besar. They have some of Malaysia's most beautiful beaches and great diving with plenty of cheap accommodation. Visitors can also explore the tropical jungle that covers much of the islands' terrain.

- **Kuala Lumpur**

  Located in West Malaysia Kuala Lumpur is the country's federal capital and largest metropolis. Commonly called KL by locals, this energetic city is a cultural melting pot, noted for its impressive skyscrapers and lively scenes of shopping and dining. KL doesn't really have a city centre but rather several hubs of activity. The former colonial district features distinctive architecture and the pleasant Merdeka Square. Chinatown is a busy tourist hub while the Golden Triangle presents the city's modern face, with the famous Petronas Towers as its most striking building.

- **Boracay**

  Boracay may be a small island, but it packs great features such as award-winning beaches, fine-looking resorts and great adventures like cliff diving, motorbiking, parasailing, snorkelling, horse riding, scuba diving and kite surfing. If that is not enough, boat tours allow visitors to watch stunning sunsets, explore volcanic caves and remote coves of turquoise lagoons. When the sun sets, Boracay night-life pulsates with many bars and restaurants serving food, drinks and fun until dawn.

- **Palawan**

  Considered the Philippine's answer to paradise Palawan is one of the top islands in the world. This island province stretches southwest to Borneo with lush limestone peaks rising from a jewel-like sea so clear, that you can almost see the expressions of the fish from above the surface. Slivers of gleaming white sand fringed with rustling palms rim many of these jungle-clad islands, whilst under the water, coral reefs put on a show with an inspiring diversity of tropical fish, offering some of the best diving in the world. Other attractions include the islands' unique emerald lakes, wildlife, and quaint fishing villages. Coron is home to plush resorts, and El Nido drips with natural beauty and is one of the most alluring islands in the chain. From there, is possible to do an island hop around the spectacular Bacuit archipelago.

- **Bohol**

  The Chocolate Hills, one of the most iconic sights in the country, is a series of hills that spread beautifully over the municipalities of Batuan, Sagbayan and Carmen in Bohol. These natural wonders are called "Chocolate Hills" because their layers of green grass turn super brown during the country's dry season, making these hills look like your favourite confections. Bohol, besides these otherworldly hills, is also well-known for its peculiar wildlife, like the Philippine tarsiers, centuries-old churches, world-class white-sand beaches and rivers.

Australia and New Zealand

The term 'Australia' is derived from Terra Australis, the name given to a southern landmass whose existence geographers deduced before it was discovered, the country has a population of circa 24 million residents and gained its independence in 1901. New Zealand (to the east) and Papua New Guinea (to the north) are Australia's closest neighbours. To the south lie the Southern Ocean and Antarctica.

The Commonwealth of Australia is a Federation with six states – Northern Territory (capital Darwin), New South Wales (state capital Sydney), South Australia (Adelaide), Western Australia (Perth), Queensland (Brisbane), Victoria (Melbourne), and Tasmania (Hobart) – and two territories, and the Australian Capital Territory, where the federal capital, Canberra, is situated.

On the other hand, New Zealand is truly one of the most picturesque and photogenic places on earth. A small island nation of just over 4.5 million people, New Zealand is made up of two main land masses (North Island and South Island) and a number of smaller islands including Stewart Island located in the southwestern Pacific Ocean. The two main islands are divided by a 22km stretch of water called the Cook Strait.

New Zealand is located approximately 1,500 km east of Australia and about 1,000 km from the Pacific Islands. Due to its relative remoteness and being water locked, New Zealand was one of the last countries to be found and settled in. The country is made up of some of the world's most spectacular landscapes, from vast mountain ranges, steaming volcanoes to sweeping coastlines. It is a natural playground for thrill seekers and adventurers and those who simply want to visit for the culture and landscapes. New Zealander's are kindly known as "Kiwis". The name derives from the kiwi, a flightless bird local to New Zealand. It is also the national symbol.

Travel in Australia and New Zealand

Australia is a unique country and an amazing country to travel around, a true land of Oz as it is called. An island continent, bathed by several seas, with a unique fauna and flora and almost 75% of its territory formed by desert. It is an Orient that looks like the West, but the same time is so unusual. Even the language of the country, which is English, is spoken in a totally peculiar way, full of slang with a well-marked accent, and is said to be one of the most difficult to understand. For all this, travelling through Australia is experiencing practices that would never be possible in any other country.

In New Zealand travelling around the country is a unique experience or a dream for the travel community worldwide. New Zealand is a remote and geologically dynamic country bestowed with diverse, often unique landscapes and wildlife. It offers outdoor adventure in great quantities, united with vibrant culinary experiences and cultural wealth, enhanced by a welcoming approach to visitors. This small country definitely deserves its reputation as one of the world's most rewarding travel destinations.

Flying Around Australia and New Zealand

Flying is considered the best way to cover Australia's large distances in a short time. Domestic airlines in Australia including Qantas (www.qantas.com) and its budget carrier Jetstar (www.jetstar.com/au), Virgin Australia (virginaustralia.com) and its budget carrier Tiger Airways (www.tigerair.com.au) as well as Regional Express (www.rex.com.au) serve all state capital cities and many regional cities. Competition between domestic airlines means that some big value fares are available, especially if booked in advance.

In New Zealand the main flag carrier is Air New Zealand (www.airnewzealand.com), based in Auckland. The airline has carried out scheduled passenger flights since 1965. There is also Air New Zealand Link, a brand name under which two regional airlines operate feeder flights for Air New Zealand, Air Nelson (www.airnelson.co.nz) and Mount Cook Airline. Air New Zealand Link mainly connects regional centres with New Zealand's three main international airports, Auckland International Airport (AKL), Christchurch International Airport (CHC), and Wellington International Airport (WLG).

There is also Barrier Air (www.barrierair.kiwi), a 100% New Zealand owned and operated airline operating scheduled passenger and freight services from Auckland, North Shore and Great Barrier Island. Additionally, Barrier Air is the only airline offering scheduled flight services between Auckland and Kaitaia. The airline offers flights to other seasonal destinations such as Tauranga and Whitianga too, along with competitive charter services throughout New Zealand.

Travel By Bus around Australia

Bus travel in Australia is comfortable, effective and reasonably expensive. Long-distance coaches on average have adjustable seats, reading lights, air conditioning, and free Wi-Fi. Nevertheless, bus travel is distinctive than in other parts of the world. While metropolitan areas are well serviced on daily basis, long-distance trains and buses to remote regions are available only a few times a week, when not once a week. It is also possible to happen cancellations or changes to bus schedules and routes in Australia may occur without notice. So, it may take time to find the right source of information and know how and when you can travel.

Australia's national coach operator, Greyhound (www.greyhound.com.au), provides hop on hop off passes for popular routes, short trip passes and flexible passes based on the amount of miles visitors wish to travel. For travellers planning on doing a lot of travel in Australia, a Greyhound Australia bus pass will reduce costs. Bus-pass discounts of 10% apply to children under 14 and Student-card holders.

Some other bus companies to consider when exploring Australia are:

- **Firefly Express (www.fireflyexpress.com.au):** Runs between Adelaide, Canberra, Melbourne and Sydney.

- **Integrity Coach Lines (www.integritycoachlines.com.au):** Main operator between Broome and Perth in West Australia.

- **Premier Transport Group (www.premierms.com.au):** Greyhound's main rival along the East Coast.

Backpacker Buses:

Backpacker-style and more formal bus tours offer a convenient way to get from A to B and see the sights on the way. Some multistate operators are:

- **AAT Kings (www.aatkings.com):** Big coach company provides numerous tours all around Australia.

- **Adventure Tours Australia (www.adventuretours.com.au):** Affordable, young-at-heart tours in all states.

- **Autopia Tours (autopiatours.com.au):** One- to three-day trips from Adelaide, Melbourne, and Sydney.

New Zealand Bus Travel

Bus travel is ideal for travellers preferring to make their way around New Zealand without the hassle of self-driving. Tourists can just sit back, relax and enjoy the vast gorgeousness that each ride offers in New Zealand. Coach bus travel is easy, flexible and considered a cheap alternative to air travel with daily scheduled passenger services available all over the country.

There is also a large amount of coach companies serving the main tourist routes. Hop-on, hop-off traveller's networks, where is possible to buy a pass for unlimited travel, offer tourists the opportunity to travel around New Zealand's major destinations very effectively.

New Zealand's most important bus company is InterCity (www.intercity.co.nz), which can take tourists to just about everywhere on the North and South Islands. Naked Bus (nakedbus.com) has almost the same routes and is considered the main competitor. Both bus lines have promotions offering fares as low as $1 NZD.

Nationwide Bus Passes in New Zealand: Flexipass is a hop-on/hop-off InterCity pass, making travel possible to practically anywhere in New Zealand, in any direction, including the Interislander ferry across Cook Strait. The pass is purchased in blocks of travel time: minimum 15 hours ($125 NZD), maximum 60 hours ($459 NZD). The average cost of each block becomes cheaper the more hours you buy. It is possible to top up the pass if necessary more time. The Aotearoa Explorer, Island Loop and Tiki Tour Hop-on/hop-off, fixed-itinerary nationwide passes offered by InterCity. These passes link up tourist hot-spots and range in price from $775 NZD to $1045 NZD.

The Naked Passport (www.nakedpassport.com) a Naked Bus pass that allows travellers to buy trips in blocks of five, which can be added to any time, and book each trip as needed. The highlights with the 5 Trip Passport starts at $159 NZD and $439 NZD the ultimate bus pass offering 20 Trip for the ultimate Kiwi experience.

For travellers feeling like clocking up some kilometres with like-minded fellow travellers, the following operators run fixed-itinerary bus tours, nationwide or on the North or South Islands. Meals and hop-on/hop-off flexibility and accommodation are frequently included.

- **Haka Tours (www.hakatours.com):** Providing 3-to-16-day tours with adventure, mountain biking or snow themes.

- **Kiwi Experience (www.kiwiexperience.com):** The main hop-on/hop-off company, with many tours offered.

- **Stray Travel (www.straytravel.com):** An extensive variety of flexible hop-on/hop-off passes and tours.

Travel by Train in Australia

Travelling by train throughout Australia is a memorable and enjoyable experience. Australia is a vast country, where distances between capital cities are lengthy, and what better way to see the Australian countryside than by train? Train travel is an affordable, convenient, and pleasant method to explore Australia.

Some of the main rail companies and services are:

- **Great Southern Rail (www.greatsouthernrail.com.au):** Operates the Indian Pacific between Sydney and Perth, the Overland between Adelaide and Melbourne, and the Ghan between Darwin and Adelaide through Alice Springs.

- **Queensland Rail (www.queenslandrailtravel.com.au):** Runs the high-speed Spirit of Queensland service between Cairns and Brisbane.

- **NSW TrainLink (www.nswtrainlink.info):** Trains from Brisbane to Sydney, Canberra and Melbourne on the modern rail and coach network right through New South Wales.

- **V/Line (www.vline.com.au):** Trains within Victoria, linking up with bus and train services around Victoria. Trains going to Albury, Ballarat, Bendigo, Geelong, and Warrnambool.

New Zealand Train Travel

Train services in New Zealand works all through the country and take travellers through some of the most spectacular scenery. Trains in New Zealand can be affordable and opportune, allowing tourists to travel almost all over the place. Railways are situated through the heart of New Zealand, providing views not seen from the road. New

Zealand trains are also available in some cities and suburbs for daily commuting.

Train travel in New Zealand is all about the trip, not about getting anywhere in a hurry. KiwiRail Scenic Journeys (www.kiwirail.co.nz) operates four main routes, and reservations can be made through The Great Journeys of New Zealand Website (www.greatjourneysofnz.co.nz) directly, or at most train stations and all services are for day travel.

- **Capital Connection:** Weekday commuter service between Wellington and Palmerston North.

- **Coastal Pacific:** Connecting Picton and Christchurch along the South Island's east coast.

- **Northern Explorer:** Linking Auckland and Wellington: Providing northbound on Tuesdays, Fridays and Sundays, as well as southbound on Mondays, Thursdays and Saturdays.

- **TranzAlpine:** Over the Southern Alps Connecting Greymouth and Christchurch considered one of the world's most famous train rides.

Driving around Australia

International travellers are allowed to drive in Australia with a foreign driver's licence for up to three months, provided that the licence is in English. If a driver's licence does not have a photo, drivers are required to carry another form of formal photo identification with them. If a licence is in a foreign language, drivers are required to obtain an International Driver's Permit.

Driving around Australia seems like such as simple undertaking, but like many things down under, it is not without major risk and should not be attempted without a great deal of preparation. Considered to be one of the best ways to see Australia, from short trips to epic self-drive holidays and 4x4 adventures, driving on Australian roads is an amazing way to see every length and landscape in the country.

Driving in Australia can be easy on most routes but tourists need to be prepared for the road rules, distances, 4WD tracks and outback roads they might travel. They must make sure they are well prepared for their road trip in Australia with all the necessary information needed. If you are thinking of driving in the Outback or remote areas, be ready for anything. The Outback is filled with lots of space but a small number of services and people, so there may be a substantial amount of time before anyone will pass you should you break down. It is a desert out there and during summer months high temperatures can reach 44°C (110°F) to over 50°C (122°F), which are indeed not circumstances you want to endure without air conditioning.

Some important tips to consider before you start driving long distances in Australia are:

- Always carry additional food for three days and at least 10 litres of drinking water.

- Carry a 20-litre jerry can of additional fuel. Do not presume fuel will be easily reached late at night, in the early morning, or in some cases even on a Sunday. Even on some major regional roads, roadhouses may be closed late at night. It is always a good idea to fill up at every roadhouse even when driving on half a tank.

- Do not expect your mobile phone to work in remote areas. Telstra is Australia's leading provider of mobile phones and the best service for travellers on the road.

Take advantage of truck stops and roadhouses for an overnight stay; at least grab a coffee, or simply pull over to take a nap if you feel drowsy.

Driving in New Zealand

Exploring New Zealand's picturesque landscapes by car, campervan or motorhome is a common way to get around the country. With a population of circa 4.5 million people, it is comprehensible that New Zealand does not have a mass easy public transport system like you can find around more urban destinations. It is ok, we don't want that anyways. Besides, let's not mix words here; the majority of tourists going to New Zealand are visiting the country for the epic landscapes and wild views.

Although travellers can get to famous spots on day trips, the best way to get around is driving when possible. Some of the much-loved surprises in New Zealand occur spontaneously on the road, pulling down at any street that allows travellers to have a picnic, located in the middle of nowhere and enjoying amazing views.

Even experienced travellers used to driving in other places, is necessary to be well aware of things like narrow, windy roads, weather extremes, and different road rules before starting their journey in New Zealand.

There are many ways to experience the extraordinary, mind-blowing splendour of New Zealand, but arguably the best way is driving through the country.

Nevertheless, before starting to drive around in New Zealand, it is highly recommended that tourists read the New Zealand Road Code (www.nzta.govt.nz/resources/roadcode). Foreign drivers are to blame for a disproportionate number of road traffic accidents in New Zealand and local people now want to take action to make the country's roads safer, by obligating tourists to understand local road codes before driving as well as using T-Plates.

The most important road rules to consider while driving in New Zealand are:

- Stay on or under the legal speed limits indicated on road signs. The maximum speed on any open road is 100km/h (62 mi/h). The maximum speed in urban areas is 50km/h (31 mi/h). Speed must be adjusted as conditions demand.

- When traffic lights are red drivers must stop. When traffic lights are amber you must stop except if the driver is so close to the intersection it is unsafe to do so.

- Drivers and passengers have got to wear seatbelts or child restraints at all times, in both front and rear seats.

- Do not drink and drive. Driving under the influence of alcohol or drugs is a crime in New Zealand.

- Signposting follows standard international symbols and all distances are in kilometres (km).

- Driving while using a hand-held mobile phone is prohibited in New Zealand.

- It is illegal to pass other cars where there is yellow line instead of a white line marking the middle of the road. The yellow line indicates that it is too risky to overtake.

Hitchhiking in Australia

In some places hitchhiking is easy, while in other places it is difficult. Australia is one of the easiest. There is a cultural tradition of hitchhiking in Australia. People are friendly and helpful most places. It is very rare to have to wait more than a few hours to get a ride. A lot of times travellers only need to wait a few minutes. There are plenty of other people, including women who have hitched around Australia for years, and it is possible to hear lots of happy stories. In a country which has some of the most expensive transport costs in the world, hitchhiking is a celebrated way to cut travel costs.

Australia poses some attractive and distinctive challenges for hitchhikers. Distances between populated areas can be enormous; by far the majority of Australians live near the sea, with the majority of those living in the state capital cities. Temperatures can exceed 45 C in summer and go well below freezing in winter. In many ways Australia is an extreme environment, with some pretty extreme pests, people and weather; when it rains, it pours, when it blows up a wind, it howls. But in saying this when Australians smile upon travellers, the heavens open up from above and tourists can find themselves taken in, taken home, and for all practical purposes adopted for life.

As long as travellers remain on the main axes or smaller tourist roads they don't have to worry more than in other countries and they can hitchhike as they generally do. However, tourists must remember to carry more water than

404

is necessary, temperatures and distances can greatly exceed expectations and water will be crucial. Travellers might find it hard to stay at the road if the sun in hot and there is no shade. Also, if walking too far from towns as it may leave hitchhikers somewhere very isolated. A single walker in the middle of nowhere might have a better chance to get picked up because people are surprised or impressed. It is important to make sure that there is a backup plan and enough water to walk back if failing to get a lift especially if the traffic isn't consistent. Another tip that makes sense is to be very careful about not annoying the driver. A hitchhiker could be thrown out of the vehicle by an irritated driver 200km from the nearest city.

Hitchhiking in New Zealand

If travellers really want to try out hitchhiking, then New Zealand is the greatest place to do it. Despite one or two cases making it into the news, New Zealand is still one of the safest places in the world to hitchhike. Of course, hitchhiking always carries some risks with it, but then so does every other activity in this world.

It is important to understand that hitchhiking has been an established part of travel in New Zealand for a long time.

Many people hitchhike or have done it in the pass, whether being foreigners or locals. Most drivers are fairly open to picking up hitchhikers, and in busy areas tourists will have a fair amount of competition when it comes to catching a ride.

However, one of the most dangerous times for hitchhikers is when they are attempting to flag down or board a vehicle, especially in poor light. Do not try to pick up a ride on an unsafe stretch of road. Ensure that an approaching driver can see you and that there is ample room for that driver to pull over without disturbing the traffic flow or accidentally colliding with you. In addition, it is very important to avoid hitchhiking if for any reason you don't feel comfortable with the situation or the person who has stopped for you. Remember that although most people in this world mean you no harm at all, there are a few bad people out there. If there is a strange feeling, and there are some warning signals, pay attention to them.

SAFE (7233) message service: The SAFE (7233) text message service is provided to anyone wishing to record their travel intentions within New Zealand. The service is provided free by Telecom New Zealand Limited, Vodafone New Zealand Limited and 2degrees Mobile Ltd. Vodafone New Zealand

and 2degrees Mobile customers can also use the service overseas.

Messages are not monitored, but are stored for 12 months (Telecom and 2degrees Mobile) or for 3 months (Vodafone) and can be retrieved later on request by police if necessary to assist in the location of a person. Messages include the date and time the message was sent. The databases store text messages only, not multimedia or video.

Top Destinations in Australia

- **Melbourne**

  The capital of the state of Victoria, Melbourne is Australia's second most populated city as well as being considered the most liveable city in the world according to the Economist Intelligence Unit's annual global liveability ranking.

  The lively city is known for its street art, small trendy bars and an overload of cultural heritage. Located near the south-eastern tip of Australia on the large natural bay of Port Phillip, Melbourne is considered the nation's cultural capital as well as an important port. A well-planned city known for its shopping, fine restaurants and sports venues, Melbourne is the ideal destination for travellers who appreciate the good life.

- **Sydney**

  Located on Australia's south-eastern coast, Sydney is the capital of New South Wales. A modern city with a long history, Sydney is defined by its scenic harbour. The region's first inhabitants lived along the harbour's bank for thousands of years. The harbour was also the landing site for convicts sent to Australia during the 1780s. Today, ferries take visitors for cruises under the famed Sydney Harbor Bridge and past the iconic Sydney Opera House.

- **Tasmania**

  The beautiful unspoiled landscapes in Tasmania are definitely an underrated attraction. Lake St Clair National Park is home to Cradle Mountain, one of Australia's most beautiful wilderness areas. It's a region that's full of natural landscapes and gorgeous mountain ranges that were formed during the last Ice Age. Tasmania is an Australian destination that will make visitors appreciate the real undisturbed beauty of Australia.

- **Adelaide**

  The capital of South Australia, Adelaide is Australia's fifth largest city, with a population of over 1.2 million. More than three quarters of South Australians live in the Adelaide metropolitan area. The city is located on a plain between the rolling Adelaide Hills and the Gulf St Vincent and is bordered by many of Australia's famous wine regions. Historically known as the City of Churches, much of the architecture in the inner city is retained from the colonial era.

- **Alice Springs**

  While there are certainly more beautiful cities in Australia, this dusty outpost in the middle of the country's red desert centre is where the true Australian Outback experience finally unfolds. Located a mere 17-hour drive from Darwin to the north and 18 hours from Adelaide in the south, Alice Springs in the Northern Territory is the spot for riding camels, dodging kangaroos, and desert motorcycling. Hiking in the nearby Arizona-ish MacDonnell Ranges is a nice way to see the sights, but the main reason it is popular is the Uluru: the iconic massive rock (also known as Ayers Rock) in the middle of the country that can be climbed or simply admired from afar. Alice Springs also has a high concentration of indigenous aboriginal Australians, who have only lived in the area for circa 50,000 years.

- **Gold Coast**

As the closest thing Australia has to Miami, Gold Coast in Queensland is an extravagant strip of modern high-rises built on 90 miles of sunshine-soaked coastline. It's a playground for water sports and hosts its fair share of yacht parties, complete with all the corresponding vulgar behaviour that comes with them. Visitors are able to enjoy the Gold Coast's nonstop playground for some serious fun. Whether spending days at a theme park, shopping, on the golf course, learning to surf, soaking up the sunshine or just dining al fresco.

- **Perth**

Located on Australia's southwestern coastline, Perth is the country's fourth-largest city and the capital of Western Australia. Isolated from other major cities in Australia, Perth has developed its own unique character. Although the area has been inhabited for thousands of years, there's a youthful atmosphere and a fun-loving attitude in this city of nearly two million people.

New Zealand Amazing Destinations

- **Auckland**

  Blessed with two sparkling harbours, Auckland, the "City of Sails" is New Zealand's largest city and the most populous Polynesian city in the world. Rainforest hiking trails, black-sand and blond beaches, charming coves, islands, and volcanoes surround the city making it a perfect base for day trips and wilderness adventures. To appreciate Auckland's spectacular location, visitors can zoom up the 328-meter Sky Tower for spectacular views across the city and hinterland. Auckland is also home to a vibrant arts scene, top-notch dining, and a revamped waterfront area packed with boutiques and restaurants.

- **Queenstown**

  Snuggled between the shores of shimmering Lake Wakatipu and the snowy peaks of the Remarkables,

Queenstown is New Zealand's adventure capital and one of the country's top destinations for international visitors. Bungee jumping, jet boating, white-water rafting, paragliding, rock climbing, mountain biking, and downhill skiing are just some of the adrenaline-fueled sports on offer, and visitors can explore the stunning alpine scenery on the excellent network of hiking trails. In addition to the adventure sports, Queenstown offers all the creature comforts with first-class spas, restaurants, hotels, galleries, and shops. It's also a great base for trips to the Central Otagoregion, where visitors can explore gold mining towns and the Middle Earth scenery from the popular "Lord of the Rings" movies.

- **Rotorua**

On the tumultuous Pacific Ring of Fire, Rotorua is one of the most active geothermal regions in the world. This is a land where the earth speaks. Boiling mud pools, volcanic craters, hissing geysers, and steaming, thermal springs, betray the forces that birthed much of New Zealand's dramatic topography. Visitors can take a walking tour of these geothermal wonders, soak in steaming mineral springs, and learn about the region's rich history and culture. Adventure seekers will also find plenty of things to do. Sky-diving, luging, and mountain biking are some of the activities on offer. Trout fishing is also popular, and Rotorua is the gateway to the ski fields of Mount Ruapehu. It's also a popular tourist attraction with colourful hot springs and the famous Champagne Pool and Lady Knox Geyser.

- **Feilding**

   Multiple times winner of Keep New Zealand Beautiful, Most Beautiful Town award, Feilding is known for its beautiful Edwardian architecture, boutique shopping, historical museum collections and rural charm. Located just north of Palmerston North, Feilding is the rural centre of the Manawatu District. It is home to the Feilding Saleyards, a livestock sale held in the town since 1880, and the weekly Feilding Farmers' Market. For history buffs and motoring enthusiasts there is The Coach House museum and Manfeild Racing Circuit, while for art lovers a walk around Eric Brew.

- **Wellington**

  Surprisingly, New Zealand's capital city is not the largest, but it has been dubbed the world's "coolest little capital". This seaside capital is a city. In a city where there is always something happening, the surrounding districts of wine, coast and mountains, and heaps of creativity, Wellington is a popular choice for backpackers to stay a while. Visitors must check out Kapiti, Wairarapa, Wellington City Center, and Hutt Valley.

Enjoy Your Trip!

There is no better time spent or money invested than into a nice trip. Whether it's travelling abroad, a close destination or even just a relaxing weekend countryside break, it is always an unique experience with stories and memories that you will never forget.

I still remember doing interstate trips with my family when I was a child. The most exciting moments of each trip were the different variety of accents of each region in Brazil, as well as the local dishes that made each experience really unique and impossible to forget. Since then I have realized that travelling is equivalent to happiness, and every single trip is an exclusive opportunity to have some unforgettable experiences.

Even when we have a job we love and an active social life, nothing can compare with the experience that travelling can provide. Visiting other places changes our perspective of the world and, through people, culture, clothing, food and music, we appreciate more how wonderful life is. People who travel constantly, like digital nomads, know how stimulating and exciting it can be. Whether you are travelling to another country or to the town next to where you live, travelling is an experience that is not only enjoyable, but also translates into benefits to our health and mood.

If you seek happiness and are not finding it, perhaps it's time to plan a trip. A wise man once said, "Twenty years from now you will be more regretful for the things you didn't do than for the things you have done." Then follow his advice: "Release your bonds. Get away from the safe harbour. Grab the wind and explore the world. Travel around and find it out."

People love to hear good stories of travel and adventure. By having these cases in your luggage, you will be a more interesting person, do not doubt it. I have written all the strategies that I have been using to travel the world in this book. This book will certainly facilitate travellers to plan and organise their trips, assisting them to find cheap tickets, travel insurance, as well as best local transport and destination options.

Whether or not you are an experienced traveller, after going through this book you will be able to travel more while spending less money, as well as exploring the best places around this beautiful world. Finally, I offer my admiration and gratefulness to you, the reader. I hope you found these pages worthy. Feel free to let me know about your own adventures and experiences travelling the world by writing in directly from www.megatraveltips.com or saying hi on Instagram (megatraveltips), or on Facebook (@MegaTravelTips).

Have an amazing journey,

Daniel N. Silva

About The Author

With a passion for exploring the planet, Daniel N. Silva has earned a reputation as an advocate for positive change, spreading his inspirational message of exploring the world. As a deeply passionate British travel writer of Brazilian origin, he is infinitely driven by his lifelong mission to empower fellow adventurers to discover the countless beauties this planet has to offer, as well as its diverse cultures. He strongly believes that the more one experiences this wonderful world, the more one's inner world transforms.

Through tried-and-true travel tips, Daniel serves as a worldly mentor to those with an unquenchable thirst for adventure, teaching them the ins and outs of smart travelling, including discovering more, spending less, travelling to the best locations, finding low-cost air fares, effective hitchhiking, and so much more!

Since starting his world-wandering journey, over the years Daniel has travelled throughout the world on various life-altering voyages, including North America, South America, Europe, Russia, Asia, Southeast Asia and Australia. He has spent most of his career exploring beautiful cities along California's coast and Las Vegas' craziness. He has savoured tacos in Tijuana, eaten the delicious acarajé in Salvador, and enjoyed the ultimate cured jamón Ibérico like a Spaniard in Seville. He has learned Russian history in Volgograd, as well as the biblical traditions in Jerusalem.

He has explored Japan by bullet train, from Sapporo to Kagoshima, as well as appreciating Australian nature with its kangaroos, coastal lifestyle and Melbourne's delicious coffees. Daniel has also tasted durian in Malaysia, dived in Palawan, as well as riding a scooter through the picturesque villages of Lombok, and so much more…

Daniel earned a B.A. in Hospitality Management from the University of Derby, and an M.B.A. in Marketing with Distinction from the University of Sunderland. Heavily inspired by his extensive travels, he is also multilingual and speaks English, Spanish, Italian and Portuguese fluently. Daniel also writes about smart travelling on www.megatraveltips.com, sharing tips and experiences while travelling the world.

www.megatraveltips.com

Instagram (megatraveltips)

Facebook (@MegaTravelTips)

Twitter (@megatraveltips)

Pinterest (megatraveltips)

21598226R00251

Printed in Poland
by Amazon Fulfillment
Poland Sp. z o.o., Wrocław